AMBER NICOLE SHAVERS

THE LITTLE BOOK *of* MUSIC LAW

Library of Congress Cataloging-in-Publication Data

Shavers, Amber Nicole.
  The little book of music law / Amber Nicole Shavers.
     pages cm
  Includes bibliographical references and index.
  ISBN 978-1-62722-147-4 (alk. paper)
  1. Music trade—Law and legislation—United States. 2. Musicians' contracts—United States. I. Title.
  KF4291.S52 2013
  343.7307'878—dc23

                                              2013027269

Discounts are available for books ordered in bulk. Special consideration is given to state bars, CLE programs, and other bar-related organizations. Inquire at Book Publishing, ABA Publishing, American Bar Association, 321 N. Clark Street, Chicago, Illinois 60654-7598.

www.ShopABA.org

Table of Contents

I wrote my first song at the age of three. It was an ode to my elbow. The song was appropriately titled "On My El-la-bow." Why I chose my elbow as the subject of my new song, I will never know. I was inexhaustible in my defense against any corrections to the pronunciation of *elbow* suggested by my parents. My masterpiece was written on a white, mini toy-like piano with rainbow-colored keys. I soon progressed from the toy piano to a real one, all the while singing at every opportunity. With this background, I began a journey through music that would take me from my roots singing in the children's gospel choir at church to the world of musical theater, pop music, heavy metal, and beyond. It would lead me to experiences such as being the frontwoman of a band, songwriting, performing with a Brazilian samba troupe, and "second lining" with the locals behind brass bands and Mardi Gras Indians on the streets of New Orleans.

When I was not singing, I was listening. I was born into a household where everything from classical to soul to country was constantly playing. My parents are not musicians, simply fans who love their music. Like many music lovers, they would speak about famous singers and musicians as real people, not distant celebrities, and would always tell me the history and story behind an artist or a song. Sometimes it would even feel as though these entertainers were a part of the family, and singers like Smokey Robinson could have easily been "Uncle Smokey," or Gladys Knight, "Cousin Gladys."

In addition to the fond memories of the many Motown and rhythm and blues records played at my house, my parents also provided some of my early exposure to rock music. One standout memory occurred when I was in elementary school and my father played me a recording of Iron Butterfly's "In-A-Gadda-Da-Vida," excitedly pointing out the song's epic drum solo.

When I was six, Elaine, my college-aged, cool, and hip cousin, began introducing me to the punk and new wave bands coming from Britain during the late 1970s and 1980s, with The Clash being among my favorites. In junior high I became enthralled by the rock music from the 1960s and spent hours entranced by the sounds of bands like The Doors and The Who. Since I was a little girl I had been captivated by Broadway musicals, but as a preteen I also became a fan of heavy metal, to my parents' dismay. I anxiously awaited new metal video releases, along with my best friend and neighbor, during our weekly slumber parties, held for the sole purpose of watching *Headbanger's Ball* on MTV. I also began attending as many concerts as possible, including one headlined by rappers NWA that some friends took me to. Although I barely knew who NWA was at the time, I pretended like I did.

I entered my sophomore year of high school the same year Nirvana's "Smells Like Teen Spirit" was released, and grunge music became a part of my high school soundtrack. A couple years later I graduated just a few months after the suicide death of Nirvana's singer, Kurt Cobain. I attended high school in Lincoln, Nebraska, where I would often lace up my Doc Martens and attend small shows in clubs and converted churches, and also checked out the nearby music scene next door in Omaha. This included seeing a show at a small Omaha theme-park stage headlined by The Red Hot Chili Peppers. The opening act was a group that nobody in the crowd had heard of, except the guy standing to my right. He informed me it was "some band called Pearl Jam."

During my college years in Madison, Wisconsin, I was exploring a wide variety of global music offerings and discovering musical styles that had developed before my time. Sitting in my ethnomusicology classes in college, I was captivated by the interconnectedness of musical genres and their relationship to the societies from which they emerged. I later became frustrated with the stories I heard about artists going bankrupt after selling millions of records or who had signed flawed contracts and were suffering as a result. These factors contributed, in part, to me co-founding an entertainment-law and sports-law student organization while in law school.

The process of selecting the cases for *The Little Book of Music Law* began with a pen and a blank piece of paper. I wrote down issues that I thought were the most common or have had the greatest effect on the music industry. Then I reflected on the many stories of recording artists and their legal battles that I had heard of but wanted to learn more about. I subsequently began talking to friends, family, and acquaintances to get their input regarding the types of cases that might be of interest. Finally, a lot of attention was paid to the music-law topics that were making headlines. I challenged myself to see the issues from all sides and to search for the human-interest side of the story. My perspective was through the lens of an entertainer, a lawyer, and a fan.

The Little Book of Music Law is written as an entertaining approach to music law. Although it is fact based, it is not a textbook and is not meant to provide legal advice. Rather, its purpose is to provide insight into music law along with a glimpse into the stories behind the music. The time period covered begins in the early twentieth century, considered to be the beginning of the modern music industry, through today. The cases, for the most part, cover developments in American music and law.

With the birth of modern popular music and the rise of everything from bluegrass to jazz and rock 'n' roll to hip-hop, music development continues. At the same time, the rise of the modern music industry has been both an economic and emotional roller-coaster ride. From the very beginning, the industry has been fraught with extensive litigation. Court battles have run the gamut from copyright infringement to invasion of privacy and even bankruptcy. These business, legal, and creative developments have made the industry's story a rich one indeed.

Some of the cases included in this book are upbeat, such as those involving singer Teena Marie and film star Olivia de Havilland. Other cases are more somber, such as "Dream Girl Deferred," which recounts the personal and financial struggles of Florence Ballard, a former Supremes member. There is a discussion of British rock group The Verve and how the band lost one hundred percent of the music publishing rights to its biggest hit song. Then there's the story of Lady Miss Kier, former lead singer for the 1990s dance-music group Deee-Lite, and her right of publicity battle against Sega, one of the largest video-game producers in the world. There are also recurring individuals, such as members of the Rolling Stones, the Beatles, and music manager Allen Klein, who make appearances in more than one chapter. This was not planned when the subject matter for the book was being selected. However, it speaks to the major influence and effect that these people have had on the music industry. Providing a breadth of real-life music law stories, the book reflects the real world of the music business. In the real world, the "good guy" does not always win, and strong music sales do not always spell success.

The book is divided into five parts, each encompassing approximately a twenty- or thirty-year period in music history. In keeping with the musical theme of the book, it is organized into chapters referred to as "tracks." Short, supplemental write-ups called "interludes" feature either an anecdotal case or an item of interest, and provide further insight into the concepts discussed in the chapters preceding them. The "interlude" designation plays upon the definition of a *musical interlude*, which is a passage or piece of music that is played in between the parts of a song, film, or stage production. As with a large musical work, the book opens with a scene-setting "prelude" and closes with some final thoughts in the "finale." The book is by no means an exhaustive write-up of music law or music history but a distillation of some noteworthy moments in pop culture and music law. In keeping with the theme of the Little Book series, each piece is written in a style that is accessible to both the lawyer and the nonlawyer.

The Little Book of Music Law is for anyone interested in working in or having a better understanding of the music business. It is for the casual observer as well as the industry insider. For a full multimedia experience, I highly recommend a visit to YouTube or another video Web site where you can find several music videos and interviews that complement the accounts in this book. I hope you will find *The Little Book of Music Law* to be a fun and informative sampling of this unique corner of the entertainment industry. So now, I invite you to sit back, relax, and hit play.

Prelude

Setting the Scene

I n laboratories around the world, pioneers of early music technology were hard at work trying to find a way to capture and play back the human voice. The foundations of the rise of the modern music industry had been laid as the nineteenth century came to a close. There was a growing demand for wider and more accessible music options that could entertain the general public beyond the exclusive walls of opera houses and orchestra halls. The demand for music for the people, that is, popular music, surged against a backdrop of changing demographics during the American Industrial Revolution. It is during these early days of the music industry that our stories begin.

In the United States, this was a period of extreme innovation that bore witness to the development of groundbreaking technology such as the combustion engine, the expansion of the railroads, and the rise of the factory system and its assembly line. The United States was transitioning into the twentieth century, and the rise of industry was propelling the country toward becoming a leading global economic power.

Urban migration picked up dramatically as many people left their agricultural trades for the employment prospects of urban life. Between 1880 and 1920 the number of employees working in manufacturing jobs increased by over seven million people.[1] Those already living in major urban centers were joined by a large influx of immigrants. Passing through the gates of New York's Ellis Island, for example, large numbers of immigrants, mostly from Europe, settled along the East Coast, particularly in New York, and soon developed thriving, ethnically rich communities. Meanwhile, there were opportunities out in the West.

A journey westward appealed to many chasing their dreams of land ownership. This quest toward the Western frontier was aided by the Homestead Act, which sought to populate the Native American lands of the Midwest. In the South, the former Confederate states continued to rebuild their cities and redefine their social hierarchies in a post slavery society following the destruction and social upheaval of the Civil War that had ended just a generation before.

The industrial boom provided a rise in income for many Americans, and along with it something that many people in earlier times had little opportunity to enjoy . . . leisure time. Yet whether one was a city dweller, in the countryside, a Northerner or a Southerner, everyone shared a common desire. They all wanted to be entertained.

The rise of sheet music as a means for distributing the musical arrangements of popular music to the masses personalized the music-listening experience. Favorite melodies could be brought into the home and played on demand. While the printing of sheet music, or music publishing, had been in practice for several centuries prior to the Industrial Revolution, it was only during that period that entrepreneurial individuals began to truly capitalize on the earning potential of selling music to the masses.

Showboats, traveling circuses, and medicine shows, which offered exotic and often adult-themed entertainment, also offered short musical variety performances on their bill of entertainment. Additionally, both the urban centers and the Western frontier were exposed to minstrel and burlesque shows that were especially prevalent after the Civil War. The minstrel shows were productions that revolved around extreme caricatures of black people. Characters like Black Sambo and Mammy were portrayed as dimwits who pranced around the stage for comic relief and spoke in an exaggerated broken English. Typically performed by white actors dressed in blackface, the minstrel shows were an extremely popular form of entertainment. There were also a handful of minstrel troupes in existence consisting of black members who performed in blackface as well. All minstrel shows would feature songs written especially for the production, many of which became popular tunes that sold millions of copies of sheet music.[2] The minstrel shows reached their peak of popularity a few decades before the Civil War but remained a viable entertainment option until the 1920s, eventually giving way to vaudeville.

Catchy tunes that struck a chord with the public were being performed at vaudeville halls across the country. The vaudeville shows, typically started by businessmen, many of whom had cut their teeth on the traveling-circus circuit, began to spring up around the country toward the end of the nineteenth century. They brought together, for example, the performances of skilled musicians and singers and put them on the same bill as acrobats. The shows were cultural melting pots themselves and attracted people from all walks of society and were especially appealing to the urban immigrant populations who appreciated the relaxed atmosphere. In some cases, the chance to hear music from the "old country" was an added bonus. These variety shows formed the foundation for the evolution of the Broadway musical.

Many of the songs performed in the vaudeville shows became popular hits, resulting in a growing demand for sheet music. Music publishers hired "song pluggers," whose job it was to frequent the vaudeville halls and convince performers to sing songs from the publisher's catalog in an effort to turn the song into a hit and drive sheet-music sales.

Recognizing the increasing demand for sheet music, several music publishers set up shop in a group of railroad flats on a New York City block, making it their unofficial headquarters. The block became known as Tin Pan Alley. As legend has it, Tin Pan Alley got its name from the sounds of piano players plunking away in music publishing offices as publishers listened, critiqued, and debated whether to publish the song being played for them. It was said that if you stood beneath the windows of the publishing offices, the plunking sounds of several pianos sounded like constant tapping on a tin pan.[3] With a basic business model revolving around measuring a hit song by the number of copies of sheet music sold, the modern music industry began to flourish.[4]

THE LITTLE
BOOK
of
MUSIC LAW

PART ONE

1900–1930s

Playback

1901	• August 4—Jazz trumpeter Louis Armstrong is born in New Orleans. • Victor Talking Machine Company is founded by Emile Berliner.
1903	• The Wright Brothers fly the first powered airplane.
1912	• The *Titanic* sinks in the Atlantic Ocean.
1914	• ASCAP is founded. • July 28—World War I begins in Europe.
1917	• The first jazz record is cut in New York City by the Original Dixieland Jazz Band.
1919	• General Electric acquires the Marconi Wireless Telegraph company and names it the Radio Corporation of America (RCA).
1920	• Okeh Records releases "Crazy Blues," sung by blues artist Mamie Smith. The song is an unexpected hit and alerts labels to the untapped "race records" market.
1926	• The National Broadcasting Company (NBC) is founded by General Electric, Westinghouse, and RCA.
1927	• Country music singers Jimmie Rodgers and the Carter Family are recorded for the first time by Ralph Peer of Okeh Records, sparking the growth of popular country music. • October 6—*The Jazz Singer*, the first motion picture "talkie," is released.
1929	• RCA buys the Victor Talking Machine Company. • October 28—The stock market crashes on "Black Monday," signaling the beginning of the Great Depression. The record industry falters, along with everything else.

1931	• Electrical and Music Industries (EMI) is created from the merger of the Gramophone Company in Britain and the Columbia Graphophone Company, the British subsidiary of Columbia Records. EMI opens Abbey Road in London, the world's largest recording studio and future recording home of the Beatles.
1932	• Thomas Dorsey's release of "Precious Lord" establishes gospel music as a genre.
1933	• Prohibition ends in the United States.
1935	• According to legend, in the early 1930s, Robert Johnson sells his soul to the devil at the "crossroads" in Mississippi and becomes a blues guitar great.
1939	• Judy Garland has a number 1 hit with "Over the Rainbow."

The Gramophone Chronicles:

Contributory Infringement and a Rogue Record Retailer

Leeds & Catlin Co. v. Victor Talking Machine Co., 213 U.S. 301 (1909).

One day when I was in the sixth grade, my mother brought home one of the best gifts I think a child could hope for. She brought home a dog. I had always wanted a dog, but my pleas went unanswered for years. He was a beautiful, smooth black and white fox terrier whom she had rescued from a life sentence in the animal shelter. The dog's name was Brew, which was short for Sethfields Miller Lite. Yes, that really was his name. We could not take credit for it though. His former owners had given him the name. Brew and I were joined at the hip, and when we were out and about people would always say, "Hey, he looks like the RCA dog!"

The "RCA dog" they were referring to is Nipper, the iconic, floppy-eared black and white dog that has been famously featured on the RCA Records logo for over a century.[5] In the logo, the small, big-eyed dog is staring into a gramophone with his head cocked to one side and a perplexed look on his face. The image became as popular as RCA itself, if not more. However, before there was an RCA dog, or even an RCA Records, the image of that cute dog was the trademark of the Victor Talking Machine Company, purchased by RCA in 1929. At the time of the purchase, Victor had become one of the largest and most powerful record labels and record manufacturers around.

Record players and other sound-producing devices were commonly referred to as "talking machines" in the early twentieth century. The Victor Talking Machine Company exclusively held Emile Berliner's patent for the Gramophone, an early form of record player, upon which Victor had built its empire. Patent litigation over new music technology was rife in these early days of the popular music industry. Continually adding to the court dockets, these cases reflected the speed and fervor with which new music technology was being produced and the increasing public demand for these items.

Having struck gold with the Berliner patent, Victor was determined to aggressively protect its prized patent. It initiated several patent infringement lawsuits against competitor talking-machine companies and record labels, including a lawsuit against record label Leeds & Catlin. This dispute led to the case *Leeds & Catlin Company v. Victor Talking Machine Company.*[6] It was the first case in which the Supreme Court upheld a lower court's application of the concept of contributory infringement to a nonstaple item in a patent dispute. *Contributory patent infringement* is a form of indirect patent infringement that involves the sale of an unpatented item for use in a patented machine. A *nonstaple item* is a product whose primary use is with a patented product and generally cannot be used outside of the patented product. In this case, the patented product was the record player, and the nonstaple item was the "record." The court agreed that the combination of the record player and the record, when engaged with one another, qualified for protection against infringement.

Leeds & Catlin was held liable for contributory infringement for manufacturing disc records that were playable on Victor machines. The implications of the decision were much broader than record players. The idea of a record manufacturer being found guilty of infringement for producing records that are playable on another company's record player seems almost inconceivable today. *Leeds & Catlin* exemplifies the challenge the courts faced in balancing the spirit of invention during the industrial age and its intersection with the music industry in the face of claims of patent infringement.

The story of the rise of Victor Records mirrors the rise of the popular music industry at the turn of the twentieth century. It was a period of rapid innovation punctuated by a race among several inventors to build the best sound-playback machine. The labors of this competitive pursuit produced cutting-edge audio technology but also created a very litigious atmosphere. The period was a Wild West of patent infringement litigation as competing companies sought to preserve their patents and force others out of the industry entirely. Talking-machine companies rose and fell, and successful ones absorbed the smaller and more vulnerable ones. The story of the talking-machine inventors is particularly fascinating.

Thomas Edison's phonograph was the first of the talking machines that could both record and play back sound. New machines based on the phonograph but containing improvements to Edison's model soon followed. These newer machines became known by their brand names, such as Charles Sumner Tainter and Chichester Bell's Graphophone and Emile Berliner's Gramophone. As time passed, all talking machines were often generally referred to as phonographs.

The following developments began in the latter part of the nineteenth century. Edison received a British patent for his phonograph on July 30, 1877, and a U.S. patent on February 19, 1878. His phonograph originally recorded and replayed sound through the use of a metal cylinder that had been wrapped in metal foil. Helical grooves were indented into the cylinder and wrapped around it during the recording process.[7] The grooves contained the recording. A flexible diaphragm, which was a small flat disc, had a metal pin attached to it and converted the sound embedded in the grooves into vibrations, similar to a common record player needle.

Edison's original intention for the phonograph was that it be used for purposes such as taking dictation. He had no idea that his recording machine would take on a whole new life as a sound-producing mechanical instrument that would form a cornerstone in the music industry. As more technically proficient machines were developed, Edison's interest began to wane somewhat, and over the next decade he turned his focus toward electric lighting.

Chichester Bell, a chemist and a cousin of Alexander Graham Bell, in collaboration with Charles Sumner Tainter began developing an improved phonograph after Edison declined an invitation from Alexander Graham Bell to collaborate on a new talking machine. The Bell and Tainter sound-producing process differed from Edison's. Instead of metal cylinders wrapped in tinfoil, Bell and Tainter used cardboard cylinders coated in hard wax on which grooves were engraved instead of indented, as in Edison's method.[8]

Their method proved more successful in providing a higher-quality recording. By 1887, the wax-coated cylinders had replaced those wrapped in tinfoil. Bell and Tainter also mounted a sound box to their machine. Edison, Bell, and Tainter had made significant strides, but inventor Emile Berliner, whose patents were at issue in the Leeds & Catlin case, was about to corner the market and set the industry standard for talking machines.

Berliner moved to Washington, D.C., at age nineteen from Hanover, Germany, having had no formal education in his early years but possessing a curious mind. He was the kind of person who would become fascinated with a piece of technology, take it apart, and tinker around with it to understand how it worked. His initial employment in the United States included working as a clerk in a dry goods store and as a "cleanup man" in a New York City laboratory.[9] Berliner's fascination with the experiments taking place in the laboratory encouraged his passion for invention.

While attending the Centennial Exposition in Philadelphia in 1876, he was captivated by a new invention, the telephone. Soon afterward, he developed an improved telephone transmitter that was designed for placement in the telephone's mouthpiece. American Bell Telephone Company was so impressed that they made him an offer to buy the rights to his invention. They also offered him a job as a research assistant. After working several years for the American Bell Telephone Company in Boston, he resigned and returned to Washington, D.C., where he worked as a private researcher and inventor.

Through many trials and error, Berliner developed the gramophone, so named to distinguish it from Edison's phonograph. Berliner's gramophone was an improvement on the talking machines that preceded it, but it did not have immediate commercial success. The few people who saw the first version, built as a hand-turned machine, viewed it as a novelty item, and it languished in the domain of amusements and exhibitions.

Berliner was losing money rapidly during this period. All of this began to change in the1890s when he met Eldridge Johnson, who later developed a spring motor for the gramophone. With the hand-crank gone and the motor in place, the gramophone became an extremely competitive addition to the talking-machine market.

Berliner applied for and received several patents for his gramophone as he continually improved it. Patent Number 534,543 is considered to be his most important.[10] Known as "the Berliner patent," it was applied for on March 30, 1892, and issued on February 19, 1895.[11] The Berliner patent contained the design that would become the standard for gramophones and would control the talking-machine market for the next fifteen years or so.

Berliner turned recording on its side when he replaced the cylinder with a flat disc record typically made of zinc, and coated with an acid-resistant material such as a mixture of beeswax and gasoline. The sound waves produced during the recording would laterally etch themselves into the metal disc by way of a stylus attached to a flexible diaphragm. The disc would then be bathed in acid which would cause the etched lines to further imprint themselves on the disc forming deep grooves.[12] This "voice etching" would serve as the master copy of the sound recording. The zinc disc was then stamped on to flat discs made of hard, durable rubber in order to make copies.

Berliner's recording methods improved upon the cylinder methods in part because they created groove cuts that were uniform and of even depth, resulting in better playback. Also, in the previous talking machines the stylus was conveyed mechanically across the record, or the record was mechanically conveyed across the stylus. Berliner dispensed with the mechanical conveyance altogether and replaced it with a stylus that was propelled across the record by the grooves alone.

Berliner set up the Consolidated Talking Machine Company of America as a holding company over the Berliner Gramophone Company of Philadelphia and later formed the United States Gramophone Company. Meanwhile, Johnson separately set up the similarly named Consolidated Talking Machine Company. Johnson changed the name to Manufacturing Machinist almost immediately after forming the company.

After Berliner was forced to stall production due to continuous litigation from talking-machine competitors, Berliner and Johnson sought to get the gramophone business moving again by merging in 1901 to form the Victor Talking Machine Company.[13] Free from legal entanglements, the Victor Talking Machine Company was able to flourish.[14] Eldridge Johnson served as Victor's first president.

The public then got its first glimpse of the trademark that would become one of the most recognizable brand images in the world, the small fox terrier staring into the horn of a gramophone with his head tilted to the side reflecting the charm of canine curiosity. Francis Barraud, an English painter, painted the image. The dog originally belonged to Barraud's brother Mark, who named him Nipper. After Mark's death, Barraud became Nipper's caregiver. One day he spotted Nipper peering into the horn of a phonograph with his head cocked to the side. He envisioned that perhaps Nipper thought the voice of his former and deceased master was emanating from the machine.[15] Inspired by Nipper's perceived longing for Mark, Barraud named his painting *His Master's Voice*.

Nipper was originally illustrated looking into a phonograph cylinder playback machine instead of a gramophone. Barraud attempted to sell his creation to phonograph manufacturers, but he was unable to generate any interest in the image. On the suggestion of a friend, he decided to create a painting of the illustration and replace his black-colored phonograph speaker horn with a brass one. He reached out to the Gramophone Company in England to inquire about borrowing one of its brass speaker horns as a model.[16] When the manager of the London-based company saw a photograph of the painting, he made an offer to buy it provided that Barraud use a gramophone instead of a phonograph. Barraud agreed and sold the rights to his painting. The English gramophone outlet, along with Barraud's painting, were acquired by the Victor Talking Machine Company shortly after the company was founded. The image soon became a regular fixture on Victor products. Little Nipper was on his way to worldwide fame.

By the fall of 1901, four of the most important and largest music chains had become customers of Victor. These included Grinnell, Wurlitzer, Lyon & Healy, and Sherman Clay.[17] The company also found success through a series of popular music record releases. To bolster their recording catalog, Victor established the Red Seal recording series. A red label placed upon the records identified recordings in this series and signified, for the discriminating listener, that the talent was of the highest caliber. The first of these releases was a 10-inch, 78 rpm disc featuring recorded music performed by the popular Italian tenor Enrico Caruso. Known as the "Caruso Recordings," the first of these records was released in 1904 to strong consumer demand. The soaring record sales further increased Caruso's celebrity. Once suspicious of the disc record, Caruso's recording success was influential in causing many celebrities to view records as being a beneficial medium for their careers.

Not only was Victor rolling out top-shelf recordings, they were changing the dynamics of the talking-machine market with new and appealing machine models. Its Victrola machines debuted in 1906. These machines differed greatly from the phonograph and gramophone models. Instead of a horn reaching into the air from a record-machine base, the Victrolas were designed in the shape of freestanding cabinets. All the mechanical components of the player were tucked away inside the cabinet doors of these fixtures, which were designed to look more like furniture than machines. The Victrolas were fashionable and in high demand. Things were looking up for Victor.

In the midst of Victor's success, there were a few companies who appeared to be feverishly cashing in on its patents without permission. One of those companies was Leeds & Catlin. In the business of selling phonographs, discs, and cylinder recordings, Leeds & Catlin has been referred to by some as "notorious record pirates."[18] The company's recording and record retail practices were highly questionable, with counterfeit or pirated recordings being a company specialty. However, there is some evidence to indicate that not all were pirated.[19]

As a result of Leeds & Catlin's actions, Victor filed the lawsuit described above. The case was filed in the Circuit Court for the Southern District of New York. Victor claimed that Leeds & Catlin had infringed upon the Berliner patent. It alleged that the company was making and selling records that were designed to be played on Victor playback machines and were based on the Berliner patent. Victor sought an injunction requiring Leeds & Catlin to cease its record sales. Leeds & Catlin argued that selling records designed for playback on Victor machines was not infringement because Victor's patent was not valid.

The trial court concluded that the Berliner patent was valid and its grant of an injunction against Leeds & Catlin was upheld on appeal to the Circuit Court of Appeals for the Second Circuit. Despite the rulings, Leeds & Catlin continued selling the questionable records, and on November 15, 1906, Victor once again sued Leeds & Catlin. This time Victor sued for contempt due to Leeds & Catlin's violation of the injunction. The label was found to be in contempt of the injunction ruling by the trial court. After Leeds & Catlin lost on appeal to the Circuit Court of Appeals for the Second Circuit, the Supreme Court, which accepted the case, began hearing arguments on January 15, 1909.

The Court began by first examining whether the lower courts had erred in ruling that the Berliner patent was valid. In its most basic form, a U.S. patent consists of a description of the invention or inventions along with several enumerated sections, each listing a particular element of the invention. Each enumerated section is referred to as a *claim*. Each claim, or element, is considered its own invention. A union of elements working together as a machine is known as a *combination*. An inventor can improve upon an already existing item and still be granted a patent. However, the inventor will be granted a patent only on the actual improvements themselves.[20] Victor was particularly concerned with two claims within the Berliner patent. One was for Berliner's use of the groove-propelled stylus, which was enumerated in the patent as claim number 5. The other was for the combination, or the gramophone apparatus itself, enumerated in claim number 35.[21]

Berliner had filed for several foreign patents as he developed his gramophone. Before receiving the U.S. patent in question, he had been granted patents in France, Germany, Great Britain, and Canada. All of the foreign patents had expired by the time Victor filed its lawsuit. Leeds & Catlin relied on Section 4887 of the Revised Statutes, which stated that a U.S. patent would expire at the same time as its equivalent foreign patent. The company argued that Berliner's U.S. patent would therefore have expired, and as such Victor did not have an actionable claim of infringement.

The Court held that although the French, German, and British patents had expired, there was no effect on the expiration date of the U.S. patent. As the lower courts had held, the European patents, although very similar to the U.S. patent, did not include any reference to claims number 5 and number 35, and as such the Court did not consider the patents to be equivalent to the gramophone model as it was covered in the U.S. patent.

However, the Canadian patent did reference claims number 5 and number 35. Considered by the Court to be similar enough to the U.S. patent, the Canadian patent's expiration date was tied to the U.S. patent expiration date. The Canadian patent had expired in 1899, approximately seven years before Victor filed its lawsuit against Leeds & Catlin. Therefore, according to Leeds & Catlin, the U.S. patent would have expired along with it, and as a result the court proceedings for infringement were a pointless exercise.

However, there was one small twist. Although the Canadian patent had expired prior to Victor's lawsuit against Leeds & Catlin, the original duration of the patent grant was for eighteen years from its issue date in 1893. This meant the Canadian patent would expire in 1911. Yet, as it turned out, the reason the patent had expired in 1899 was because under Canadian law, the patentee was required to pay an administrative fee every six years to keep the patent active. The fee was not paid after the first six-year period, and the patent subsequently expired in 1899.

The Supreme Court clarified that the failure to meet an obligation abroad, such as payment of administrative fees, would not shorten the lifespan of the U.S. patent. The life of the U.S. patent would still run equivalent to the full duration originally granted in the foreign patent. Therefore, Berliner's U.S. patent was entitled to the full eighteen-year period and had not expired at the time of the lawsuit. As a result, the patent was held to be valid and the Supreme Court held the grant of the injunction against Leeds & Catlin to have been correct.

Next, the contempt ruling was reviewed. The unique elements of particular concern in Berliner's gramophone were the "traveling tablet" referring to the record and the "reproducing stylus" that was propelled by the grooves etched into the record. The joint actions of these elements were features that made Berliner's patent stand out from other records and talking machines. Leeds & Catlin had been enjoined from selling, using, or manufacturing talking machines or records created to work with these distinct features.

Additionally, after the court of appeals affirmed the injunction against Leeds & Catlin, the label began selling a "feed device machine," a different style of talking machine, supposedly so that customers could play the infringing records on that machine instead of Victor's gramophone. Leeds & Catlin's goal was to avoid the perception that the records they sold were to be used on a gramaphone The records could be played on the Leeds & Catlin feed device machine, but as the court pointed out, Leeds & Catlin took advantage of Victor's popularity with consumers and hardly made an attempt to restrict the use of the infringing records onVictor machines. For example, it did not put notices on the records informing consumers that they were only to be played on Leeds & Catlin machines and not on Victor's gramophone.

Leeds & Catlin argued that even if the records they were selling were considered a part of the combination invention, the sale of a Victor Talking Machine to a customer gave that customer an implied license to buy suitable records. That right, they reasoned, extended to situations in which the customer wanted to purchase from a retailer other than Victor. The Court noted that this would be permissible only if the owner of a patented machine were purchasing an unpatented item for the purposes of resupplying an element due to its deterioration. However, in this case, the Supreme Court found that customers purchased the infringing Leeds & Catlin records to refresh their music collections rather than repair the gramophone. As such, owners of the gramophone were committing acts of direct infringement each time they used non-Victor records, and Leeds & Catlin, as suppliers of the infringing records in question, committed contributory infringement.

In fact, the actual records themselves were not patented. Leeds & Catlin believed that because the records were unpatented, they should be able to be freely sold without restriction or concern of infringement. The Court saw things differently. It held that although the records were unpatented articles, they were intended for use on Victor talking machines based on their design and had been marketed that way. The records were considered elements of the gramophone working in conjunction with the other working parts of the gramophone, such as the stylus, to reproduce sound. Effectively, this meant that the records, when engaged with the gramophone, fell squarely within the Berliner patent. The Court made clear that Leeds & Catlin had not been enjoined from selling *all* records, just records designed for use in Victor machines. The sale of records designed to engage with the Victor talking machines by anyone other than Victor would qualify as contributory infringement. Generally speaking, a person may be guilty of contributory infringement if he or she knowingly sells an unpatented item for the purpose of using it in a patented item. The fact that the records were unpatented was immaterial in the Court's eyes.[22] It acknowledged that combination-type inventions, like the gramophone, consisting of unpatented elements were common.

A hard battle had been waged before the Supreme Court, with the injunction and the contempt charge being upheld against Leeds & Catlin. The Court's decision rounded out several court victories that allowed Victor to fight off competitors and ensure the validity of the Berliner patent. With renewed optimism, the company took out ads warning consumers that the purchase of products found to be infringing upon the Berliner patent could lead to legal action against them. Ads heralding the company's legal triumphs were also taken out. One ad boldly stated that although the Victor Company hesitated to brag, it felt it was necessary for everyone to fully understand that the "Victor Company is on Top."[23]

Meanwhile, back at Leeds & Catlin headquarters in Middletown, Connecticut, the Supreme Court's decision proved devastating. The company filed for bankruptcy in 1909, just a few months after the decision. Payments from record retailers to whom the label had sold records prior to the Court's decision remained outstanding because no one wanted to become embroiled in any further litigation. A large inventory of unsold records, all dressed up for shipment with nowhere to go, filled the Leeds & Catlin warehouse and became practically valueless. At the time of the bankruptcy filing, the company's liabilities amounted to approximately $1 million. Victor may have taken out "Victory ads," but Leeds & Catlin could also be found in the papers. Reduced to bankruptcy, its epilogue could be found buried in the newspaper bankruptcy-notices section with the simple headline, "Leeds & Catlin Co. Fails."[24]

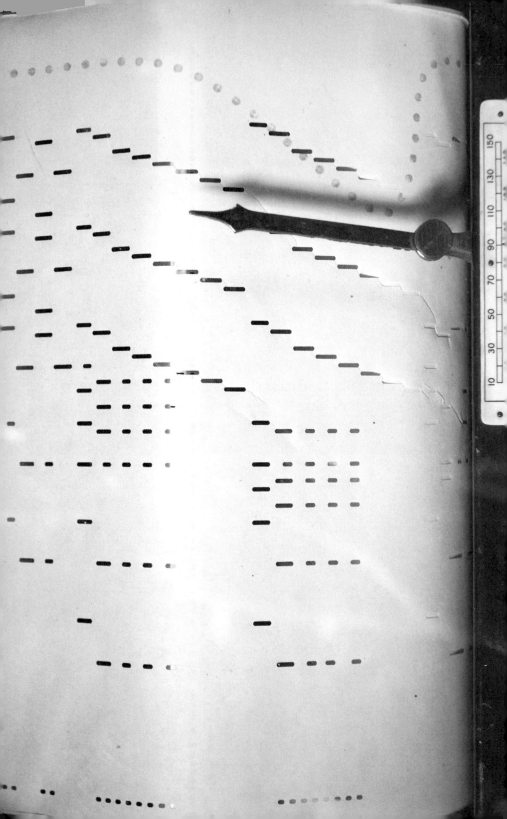

The Piano-Roll Rag:
Copy or Component?

*White-Smith Music Publishing Co. v.
Apollo Co.*, 209 U.S. 1 (1908).

Ey 1900 the American popular music business was in full swing. The sheet-music trade dominated the marketplace, and an emerging market was forming around audio playback machines and sales of sound recordings. Player pianos had recently hit the market following the new audio technology wave that started with the "talking machines." A welcome development for music lovers and player-piano retailers, the player-pianos were also rustling feathers in the world of music publishing.

A player piano was a marvel audio-playback machine when it debuted. Through the use of a piano roll, made from strategically perforated cloth or paper, a player piano mechanically reproduces a song without human involvement. These pianos were a hit with the public. Player-piano retailers offered an array of piano rolls, containing popular songs in a range of musical styles including classical, jazz, and ragtime. In 1902, approximately 75,000 player pianos were being used in the United States.[25] The production of perforated music rolls was robust; an estimated 1.5 million were made that year.

The music publishing community was mixed in its reception of the player pianos. On one hand, many publishers saw this addition to the audio-playback machine offerings as a welcome development because the popularity of the piano rolls helped to increase a song's popularity. On the other hand, there was a growing concern that the sales of piano rolls were a threat to the publishers' thriving sheet music business. Adding to the discontent of publishers was a lack of clarity as to whether, under U.S. copyright law, piano rolls could be considered copies of a copyrighted work. If so, the piano-roll retailers would be required to seek permission from a song's copyright holder, who in many cases was a music publisher, before they could sell that song as a piano roll, and this was not being done. This issue soon found its way to the courts when Boston-based White-Smith Music Publishing Company accused The Apollo Company, a player-piano retailer, of copyright infringement of two songs being sold as piano rolls: "Little Cotton Dolly" and "Kentucky Babe."

Apollo was a piano manufacturer known for its high-grade grand pianos and player pianos. Its piano-roll catalog was large and contained music of some of the world's greatest composers and pianists. Adam Geibel, the composer of the contested songs, had assigned his copyright in the songs to White-Smith Publishing. Geibel, a German-born and Pennsylvania-raised composer who had been blinded by an eye infection at the age of eight, wrote mostly nonsecular songs but had a few secular successes, "Little Cotton Dolly" and "Kentucky Babe" being two of them.

The popular "Kentucky Babe," for example, was a "negro lullaby" that evoked minstrel imagery of a young black child being lulled to sleep in his "Mammy's" breast amid the "skeeters" and honeysuckles. This plantation lullaby is still performed today, with popular versions recorded by Perry Como, Dean Martin, and Eddy Arnold.

White-Smith brought its copyright infringement challenge against Apollo in the U.S. Circuit Court for the Southern District of New York in 1905. The case was dismissed on the grounds that White-Smith failed to show a legal basis upon which it could prevail. The publisher appealed to the U.S. Court of Appeals for the Second Circuit, which also ruled in favor of Apollo, affirming the trial court's dismissal.[26] The case was subsequently argued before the U.S. Supreme Court in January 1908 and decided in February 1908.

U.S. copyright law has evolved throughout its history. When the law was first codified, music was not included among the items garnering copyright protection. The first federal copyright law, enacted on May 31, 1790, provided protection only for books, maps, and charts.[27] Musical compositions were not added until February 3, 1831.[28] On January 6, 1897, the protection against unauthorized public performances of music was added to the bundle of rights available to the owner of a copyright.[29] This new protection meant that copyright owners held the exclusive right to grant a public performance of their copyrighted work. However, the court in *White-Smith* disregarded this amendment remarking that the public performance of copyrighted music was not at issue. Instead the issue was whether the piano rolls were copies of copyrighted music and therefore eligible for copyright protection.

The question of whether a piano roll was a copy did have some precedence. In *Kennedy v. McTammany*, a case brought in the Circuit Court of Massachusetts, the court held that the thousands of songs available for use on an organette, a small, hand-cranked organ, were not considered copies of an original song, and therefore copyright infringement had not occurred by their use.[30] Several years later, in *Stern v. Rosey*, an injunction was sought to stop the manufacture of phonograph records, based on the charge of copyright infringement. Again the court concluded that a phonograph record was not a copy of a musical composition.[31]

In order to settle the dispute in *White-Smith versus Apollo*, the Supreme Court looked to the definition of just what qualified as a *copy*. Under the Copyright Act, the copyright holder has the exclusive right to make or authorize copies of his or her work. According to the Court, "a copy of a musical composition within the meaning of the statute is a written or printed record of it in intelligible notation."[32] The Court then dug deeper into the meaning of a copy in order to clarify Congress's original intention when drafting the act. The statute did not specifically state what items could be considered a copy. The Court further interpreted the statute by analyzing the concepts of "tangible expressions" versus "intellectual conceptions."

The Court stated that the statute "provided for the making and filing of a tangible thing," but that the intellectual conception of that item was not covered under the act. That meant that in this case, the music actually emanating from the player piano was the intellectual conception whereas, on the other hand, the sheet music itself was the tangible expression. White-Smith had argued that the statute did cover the intellectual conception and that the melody, the resulting aural product of the notes carefully selected by a composer, is the real invention and should be protected. The publishing company poetically stated, "music is intended for the ear . . . as writing is for the eye."[33]

Although the Court saw merit in White-Smith's argument, it strictly construed the statute to limit protection only to what is tangible. The music heard when a perforated roll is played was viewed as intangible. It was found to be intangible because, in spite of the skill required to cut the perforations and design each piano roll, the final product was not sheet music. In the Court's view, it looked nothing like sheet music, was not readable as sheet music, and was therefore not a copy. Additionally, the Court stated that the piano roll, when used in the player piano, became a part of the machine and that the sound produced by the machine was intangible.

The Court's conclusion was that the piano roll was neither identical to nor used for the same purpose as sheet music. It becomes part of a sound-reproducing machine whose product, the song, is an intangible intellectual conception and therefore not protected as a copy under the statute. Specifically, it held that piano rolls were not copies and as such not protected under the Copyright Act, making Apollo not liable for copyright infringement.

The decision in *White-Smith* did not sit well with music publishers, although they could take some solace in Justice Holmes's concurring opinion. Holmes agreed with Justice Day's majority opinion for the Court but he also recognized the limitations of the statute. He pointed out the growing gap between the notion of copyright as a traditional property right and its evolution into a unique property right that was becoming more and more abstract in nature. In his concurring opinion, Holmes politely but directly prodded Congress to widen the scope of the statute to include protection for "machines or anything capable of reproducing the result which gives the invention its meaning and worth."[34]

Fortunately for the music publishers, the wait for their concerns to be incorporated into the law was a short one.

The audio playback of a piano roll in a player piano is a mechanical reproduction of a piece of music. The exclusive right to grant permission to reproduce musical works mechanically was not included in federal copyright law at the time of White-Smith's lawsuit. Beginning in 1905, several music copyright owners turned to Congress and sought the exclusive right to authorize the mechanical reproduction of their works. They noted that under the current law, manufacturers of perforated rolls were allowed to use musical compositions without payment to the copyright owner.

However, prior to the passage of the Copyright Act of 1909, a strategic and somewhat clandestine maneuver executed by a major player-piano retailer with the support of several music publishers came to light in Congress. That crafty move was the bankrolling of publisher White-Smith's case against Apollo by The Aeolian Company, a pioneer in the player-piano industry. This made many in Congress concerned about the possibility of a burgeoning music publishing monopoly.

Founded in July 1887, Aeolian grew to be one of the most successful "Pianola" manufacturers in the industry. Through color advertisements, the company pushed the idea that every home should have a Pianola. Aeolian was also a leader in the manufacture of perforated rolls. The Aeolian Company's involvement in the mechanical sound reproduction issue began in 1902, when it was apparent to many music publishers that piano-roll manufacturers were gaining the financial benefit of the sales of piano rolls without any compensation flowing to the music's composer and/or publisher. Aeolian's motivation behind bankrolling White-Smith was that composers would soon become aware of the potential infringement caused by the piano-roll sales. Aeolian contemplated a possible music publisher victory over the player-piano retailers in the courts that would drastically upset the status quo, causing financial losses to Aeolian as well as a loss of the ability to use compositions to make piano rolls. To avoid this outcome, the company approached the leading music publishers and offered to finance any litigation that would ultimately settle this question in the Supreme Court.

Aeolian offered to pay a royalty to the publishing companies who had entered into the arrangement if the Supreme Court were to determine that piano rolls were copies of musical compositions and their use represented infringement, although no royalty would be paid for past use of copyrighted material. The agreement also stated that if royalties were to be paid, the Aeolian Company would be granted the exclusive right to use the publisher's compositions for its perforated rolls.[35]

Aeolian was successful in getting approximately eighty-seven of the leading music publishers to sign an agreement, although the majority did not. These signatory publishing companies were very interested in the proposal, especially considering that they received no compensation under the then-current copyright and licensing structure. Additionally, many of the publishers were small and had insufficient funds to pay for the litigation required to settle this issue in the courts. Aeolian was hedging its bet while at the same time attempting to corner the piano-roll market.

The existence of contracts with several of the largest music publishers, who together controlled more than 300,000 compositions, demonstrated to Congress the potential for a monopoly in piano rolls. If Aeolian, one of the largest manufacturers, had exclusive control of the compositions of the largest publishers, consumers would gravitate toward Aeolian products. In addition to the broad offerings, there was no industry standard for piano rolls. This meant that a purchaser of Aeolian rolls might be forced to use only Aeolian player pianos, for example. The issue of mechanical reproduction and the possibility of a virtual music publishing cartel holding a monopoly over the music trade, as seen in the Aeolian deal, were included among the hotly discussed topics during the congressional hearings leading up to the passage of the Copyright Act of 1909.

Recording-industry businessmen and musician celebrities, including composer John Philip Sousa, passionately asserted their position on whether there was a need to expand protection. Sousa, famous for marches such as "Semper Fidelis" and the "United States Marine Corps March," had great disdain for mechanical sound reproducers and testified that it was ridiculous that a mechanical reproduction of a song was not protected but the printing and public performance of a song were.[36] Conversely, several congressmen who were against protection for mechanical reproductions of sound believed it to be against the intent of the Constitution's Copyright Clause because it would inhibit the "progress of science."[37] All the while, the burgeoning talking-machine industry was staunchly against such protection. The industry essentially viewed any payment to the music publishers as unjust, because from its perspective the specific act of reproducing a song on a talking machine was more a result of the sound-reproducing technology than any composition.[38]

Finally, when the Copyright Act of 1909 was passed, it included a provision that allowed anyone to make a mechanical reproduction of a copyrighted work without the copyright holder's consent. Fearing a possible publishing monopoly, the mechanical license, which was compulsory, meant that anyone could mechanically reproduce a copyrighted work without having to get permission from the copyright holder, provided the copyright holder was paid a royalty, thus overturning *White-Smith*. The music publishers' argument had been heard and won the day. The mechanical royalty, as it is commonly known today, was firmly in place.

However, one of the big winners may have been the Aeolian Company and the manufacturers of piano rolls. If publisher White-Smith had prevailed over the Apollo Company, Aeolian had agreed to pay a royalty of 10 percent on the sale of perforated rolls to the music publishers who had signed its agreement. Yet the Apollo Company had prevailed, and Congress, after discussing the validity of instituting a mechanical royalty based on sales, instead decided on a statutorily determined royalty rate specifically for mechanical reproductions of sound. As it turned out, the initial statutory rate of two cents was much lower than the royalty rate under Aeolian's offer to music publishers. That initial statutory rate, set in 1909, was unchanged until 1978, when the revised U.S. Copyright Act of 1976 took effect.

Ragtime, Blues, and Jazz: The Birth of Modern Popular Music

Interlude

Though popular music today is a collection of songs offering a vast array of musical genres and styles, much of its core is rock 'n' roll roots and R&B refrains. These indelibly influential genres were themselves borne out of musical styles that were the result of a musical concoction of foreign influences. Each stylistically reflects the arrival of new cultures to American shores during the formative years of the country. This musical mixture, consisting heavily of European and African influences, was sometimes resisted, sometimes welcomed, but its impact on popular music is undeniable. Initially a blend of imported musical cultures, the resulting sounds developed into lasting musical genres that were distinctly American. The blues, ragtime, and jazz were among these primary genres that defined American music.

Captive individuals transported from Africa to the Americas during the transatlantic slave trade first appeared on American shores in the early seventeenth century. By 1860 there were nearly 4 million slaves in the United States.[39] Several elements of various African cultures were transported to America with slaves who survived the middle passage. The brutality and identity-crushing nature of slavery included deliberate attacks, both physical and psychological, designed to erase any connection to Africa or a native culture that a slave might possess. Cultural expressions such as music, song, and dance were not spared.

New musical traditions, linked to their African cultural antecedents, developed within black communities during the nearly three centuries that slavery existed in North America. These traditions were passed down from generation to generation. Though it is certain that many were lost during the years of slavery, many survived.

Slaves and free blacks were often called upon to entertain. They would play for their masters, play music at functions, or entertain white crowds in public. Many in the crowds possessed a curiosity about the seemingly dark and mysterious culture of black people. Slaves on many plantations also found ways to congregate among themselves and sing, dance, and share oral traditions. Common threads existed in the music of African diasporic culture, with the most prominent being the arts of call and response, improvisation, and the playing of an instrument as expressively as the voice.[40] All of these elements could be traced to their African origins as defining features of African oral and musical traditions.

An uncomfortable dichotomy within white slave-holding society toward these black musical traditions existed. Fascination about the culture went hand in hand with blatant disgust and disregard for the culture as being inferior. Furthermore, black awareness of the African origins of their musical culture was viewed by many in white society to be a means of power through identity. Slave owners involved in this continuation of human captivity sought to eradicate any means by which a slave could draw power, because power was a threat to the status quo.

Resourceful slaves, however, utilized any available materials to create musical instruments. Many of these instruments were designed in the vein of instruments some slaves had remembered playing in Africa, or that had been part of traditions passed down from elder slaves. The results were similar to African instruments but constructed out of found and available materials on the slave plantation.

African vocal traditions incorporating group participation and improvisation flourished in slave communities. Hymns adapted from the Christian hymnals of white churches were sung with a new expression. Voices joined in and new harmonies and syncopated rhythms were improvised, and together these elements created music far different from what was written on the hymnal page. Many slaves laboring in the fields of their masters sung "work songs." Often under a hot sun, the slaves performed backbreaking work such as picking cotton, or whatever crop the slave master was trading, from sun up to sun down as the slave overseer stood by to ensure that nobody was slowing down or stopping. The work songs, with their rhythmic call and response form, helped the slaves get through the grueling days.

As with the evolution of most musical traditions, the transition from the music of slavery to the popular musical traditions that derived from it did not follow a clear path. This is true of the birth of blues music, the exact origins of which are probably lost to time. The earliest examples are to be found in recordings made in the 1920s and later.[41] It is likely that the blues tradition itself extends further back into the days during and shortly after slavery, but documentation contemporaneous to the period speaks little of it.

The evolution of the blues began with the solitary singing and self-accompaniment of the "country bluesman."[42] Robert Johnson, Charlie Patton, and Blind Lemon Jefferson are some of the best-known examples of this tradition. Noted for expressive guitar playing and soulful vocal expressiveness, their music tradition is often compared to that of the African griot. The griot, in many African cultures, plays his kora, a stringed instrument made from a carved-out calabash, while singing the stories and history of his village to his people. However, though the bluesmen share similarities with the griot, the style itself is distinctly American.

The early bluesmen also took liberties within a free-flowing genre that would soon define itself structurally. This structure developed as a result of the popularity of the early bluesmen. Typically playing alone, bluesmen like Patton and Johnson did not need to follow a set musical format, because there were no other musicians or vocalists relying on any communicated chord or time changes in the music. As the blues spread beyond the Mississippi Delta region, more instruments were added, and women began to appear at the forefront of these new ensembles. The formation of groups necessitated a formalized musical structure that the band and singer could follow. Hence the twelve-bar structure, a signature chord progression of the blues.

Many female singers, like Mamie Smith, were leaders of this next generation of the blues. It was Mamie Smith's 1920 recording of "That Thing Called Love," a blues tune on the Okeh label, that demonstrated to record labels that there was a market for "black music." Smith's follow-up recording for the Okeh label, "Crazy Blues," sold over one million copies in 1920 and solidified the existence of a market consisting largely of previously ignored black record consumers.[43] Most other record labels set about turning out recordings directed toward this new market.

Ralph Peer, who was a recording director at Okeh records, first coined the term "race records."[44] The name was used to define records that were recorded by black artists with the intent of being sold to black people. Okeh became a leader in the race-record market, although most large record labels created race-record divisions of their own, including Columbia and Victor records. The recordings were not only geared toward a segregated audience but the recordings themselves were contained in a segregated list in a record company's catalog of available titles. This was also true of other recordings within other sidelined traditions such as "hillbilly" or "country" music. Of course, the market for race records was more diverse than the category name would imply. Many white and nonblack consumers were regular purchasers of race records and some were very accessible, with the Sears, Roebuck and Company catalog, for example, carrying several such recordings.[45]

Legendary singer Bessie Smith is recognized as being at the forefront of the intersection of blues and early jazz. She often sang her bluesy style of vocal expression over the more rhythmically complex and improvisation-prone style of a jazz band. However, to move straight from blues to jazz is to leave out an important tradition in this chronology of early popular music: ragtime. To understand ragtime we must journey to New Orleans.

Famously known as the birthplace of jazz, New Orleans was truly a musical melting pot. African cultural expression, a collective expression formed from the many African societies from which the slaves were transported, was able to flourish, in a manner of speaking, in this city. This differed from the other states in the union, where a colonial "protestant ethos," with a strict resistance to any traces of African culture, had been transported from England.[46] This rigidity was a dominant force in the majority of slaveholding states. Generally, efforts to remove the cultural representations of slaves' African identity were systematic and endless. However, New Orleans was just different enough to keep several cultural links in tact.

The African-inspired drumming and singing seen on plantations throughout the South could also be witnessed every Sunday in New Orleans's Congo Square. It was a public square where slaves were allowed to gather, sing, dance, play music, and worship. What was different about New Orleans was that this type of African expression was somewhat more tolerated by white society than in other parts of the country.

New Orleans, the only city in America to have been owned at one time by the French, Spanish, and now the United States, has always been unlike any other American city. While under both French and Spanish rule, New Orleans was a slave city, but it was also a Catholic city. The French and Spanish, just like the British, had been involved in the vulgarities of the slave trade. They too were guilty of gross indignities and violence toward slaves in the New World. However, although tirelessly examined, the reason remains unknown why they, along with the Portuguese in Brazil, were more tolerant of some retention of African culture among the slaves.[47] This "tolerance" permitted the growth of mixed musical forms that were rooted in African culture but also blended European music and other forms as well.

By the late 1890s, New Orleans was brewing musical concoctions that were becoming distinctly American. This musical syncretism can be seen with the mixture of military-style marches combined with the music of the French quadrilles, a type of formal square dance played at high society dances and octoroon balls. This style, mixed with Spanish influences and the pulsating African percussive rhythms and improvisatory stylization, loosened the tight syncopation of the classically rooted quadrille form, creating a new sound that had a swing—ragtime.

Jelly Roll Morton was a New Orleans piano virtuoso who specialized in ragtime and early jazz styles. The combination of his rhythm-pounding left hand and the dexterity-rich melodies he played with his right hand helped create an infectious sound that took hold in popular culture. Early on, this style of playing was known as "ragging" or "ragged time."[48] Scott Joplin, composer of the seminal ragtime tune "The Entertainer," was another great and well-known ragtime player.

The rise of ragtime, a piano-based tradition, seemed to be in lockstep with the rise of the home piano and the soon-to-follow player piano.[49] The prosperity of the industrial age allowed many households to invest in more leisure items such as pianos. Ragtime's popularity lasted from the late nineteenth century until the early 1920s, leading the way for the arrival of the Jazz Age.

Jazz in its earliest forms was rooted in the musical traditions of Africa and New Orleans. F. Scott Fitzgerald once referred to the evolution of jazz in terms of its changing level of respectability as "sex, then dancing, then music."[50] Before jazz was a musical-genre-defining name, some historians believe it was a word used to describe the act of sex.[51] That is, *to jazz* was to have sex. How the term came to describe a style of music is not entirely clear. However, some suggest that the word *jazz*'s supposed sexual connotations and the stimulatingly aggressive music of ragtime were likely, well, bedfellows, though the earliest documented use of the word was decidedly asexual. These early uses came from California newspaper publications using the word to describe "lively" and "energetic" aspects of baseball at the turn of the twentieth century.[52]

It follows that early jazz and ragtime were often indistinguishable. Later, in the 1930s, commenting on jazz music, Jelly Roll Morton stated, "if you can't manage to put tinges of Spanish in your tunes, you will never be able to get the right seasoning, I call it, for jazz."[53] Jazz started coming into its own by combining ragtime musical structures with a full band and more complex improvisation. The great Louis Armstrong, also a product of the culturally rich musical surroundings of New Orleans, brought jazz to new heights. Armstrong, a trumpet player and vocalist, possessed a natural ability to improvise. He built upon his technique to create new and advanced forms of solo improvisation that focused on chord development as opposed to just melody lines.

A defining cultural element during the age of Prohibition in the 1920s and early 1930s, jazz flourished and began to evolve in many directions. Big-band orchestrations like those of Count Basie soon followed. Bebop would later arrive on the jazz scene, as would more experimental and introspective forms of jazz. And it was the groundwork laid by the early forms of the blues, ragtime, and jazz that gave birth to rhythm and blues and later, combined with country music traditions, rock 'n' roll. A musical legacy that started with a collective of African musical elements adapted to a new environment and blended with European and folk traditions gave rise to the rich genres that help define American culture. The legacy of the blues, ragtime, and jazz is lasting and continually evolving.

ASCAP Goes to Court for the First Time

Herbert v. Shanley Co., 242 U.S. 591 (1917).

This story opens with a simple question from a composer to a music publisher. The recipient of the question was a man by the name of George Maxwell, who was the American representative for Recordi, an Italian music publisher. The client was the legendary operatic composer Giacomo Puccini, famous for his operas, including *La Bohème, Tosca,* and *Madame Butterfly.* In 1910 Puccini asked Maxwell to explain to him why he was not receiving royalties when his music was being played inside restaurants and hotels in the United States. Maxwell explained that there was not an organization in existence or the legal authority to collect any performance royalties. Dismayed by this answer, Puccini touted the advantages of his membership in the Italian Society of Authors and Publishers. This simple conversation planted an idea in Maxwell's mind. He needed to find a solution to this problem, which plagued the livelihoods of composers and music publishers.

Nearly one century ago, in New York City, the bright lights of Broadway were just beginning to shine as new theaters and restaurants began to open up throughout the emerging theater district.

Discriminating diners feasted on haute cuisine in grand dining rooms at the finest hotels. It was common for an orchestra or live music ensemble to accompany these fine meals. Music filled the room in restaurants and nightclubs as patrons enjoyed the public performances of their favorite tunes.

All was not well, however. Several composers of those songs filling the air in these busy venues believed they deserved compensation for the public performances of their music. The dilemma that would soon face the courts was whether composers and music publishers were going to be compensated for public performances of their music. Or had the payment already been made with purchase of the sheet music?

By the time Puccini had his conversation with Maxwell, New York City had been gaining significant momentum and was becoming the theater mecca that it is today. In the 1910s, operettas, light and often comedic musical productions, were being performed on the city's stages. Meanwhile, in nearby Tin Pan Alley, music publishers were supplying a steady stream of new tunes to the early Broadway stages and providing sheet-music songs to meet increasing demand. These popular songs were also appearing on records and piano rolls, and they could be heard at nightclubs, restaurants, and hotels, where orchestras entertained guests playing the songs.

George Maxwell, along with several of his fellow music publishers and composer associates, was becoming concerned that many compositions were being played regularly in public venues without permission or compensation for the composers and publishers. These composers and publishers believed that they, as the song's copyright holders, should be receiving some compensation for the public performance of those songs.

They had good reason to feel optimistic about voicing their complaints because just one year prior to Maxwell's conversation with Puccini, music copyright holders had received a victory in the form of the Copyright Act of 1909, which widened the scope of protected works. The newly revised act offered protection to the mechanical reproduction of sound, which at the time included the sound produced by player pianos and phonographs. A compulsory license provision had been created that allowed those wishing to record copyrighted songs to do so, as long as they paid a royalty to the copyright holder. Though this was a welcome development for copyright holders, it did not apply to the public performance problem at hand.

According to music lore, one evening in the fall of 1913, composer Victor Herbert was inside Shanley's Café, a staple Times Square restaurant at the time, when he heard his song "Sweethearts" being played by the house orchestra. Herbert was one of the most prolific composers on Broadway, and "Sweethearts" was a tune from one of his operettas that was enjoying its run in 1913. Herbert was now hearing it played at the restaurant without his permission. He apparently exclaimed in his strong Irish accent, "If they'll do this to my stuff when I can afford expensive lawyers, what aren't they doing to the others? We've got to look after the b'ys[sic]."[54]

Herbert's contributions to the early American musical stage cannot be overstated. Moving to New York City from his native Dublin, Ireland, in 1886, he quickly became a sought-after conductor. His wife had traveled with him from Dublin and was an operatic soprano from Vienna who had been given a contract with the Metropolitan Opera. In addition to his conducting abilities, he was a cellist and a composer. His cello playing was featured on several recordings released by the Victor Talking Machine Company. Original compositions included well-known contributions to the American songbook, including the sweeping "Ah! Sweet Mystery of Life," "Gypsy Love Song," and the holiday favorite "Babes in Toyland." In 1927, three years after Herbert's death, a statue of him, commissioned by ASCAP, was unveiled in Central Park, where it stands to this day.

Herbert knew George Maxwell because they were both immersed in the inner circle of music publishers and composers. Maxwell had previously told his lawyer, Nathan Burkan, of his conversation with Puccini. Herbert organized a meeting inviting concerned composers and publishers to find a solution to their copyright problem and discuss the possibility of forming an American collection society for the benefit of music publishers and composers. Maxwell and Burkan were among the invitees. The first meeting was held in October of 1913 at Luchow's restaurant in New York City. Luchow's was *the* place for the theater set and one of the largest dining rooms in the city. Unfortunately, inclement weather and blustery winds limited the attendance to only five people.

Herbert tried again and convened a meeting on February 13, 1914, at the Hotel Claridge in New York. This time more than one hundred music publishers and songwriters attended. It officially became the charter meeting of the new American Society of Composers, Authors, and Publishers, or as it is commonly known, ASCAP. Founding members of this new royalty-collection society included music luminaries such as famed composers Irving Berlin and John Philip Sousa. George Maxwell became the first president of ASCAP, with Victor Herbert serving as the vice president and Nathan Burkan as general counsel.

ASCAP set up an office near Times Square shortly after its charter. The goal was to serve as a clearinghouse for music-copyright holders and provide licenses for public venues, particularly the offending hotels and restaurants, to use the work of their members. The licensing process involved music-copyright holders giving their permission exclusively to ASCAP to license their music for use by the venues. The venues would in turn pay for a license from ASCAP that would allow them to play all of the music in the ASCAP library.

ASCAP was now up and running. However, for as much passion as there was behind the objectives, there was very little enforcement power to match. Initial efforts to implement the licensing system with venues had limited success. Since there was no legal authority to enforce the licensing system, the strategy became one of trying to persuade the venues to enter voluntarily into the licensing agreements. Some hotels and restaurants acquiesced and willingly purchased licenses from ASCAP. However, the income derived from the licenses was minimal, barely enough to maintain the ASCAP office and definitely not enough to pay out royalties to its members.

To make matters worse, many venues were adamantly against having to pay for a license at all. Generally, those venues did not believe that they should have to compensate copyright holders for playing their music.[55] After all, they paid for the sheet music—wasn't that compensation enough? Didn't the sheet-music purchase give the venue an implied license to use the song?

Turning to the courts appeared to be the only way to try and gain any real persuasive power in the form of legal backing for ASCAP. Several months later, music publisher The John Church Music Company, on behalf of John Philip Sousa, filed suit against the Hilliard Hotel Company in the U.S. District Court for the Southern District of New York.[56] Nathan Burkan served as the music publisher's lawyer. The lawsuit was filed on the grounds that one of Hilliard's properties, the Vanderbilt Hotel in New York City, had an orchestra play one of Sousa's songs in the dining room during meal times. The song was titled "From Maine to Oregon" and was from an operetta by Sousa.

The question before the trial court was whether the hotel had performed Sousa's song for profit. Under the Copyright Act of 1909, the copyright holder had the exclusive right to publicly perform his or her work if the performance was "for profit." Also, the song was protected as part of Sousa's full operetta in the dramatic-work category of the act.[57] But Sousa, like many other composers, also held a copyright on the song alone, separate from the operetta music book. The song had also been released as a single on sheet music.

The court granted a preliminary injunction against the hotel and eventually ruled in favor of the music publisher, finding that the hotel did perform the song "for profit." The Hilliard Hotel Company appealed, and in February of 1915, the Circuit Court of Appeals for the Second Circuit instead ruled in favor of the hotel. The reasoning was that customers came to the hotel not for the music but to dine and pay only for the food.[58] In reaching this conclusion, the court drew an analogy to the public performance of music with coin-operated machines. The court did so citing what later came to be known as the "jukebox exemption."[59] This exempted the public performance of music from these machines from being considered for profit unless an admission fee was charged.[60]

Jukebox as a colloquial term would not be prevalent until the 1940s. In the early 1900s, the coin-operated machines referred to by Congress were film, game, and novelty machines, as well as player pianos, found in "penny arcades," which as the name suggests were establishments that charged a penny to operate a machine. Drawing similarities between the music in a penny arcade and the venues where the public performance of music occurred, the circuit court found that the music played in a restaurant, nightclub, or hotel was a part of the general ambience of the establishment and that further, because there was no admission fee, the music was not a public performance for profit.

The ruling was a blow to ASCAP and was perhaps particularly poignant because it was the first case supported by the new organization. However, things were just getting started. A few months after the ruling was announced, a second lawsuit was filed. Victor Herbert, with the support of ASCAP, filed a lawsuit against Shanley's Café, the restaurant where he had heard his music being played without his permission two years earlier. Once again Nathan Burkan took the helm as lawyer. The song at issue was Herbert's "Sweethearts," which, like Sousa's song in *Hilliard*, was from an operetta of the same name as the song. "Sweethearts" had also been separately copyrighted and released as a single on sheet music.

Like Sousa's challenge, Herbert's case was filed in the U.S. District Court for the Southern District of New York. Though the circuit court of appeals had ultimately ruled against the music publisher in that case, Herbert was determined to show that his case could be victorious under the law. Since the appellate court had recently ruled that the "for profit" analysis would not apply to a situation like Herbert's, Burkan instead argued that under section (d) of the Copyright Act, Herbert's song would be protected because section (d) gave the copyright holder the exclusive right to perform dramatic works publicly. Burkan believed that because this section would apply to the entire *Sweethearts* operetta, it should logically apply to the public performance of just one song from it, even though that song had been copyrighted separately as a single.

The Shanley Company, using the court's ruling in *Hilliard*, responded by arguing that because it did not charge an admission fee, the playing of Herbert's music could not be considered a performance for profit. The company also stated that not only was the hired singer who performed the tune not a professional actress, but the platform upon which the orchestra played was not truly a real stage, so again it was not a true performance. Lastly, Shanley emphasized that the orchestra played "Sweethearts" from sheet music that had been published as a musical composition separate from the full songbook for the *Sweetheart* operetta and was therefore not protected as a dramatic work.

In a ruling delivered by Judge Learned Hand, the district court held that although a performance in a restaurant is not a performance for profit, the entire dramatic work, the operetta, is protected under the copyright act. However, the court also said that by publishing the song separately, Herbert had given up his "dramatic" rights in the song. As such, on its own, Herbert's song would be infringed upon only if Shanley's had played it for profit, and the court found that it had not. Herbert's lawsuit was dismissed.

Herbert appealed the decision only to have the circuit court of appeals affirm the trial court's decision.[61] In January of 1917, both the John Church Company case and Herbert's case were consolidated and heard by the Supreme Court. In perhaps one of the shortest Supreme Court opinions on record, Justice Oliver Wendell Holmes Jr. delivered a three-paragraph opinion that reversed the lower courts and held in favor of the John Church Company and Victor Herbert.

The Court expressly stated that it did not find it necessary to look at the issue of the separate copyrights held for each of the songs as singles. Instead, Justice Holmes got right to the point and stated that the purpose of the restaurants and hotels engaging musicians to play songs in their establishments was to add to the venues' ambience, and any benefit the music provided was not separable from the food or service that the patron had paid for. The opinion may have been short, but Holmes still managed to sprinkle in a touch of his celebrated wit. The opinion read in part:

It is true that the music is not the sole object, but neither is the food, which probably could be got cheaper elsewhere. The object is a repast in surroundings that people having

48

> limited powers of conversation, or disliking rival noise, give a luxurious pleasure not to be had from eating a silent meal.[62]

Justice Holmes's opinion was direct, to the point, and written without citing any case law or statutes. The Court found that the hotel and restaurant were using the music for their own profits, and as such, these types of public music performances fell under the protection of the Copyright Act.

This decision was the victory that both Victor Herbert and ASCAP sought. ASCAP was now emboldened with the legal backing to procure licenses from hotels and restaurants for playing the music of ASCAP's members. What developed out of this practice was the "blanket license." This renewable license allowed a venue to play songs from the entire ASCAP catalog in exchange for the payment of a fee. The blanket license practice is still used today.

ASCAP has continued to grow and now boasts a membership of over 450,000 members.[63] In the years following the Supreme Court's decision, the scope of the for-profit designation for public performances of musical compositions has widened dramatically. First to be included within the for-profit designation following the decision were the live piano accompaniments played along to silent films. This was followed by the inclusion of music playing within the films once "talkies" hit the big screen. The for-profit designation has since widened to everything from music played on the radio to the ambient music in shopping malls. In just three short paragraphs, Justice Holmes's words had a profound effect on copyright law as applied to the music industry.

He aptly completed his opinion by stating, "If music did not pay, it would be given up. If it pays, it pays out of the public's pocket. Whether it pays or not, the purpose of employing it is profit, and that is enough."[64]

Edwin H. Armstrong:

The Ballad of the FM Radio Patent

The twentieth century opened with optimism in the American dream that became, for many, a feverish passion arguably unmatched in any previous period. A slice of the American dream seemed tangible and within reach, provided one had a competitive spirit and a desire to rise to the top. For some, their desire led them to look upward and envision the possibilities of wireless communication. They knew that the air and sky would be the new roads for transporting sounds and voices from distant origins into intimate spaces in the home. For these innovators, radio was the future.

The story of radio's rise begins innocently enough, with a fascination with wireless telegraph communications leading to entrepreneurial dreams of expanded global communications. At the center of the story is Edwin H. Armstrong. His contributions to radio technology included the creation of FM radio, which resulted in the clearest radio reception then possible. FM radio, however, which is now an essential element of radio broadcasting, almost never saw the light of day. Armstrong's efforts to disseminate his technology were frustrated by the bruised egos of his competitors, betrayal of a former close friend and ally, long-lasting legal battles, and ultimately Armstrong's tragic death. As a result, the man who is considered by some to be to radio what Thomas Edison was to the light bulb remains largely unknown.

Edwin H. Armstrong was born into a large family living in the Chelsea district in New York City prior to the turn of the twentieth century. It was by all accounts an idyllic childhood. He was surrounded by his extended family, who lived in the brownstones near his own, and he spent a large portion of his time attending church, where his family members were also very active. As the Chelsea neighborhood began to change with the arrival of more commerce and the increasing crowds of newly settled New Yorkers, the family relocated to nearby Yonkers, New York, where they had purchased a large Victorian house. It was in that house that Armstrong would spend many hours in the attic fascinated with technology.

Although Armstrong's childhood was happy, he was largely a solitary youth. His preference for solitude is in part attributed to a bout with rheumatic fever when he was a small child.[65] The illness left him with a permanent tick that became more pronounced when he was excited or agitated.

When he was thirteen years old, a popular science book called *The Boy's Book of Inventions* became a fascination. The book detailed the major progress in science from the late nineteenth century to the early twentieth century. Complete with illustrations, it told the story of scientific luminaries such as the Wright Brothers and their invention of flight. Armstrong was mesmerized by it all, but what caught his attention in particular were the developments in the field of wireless communication. From the moment he read about wireless, he was hooked, and he knew that wireless technology would be his field of pursuit.

From his attic room Armstrong, like many other amateur radio enthusiasts during that era, spent hours tinkering around with crystal sets, rudimentary radios that could receive sound waves from far distances. Armstrong could often be found climbing the roof of his house or nearby poles installing antennae to increase the reception of these sound waves. At one point he installed a 125-foot antenna at his home in order to get reception from far-away locations.

In 1909 he went to college at Columbia University. A towering figure in stature, Armstrong was confident and exuberant. He lived at home in Yonkers while attending college but could easily be spotted on the road to Columbia on his red motorcycle, which he rode to school every day. In class Armstrong, who was majoring in engineering, was keen to learn but also willing to question his professors' theories and assertions. Most professors found this to be bothersome, but one professor, Michael I. Pupin, saw in Armstrong a strong and adventurous mind, and he supported Armstrong's drive and curiosity.

One night in 1912 while in his attic room in Yonkers, Armstrong had his first major breakthrough. "I've done it!" he shouted as he danced and jumped around into his sister's bedroom.[66] Armstrong was celebrating his success in creating the best radio amplification at the time. He had created the regeneration circuit. His bedroom invention, the result of experiments conducted on an Audion tube given to him by Pupin, is considered to be the most important development in radio. By feeding a radio signal through a radio tube multiple times, the signal increased in power with every pass through the tube. Armstrong knew his discovery was groundbreaking.

He would soon also discover that by increasing the feedback beyond its critical level, the tube would oscillate and create its own radio waves, which made it possible to both transmit and receive radio waves. Yet while he celebrated his discoveries, a serious problem was brewing. His regeneration circuit invention was based on an already existing piece of technology invented by Lee de Forest. De Forest had invented his Audion tube nine years earlier, in 1903. A wireless innovator himself, de Forest's invention was created as a radio-signal detector and amplifier. His Audion tube was based on a vacuum tube developed by John Ambrose Fleming.[67] Unfortunately for de Forest, he did not fully understand the capabilities of his invention. Instead, Armstrong would improve on the existing features of the Audion tube, as well as make it possible for the tube to transmit radio signals, ensuring that the wireless sound transmission would reach its full potential.

After graduating from Columbia, Armstrong continued his work in radio development. On February 1, 1914, he spent the evening demonstrating his regeneration circuit to a sharp, up-and-coming executive from the powerful Marconi Company at the company's lab in Monmouth, New Jersey. The executive, David Sarnoff, was a self-made man. He had immigrated to the Unites States as a child, having grown up in a shtetl in Russia. Emboldened with a deep drive and desire for success, Sarnoff started his career as a newspaper boy on the streets of New York. By the time he was fourteen, he called the shots as the owner of his own newsstand. Shortly thereafter he became the best telegrapher at the Marconi Company, where he so immensely impressed Mr. Marconi himself with his drive and abilities that by the age of twenty-one, Sarnoff had his own office in midtown New York. He was chief inspector for the Marconi Company in charge of new technological acquisitions.

That fateful February night, upon seeing the circuit's capability, Sarnoff knew he was witnessing the future. He went back to Marconi and tried to advise him to buy the regeneration circuit. However, Marconi, lacking the visionary abilities of Sarnoff, declined. Seemingly sharing a similar drive and interest in promoting radio technology, a deep friendship formed that night between Armstrong and Sarnoff. Yet the relationship of the two kindred spirits would grow strained and rancorous over the following decades.

Meanwhile, de Forest was very aware of and extremely angry about Armstrong's experiments and success with the regeneration circuit. He was angry because he believed that Armstrong had stolen his invention, and he was also embarrassed that he had not discovered its capabilities. This was particularly upsetting for de Forest because though he had demonstrated superior intellectual abilities throughout his life, he had also struggled greatly in the social arena. He did not seem to fit in anywhere. In fact, his college classmates voted him the "nerdiest and homliest" member in the class.[68] His intellectual pursuits were one of the few areas where he saw the potential to find success and achieve recognition.

Like both Sarnoff and Armstrong, de Forest's goal was to bring radio into the home and make money doing so. When Armstrong received his patent for the regeneration circuit in 1913, de Forest was livid to say the least. De Forest tried twice to obtain a patent on a slightly altered version of the Audion tube called the "ultra-audion." He was denied a patent because the ultra-audion was considered to be too similar to Armstrong's regeneration circuit. De Forest then turned to the courts. He argued that the regeneration circuit was in fact his own invention but he had simply not taken the time to get a patent for it. His patent lawsuit against Armstrong, which began in 1915, would turn out to be the longest patent lawsuit in history.

Just prior to the filing of de Forest's lawsuit, World War I erupted and the United States was flung into the global conflict. The government froze all patent lawsuits. Wireless communication played an essential role in the war effort, and the government commandeered all wireless transmitters. Throughout the war Armstrong continued his work. He had also enlisted in the U.S. Army and was stationed in Paris, where he served in the Signal Corps.

While the war pressed on, Armstrong developed the super-heterodyne. This invention "captured radio waves of very high frequency and combined them with low frequency waves to create a new wave which was amplified several times vastly increasing the sensitivity of all receivers."[69] The superheterodyne was another major development in wireless communication, and Armstrong received a promotion to major for his efforts. It is a standard piece of radio technology to this day. He sold the superhetero-dyne to RCA, the head of which was his friend Sarnoff. The sale made Armstrong the largest single shareholder in the company. A little while later he married Marion MacInnis, Sarnoff's secretary.

After the war, the de Forest patent infringement lawsuit against Armstrong resumed. Armstrong won the first of many court battles. To say that he was pleased by this turn of events would be an understatement. He let his victory flag fly, literally. In celebration of his win over de Forest, he flew a flag in front of his home that had the number of the contested patent on it.

In 1920 Westinghouse, which had a patent-sharing arrangement with RCA, used the superheterodyne to broadcast the first entertainment radio broadcast on Pittsburgh's KDKA, the nation's first licensed radio station. Radio broadcasting was about to explode. However, it was a broadcast that took place a year later that would establish radio programming as a permanent fixture in leisure activities.

RCA, in possession of Armstrong's superheterodyne patent, was in position to supply the increasing demand for home radio sets. In 1921, Sarnoff arranged for a live radio broadcast of the highly anticipated heavyweight boxing championship fight between defending champion Jack Dempsey and challenger Georges Carpentier. Sarnoff, correctly predicting the interest in a live radio broadcast, was elated when the fight drew hundreds of thousands of home radio-set listeners. Listeners were riveted as Carpentier went down in a fourth-round knockout and Dempsey held on to his title. After the fight, the sales of home radio sets skyrocketed, and Sarnoff was hailed a hero in the radio business. A few years later he helped to create the National Radio Broadcasting Company, NBC, and coordinated live coverage of international aviator Charles Lindbergh's historic return flight to the United States from Paris.

By 1930 the stock market had collapsed and America was enduring the Great Depression. However Armstrong was a very wealthy man during this time. He was on the faculty at Columbia University but received an annual salary of only one dollar, which enabled him to focus solely on his research and not have to worry about teaching classes and publishing papers. All appeared to be going well. He was happily married, his inventions were doing well in the public sphere, and his friendship with Sarnoff, the star-broadcasting executive with the Midas touch, seemed solid.

In 1933 Armstrong's peace of mind was shattered, when de Forest's lawsuit against him was resumed on appeal to the Supreme Court. On an "arcane legal question," the Supreme Court found in favor of de Forest. It held that de Forest was the inventor of the regeneration circuit and not Armstrong. Armstrong's peers were shocked, with several pointing out that Lee de Forest, according to his own testimony, did not even fully understand how the regeneration circuit worked. Nevertheless the decision was final, and at the end of this nearly twenty-year patent battle, Armstrong had lost his regeneration circuit patent. He was devastated.

At an engineering convention soon after the Supreme Court's decision, Armstrong attempted to return a medal that had been given to him for his work. The convention body would not take it back and instead gave Armstrong a standing ovation. The general consensus was that Armstrong had been robbed of his invention.

Despite the regeneration circuit setback, Armstrong kept pressing ahead. On Christmas Eve, 1933, he invited Sarnoff to his laboratory in Columbia's Philosophy Hall. There he demonstrated his new invention, radio without static. He called his new invention FM radio. FM, which stands for *frequency modulation*, was capable of providing a clear broadcast. *AM* stands for *amplitude modulation*. Prior to FM's invention, AM had been the broadcasting standard, but it always delivered static-filled transmissions. Most in the field of radio at the time believed that static was an inevitability, and that there was no way of removing it from a transmission. Armstrong discovered that if he widened the frequency band, the reception would improve. The improved sound was so clear that if a match was struck on air "you could tell if [it] was a paper match or a wooden match."[70] FM was the real game changer and Sarnoff knew it. However, this time Sarnoff would not be supportive of this new creation, or Armstrong.

Sarnoff had previously given Armstrong space on the top of the Empire State Building to conduct field tests of his FM system, which included sending out transmissions from the Empire State Building to trusted locations. Sarnoff was threatened by Armstrong's revolutionary FM development, and his company, RCA, was strained financially because it was spending a large amount of money on the development of television. The National Broadcasting Company, NBC, a subsidiary of RCA at the time, was the primary source of its income due to its radio-set sales. All of the radio sets were built for AM transmissions. So FM, in Sarnoff's mind, was a direct threat to his income stream and therefore his plans for television. He was determined to protect his business interests and aspirations, which, in his mind, meant stopping Armstrong from exploiting FM. His first move against Armstrong was reclaiming the space in the Empire State Building. Sarnoff told Armstrong that he needed the space for greater TV trials.

Armstrong applied to the FCC for permission to build an experimental FM station. There was a general belief at the time that people would not pay for high-fidelity programming. Amazingly, the FCC was successfully lobbied to deny Armstrong's request. His FM radio permit was denied for being a "visionary development" and of no real practical value.[71] Yet still determined, Armstrong was granted a permit when he threatened to take his FM trials overseas.

He set up camp on the New Jersey Palisades, where he built a radio tower in Alpine. In 1939 his new network, the Yankee Network, began broadcasting from Alpine. Armstrong hoped that his network would grow to be as large as NBC. It certainly had the potential to do so.

FM was catching on quickly. After the Yankee Network was up and running, Sarnoff offered Armstrong one million dollars for the rights to have RCA manufacture FM radios. Armstrong denied Sarnoff's request, believing that Sarnoff should pay royalties for the privilege of manufacturing FM radios, just as other companies were doing. However, Armstrong's declination of Sarnoff's offer did not really matter in the end. RCA established its own FM radio development team and began selling FM radios without paying for a license from Armstrong, therefore ignoring Armstrong's FM radio patent.

Once again war intervened and interrupted daily life. When the United States entered World War II, Armstrong, who was commonly referred to as "the Major," gave the U.S. government a license on his patents and also waived any royalty payments to assist with the war effort. During the war, commercial radio-set production was halted in order to meet the demands of the war. When the war was over, commercial production resumed, but now several companies were moving ahead with FM radio sales and opting to ignore Armstrong's patent and failing to pay him royalties.

By this time, Armstrong's patent was nearing its expiration date, which was in 1950.

Then the ax fell. In January of 1945, the FCC delivered a shocking proposal. It proposed to move the FM frequency to the 100-megahertz range. Up until this point FM had sat comfortably between 42 and 50 megahertz. A move to the upper range would have an immediately devastating effect on FM radio because the overwhelming majority of radio sets were built for a lower range. The reason given for this proposed move was to protect the FM frequencies from sunspots. The FCC stated that it needed to be done quickly because the "height of the sunspot cycle was supposed to occur between 1948–1949."[72] The megahertz frequency where FM had been located was scheduled, not likely by coincidence, to be given to television.

The FCC held hearings over the issue and established a Radio Technical Planning Board. It voted twenty-seven to one in favor of not moving the FM frequencies. Yet the board's determination made little difference. The FCC approved the move in 1945 for FM's "own good."[73] The growing portion of the radio industry that had been built around FM technology was instantly flung to the brink of extinction and faced with having to rebuild itself all over again. This was good news for Sarnoff, however. His RCA/NBC companies were now secure because the decision "protect(ed) the status quo in radio while providing spectrum space for the expansion of television."[74]

Determined as ever not to back down, Armstrong appealed to the court for a resolution to his grievances. In 1948 he sued RCA and NBC for conspiring to influence the FCC to stifle the development of radio. Sarnoff was prepared for a legal battle and established a team of lawyers to fight the claims. The litigation lasted for several years. Sarnoff's litigation strategy included subjecting Armstrong to extensive and largely unnecessary interrogatories. This contributed to the length of the already long and drawn-out prelitigation proceedings. At the same time, RCA and NBC were growing by leaps and bounds. By the early 1950s, radio, although waning, was still popular, but TV was being beamed into living rooms around the world. RCA and NBC were at the forefront of the industry. Flush with cash, Sarnoff and his lawyers could keep Armstrong tied up in litigation for a long time.

Armstrong on the other hand was suffering. His FM radio patent had expired in 1950. He had not received royalty payments from the many companies who profited from his technology. Slowly his wealth began to disappear as he fought his extended legal battles with RCA and NBC. His health was deteriorating and the strong and innovative spirit that had served him well through the years was rapidly fading. He once exclaimed, "They will stall this along until I am dead or broke."[75]

By 1953 he had already spent another one million dollars fighting his case. His legal team believed he would ultimately win, but that it would take another nine years or so. This prognosis proved to be a breaking point for Armstrong. On Thanksgiving night in 1953, he uncharacteristically had a fight with his wife Marion and swung a fire poker at her, which hit her on the arm. Marion, who had been driven to the point of mental exhaustion from Armstrong's legal ordeals, left her husband to go and live with relatives.[76] Days passed during that dark holiday season, and Armstrong was truly distraught.

Sunday night, January 31, 1954, Armstrong wrote a letter to his wife. "I deeply regret what has happened to us . . . I would give my life to turn back to the time when we were so happy and free," he wrote. "God keep you and may the Lord have mercy on my soul."[77] Dressed for the cold air outside, he put on his coat, scarf, hat, and gloves. He then stepped out the window of his thirteenth-floor apartment. A maintenance man on a third-floor terrace found his body the next morning.

Shocked upon hearing of Armstrong's death, Sarnoff stated, "I did not kill Armstrong!" Once friends, Sarnoff and Armstrong's alliance had ended tragically. The morning of Armstrong's death was February 1, 1954. Just forty years prior to his death, on that same date in 1914, an exuberant Armstrong had spent the evening with Sarnoff, then a rising executive, in Monmouth, New Jersey, as Armstrong demonstrated his regeneration circuit by picking up signals from around the world. Over the years they had both commemorated that fateful February night in 1914 by sending telegrams to one another, always on February 1, reminding each other of that night when their friendship was forged. One such telegram from Armstrong to Sarnoff sent in 1934 read, "This is the night we first met and how wonderful it was and it's created this long and enduring friendship."[78]

After Armstrong's death, his widow, Marion, took up his legal battles. In addition to his battle with RCA and NBC, Armstrong had filed lawsuits against twenty-one companies that he believed owed him royalty payments for the use of his FM technology. By 1967 Marion had won every single one. Although Armstrong did not live long enough to see it, he was victorious in the end. The father of modern radio as we know it, Armstrong's innovations brought radio into the homes of millions, but the Armstrong name, as of now, is not a household name.

PART TWO

1940s–1950s

Playback

1940	• U.S. President Franklin Delano Roosevelt is elected to a third term.
1941	• Japan bombs Pearl Harbor and the United States enters World War II.
1942	• Bing Crosby's recording of "White Christmas" becomes the bestselling record of all time—a title it will hold for the next fifty years.
1943	• Rodgers and Hammerstein's musical *Oklahoma* debuts on Broadway.
1945	• Bluegrass-style music becomes popular following the release of Bill Monroe's "Kentucky Waltz." • World War II ends.
1947	• Chess Records and Atlantic Records are established and focus on R&B and black music.
1948	• *The Ed Sullivan Show* debuts with its original title –"Toast of the Town" • Columbia Records introduces the 33⅓ rpm record.
1949	• RCA Victor Records introduces the 45 rpm record.
1951	• "Rocket 88," considered the first rock 'n' roll song, is released by Jackie Brenston and his Delta Cats.
1953	• Elvis makes his first demo recordings at Sun Records in Memphis, "My Happiness" and "That's When Your Heartaches Begin."
1955	• Rosa Parks is arrested in Montgomery, Alabama, after refusing to give up her seat to a white passenger on a city bus.

1956	• Verve Records is founded to promote jazz.
1958	• Iconic photo *A Great Day in Harlem*, featuring jazz greats, is taken. • Recording Industry Association of America (RIAA) establishes the "gold" record designation for singles or albums selling over 500,000 copies.
1959	• Motown Records is founded in Detroit, Michigan. • Buddy Holly dies in a plane crash at the age of twenty-two, along with Ritchie Valens and the Big Bopper.

What Monopoly?
Radio Music Licensing Battles and the ASCAP "Boycott" of 1941

U.S. v. ASCAP, 1940–43 Trade Cas. ¶ 56,104 (S.D.N.Y. 1941).

U.S. v. Broadcast Music, Inc., 1940–43 Trade Cas. ¶ 56,096 (E.D. Wisc. 1941).

It was the 1930s and popular music was more accessible than ever. Radio, which had been broadcast for the first time just a decade earlier, was garnering fans by the millions and becoming a stronghold in American entertainment. The music played over the airwaves seemed to be changing just as quickly as the technology upon which it was played. The exuberant Jazz Age of the 1920s, which brought with it the birth of jazz music and party dances like the Charleston, had been replaced by the Great Depression, a period during which many struggled to survive after the stock market crash of 1929.

The economic decline lasted almost four years. During that time, record sales suffered more than the overall economy, declining almost 90 percent from their 1929 peak to the bottom in 1935. The recovery in record sales was slow, and sales did not return to pre-Depression levels for another ten years. Even during those trying times, recording artists such as Billie Holiday, Judy Garland, Glenn Miller, Duke Ellington, and the Carter Family continued to release music demanded by the public. Despite approximately one-third of households having access to a record player, few could afford the cost of records. However, there was no medium that both satisfied and continued to stimulate the appetite for popular music like radio.

Since the first commercial radio broadcast in 1920 on Pittsburgh's KDKA, radio had been on an upward trajectory in popularity. It had established itself as a primary form of entertainment around the world. Through radio, people could hear a wide variety of programming, ranging from their national and local news to the latest celebrity gossip. The radio listener could tune in to hear actors performing dramatic and comedic plays and short stories. The stories were brought to life with colorful and descriptive dialogue, combined with creative in-studio sound effects. These characterizations helped create detailed visualizations that were limited only by the listener's imagination. Radio broadcasts could be enjoyed anywhere. Many families spent time gathered together around the radio enjoying their favorite programs. The constant airplay of music was a common thread among radio programs. In these early days, as radio was coming into its golden age, the music used for programming was licensed, in large part, by the music catalog of the Association of Composers, Authors, and Publishers (ASCAP).

ASCAP had been in existence since 1914, when it was formed out of a need to protect and police the right of public performance belonging to the composers and publishers of a song under U.S. copyright law. It monitored the public performance of music belonging to its members. To control the public performances, members would exclusively grant ASCAP the public performance right of their compositions. Although the public performance right was transferred to ASCAP, the member and copyright owner retained the separate rights of reproduction, making new versions, distribution, and inclusion in media such as film or television. With the public performance rights, ASCAP could then issue a license to a profit-making organization that wished to use the music in its catalog. Upon payment of a negotiated fee, ASCAP would grant the organization a "blanket license," giving it the right to play any song in the catalog.

The benefits of a blanket license were very desirable for radio stations, considering that ASCAP held the public performance rights for more than 75 percent of popular music at the time.[79] The blanket licenses were priced on an annual basis. In the infancy of commercial radio, the licenses were granted to individual radio stations for free or for a very low cost. As radio's popularity grew, ASCAP began to require more substantial licensing fees from radio stations. Although the annual licensing fee remained a flat fee, disputes arose between radio stations and ASCAP over what amount constituted a fair licensing fee. These disputes were typically settled on a station-by-station basis. In 1932, the disputes between ASCAP and the stations reached a boiling point that threatened to disrupt access to the ASCAP catalog and alter the way the business of music licensing was conducted.

ASCAP attempted to streamline the radio blanket-license process while at the same time increasing the blanket-license fee in 1932. Until this time, ASCAP had earned approximately $1 million per year from the annual blanket-licensing fees.[80] The radio stations were notified that, going forward, in addition to the annual fee, the total cost of the blanket licensing fee would now include a percentage of the station's gross receipts. The percentage was to be determined on a sliding scale, with payments equaling three percent of the station's gross receipts in the first year of the contract and then increasing one percentage point each year during the remainder of a three-year term. This gross-receipts rule applied to all of a station's programming, even if it used no music from the ASCAP catalog.

The radio stations, unsurprisingly, were taken aback by this new fee structure and scrambled to avoid the increase. They were able to stall the effective date of the new blanket license by about four months but had to face the realization that no other sources provided the wide variety of popular music in the ASCAP catalog. Most importantly, the radio shows had to go on. Reluctantly, the stations agreed to the increase and signed the new three-year contracts.

Despite the existence of signed contracts, the tension between the radio industry and ASCAP remained. Radio stations resented the fact that ASCAP controlled such a large share of popular music. The contract disputes sent up red flags, which garnered the attention of the U.S. Department of Justice. Concerned that ASCAP was becoming a monopoly with the power to dominate the radio industry, the Department of Justice filed a lawsuit against ASCAP under the Sherman Antitrust Act in 1934.[81] ASCAP proposed locking in the terms of the 1932 contract and extending its term for five years out of concern over the ramifications of a negative court ruling.

The only difference between the five-year contract and the previous three-year contract was that the percentage owed to ASCAP from the gross receipts would be set at 5 percent for each year instead of on a sliding scale.[82] The radio broadcasters agreed to this offer and entered into the extended contracts. The last-minute deal occurred just as the antitrust trial was to begin. With the deal in place, the trial was scuttled.

Even with the new contract, the radio broadcasters remained upset with what they perceived to be ASCAP's rapidly increasing powers as a music-copyright monopoly. Because immediate action by the federal government against ASCAP appeared unlikely, the radio broadcasters turned to the National Association of Broadcasters (NAB) to make their case.

The National Association of Broadcasters, a trade association for radio broadcasters, was working to curb ASCAP's continuing licensing fee increases. The organization, founded in 1922, was an umbrella organization that served the interests of the major radio networks such as NBC and CBS. NAB viewed ASCAP as a powerful and influential organization possessing too much leverage in its ability to set prices for music licensing, and as such ASCAP was an obstacle to greater revenue for the networks. NAB lobbied tirelessly and forcefully at the state level for the passage of laws that would prevent ASCAP from being able to grant licenses in those states. NAB's strategy was to cut off ASCAP's source of income and eventually cause its collapse. NAB's efforts were partly successful in several states.

In Nebraska, for example, NAB successfully lobbied the state legislature to pass a law effectively barring ASCAP from doing business in the state. The law, passed in 1937, banned "declared associations of a substantial number of the total number of composers, authors and owners of musical copyrights in the United States to be unlawful if one of the purposes of the organization was to fix prices."[83] ASCAP moved into fighting mode and began a state campaign of its own to push back on the attacks.

In response to the Nebraska statute, Gene Buck, the president of ASCAP, was able to secure an injunction preventing the enforcement of the statute. The U.S. District Court for the District of Nebraska granted the injunction on the basis that a section of the Nebraska statute was unconstitutional because it allowed people to freely use copyrighted material without liability if the copyright holder did not first comply with certain steps prior to the sale of the copyrighted material.[84] Furthermore, the court found that the statute was not separable and therefore, because one part of it had been held to be invalid, the statute failed as a whole. The U.S. Supreme Court soon overturned the lower court's decision on review.[85] The Court found that the statute was indeed separable and within the state's power to prohibit monopolies. Although the statute was left to stand, the Court left open the question of whether the statute was constitutional.

The Supreme Court ruling was a victory for NAB. However, the victory was short-lived. Soon after, a music publisher that was also a member of ASCAP, filed an independent infringement action at the state level against Nebraska residents who it believed had used music from ASCAP without paying a licensing fee.[86] This time the district court in Nebraska was very careful with its findings. Emboldened by the Supreme Court's confirmation of the states' power to regulate monopolies within their borders, the district court specifically ruled that the section of the anti-ASCAP statute that had permitted the use of the copyrighted music without permission from the copyright holder was invalid. The statute, being separable, would still stand, but it was now completely gutted and ineffective. It would eventually be repealed and replaced with a law requiring a "3% tax on the gross sales of performing licenses and [the] registration of copyrighted material licensed in the state."[87]

In 1939, radio was in its golden age. Popular shows featuring the comedy duo Abbott and Costello and the comic-book hero Superman were huge hits, but the majority of on-air time was spent playing music. These programs continuously churned out the popular songs of the day over the airwaves. Radio stations played selections such as swing recordings of popular big-band orchestras, as well as recordings featuring a "new" Latin beat that had made its way from Cuba to achieve great popularity stateside, mambo. As before, ASCAP remained the major source of music for the stations. Aware of the impending expiration date of the five-year contract on December 31, 1940, NAB attempted to head off any major increases in the licensing rates by negotiating with ASCAP prior to the release of ASCAP's new fee schedule. Additionally, NAB wanted to pursue a "per-use" fee payment structure that would allow radio stations to pay only for the music that they actually used.

NAB notified ASCAP in the spring of 1939 that it was interested in discussing the terms of a new contract. NAB appointed a copyright committee to handle the negotiations. It was apparently understood by NAB that ASCAP would be appointing its own negotiating committee as well. According to NAB, when in the fall of 1939 NAB notified ASCAP that it was ready to hold talks, the response was that ASCAP's president had not appointed the committee.[88] Furthermore, he was said to be out of town on vacation and would not return for about a month. NAB believed these roadblocks to the negotiations were stalling tactics employed by ASCAP to push the negotiations to a date that would be as close as possible to the contract expiration date of December 31, 1940, therefore giving ASCAP the upper hand. NAB quickly took responsive action to the perceived stalling tactics.

In September of 1939, shortly after it was apparent that the ASCAP negotiations would not be taking place anytime soon, the NAB copyright committee developed plans to establish its own music-licensing organization. This new entity would have no connection whatsoever to ASCAP, and its goal would be to provide the same services to radio stations that ASCAP had provided, but with terms that were more agreeable to the radio industry. The plan for the new licensing organization was ratified and authorized by a hastily called copyright convention consisting of NAB members. This new music licensing house would be known as Broadcast Music, Inc. (BMI).

The initial funding required to get the new organization started came from broadcasters. Each participating organization pledged fifty percent of the amount paid to ASCAP in 1937 for the use of its copyrighted music. In exchange, these organizations received non-dividend paying stock.[89] With the initial funding in place, BMI began the process of building its offering of music catalogs. Composers and publisher members of ASCAP were off limits to BMI because membership in ASCAP meant that it held an exclusive public-performance licensing right in member compositions. Additionally, ASCAP members were typically those who had achieved a certain measure of success in the music industry. This meant that the door to BMI membership was open to lesser-known composers and publishers.

Initially, BMI's repertoire was composed primarily of this group. ASCAP still held the lion's share of songs, but BMI was making a small dent in the market. The radio broadcasters were hoping that BMI would be able to provide an array of music broad enough to reduce their exposure to ASCAP's increasingly higher fees.

Until this point, the burden of fee payment had fallen upon each individual station, even if it was under a network umbrella. Radio stations earned their income from advertising sales, with the large networks retaining a significant portion of a subsidiary station's gross receipts. From these receipts, the networks distributed about 25 percent of the income among the independently run stations that were affiliated with the network. The most competitive stations received the largest distributions. All stations, in turn, traditionally paid a percentage of the network distributions to ASCAP for a blanket license. The networks themselves paid nothing to ASCAP.

In 1939, for example, all radio broadcasters combined earned approximately $171 million from advertising sales.[90] The major networks, CBS and NBC, accounted for nearly one quarter of this amount. Network-affiliated stations were paid approximately $12 million that year, which was distributed among more than 250 stations. ASCAP received about 5 percent of the distributed income from the network-affiliated individual stations as a license-fee payment. In the aggregate, considering the total radio-broadcast gross receipts that year, ASCAP received just over $4 million, or 2.5 percent, of the $170 million total earned that year. CBS and NBC retained about $32 million after paying out their station distributions. The networks did not pay ASCAP, because payment was left to the individual stations.

Finally, in March 1940, ASCAP announced its new licensing rates, which would be effective January 1, 1941. As expected, a dramatic increase in fees paid by individual stations was declared, and for the first time, the networks were required to pay as well. Networks were scheduled to pay a fee to the tune of 7.5 percent of their gross income. This increase would, in part, make up for the reduced amounts being paid by unaffiliated independent stations, whose income was much less than network stations. Additionally, ASCAP was unwilling to institute a per-use fee arrangement as the stations had hoped.

Disputes between radio broadcasters and ASCAP had been going on for over a decade by this point. However, with the income from radio networks now earmarked by ASCAP as a source of payment, the network gloves came off. The radio broadcasters resisted entering into a new contract with ASCAP, fearing that doing so would spell an end to an independent system of broadcasting and that the radio industry would be at the mercy of ASCAP. However, ASCAP felt justified in raising its fees and requiring the networks to pay. It reasoned that radio broadcasters were successful in large part because of the music made available through ASCAP.

Instead of entering into the new contract with ASCAP that would have gone into effect on January 1, 1941, the majority of networks and radio stations refused to play any ASCAP music. They opted instead to play music that was already in the public domain and the limited selections in the BMI catalog. During this time, public domain tunes such as "Jeannie with the Light Brown Hair" were played in constant rotation. That song was played so much that the joke going around was that Jeannie's hair had turned gray.

BMI began recording fresh new arrangements of public domain music and often let the radio stations play them for free. In need of music, some mainstream stations began to turn to R&B and country music, genres that had been mostly ignored or relegated to very small stations. This created an opportunity for both genres to have a wider exposure and develop a larger fan base.

This period of ASCAP-free radio programming, which began in January 1941 and lasted until October of that year, became known as the "ASCAP boycott." Although, depending on which side you asked, it was either a boycott or an act of reasonable commercial defiance.[91] The radio industry viewed its refusal to play ASCAP music as a reasonable response to what was perceived as an attempt to engage in price-fixing. ASCAP saw the situation as a boycott conducted by the stations in an effort to use ASCAP's music to earn large profits while avoiding payment. ASCAP was successful in getting only a handful of independent, unaffiliated radio stations to sign the new contract.

ASCAP believed that the boycott would not last. It thought the public would soon demand that radio stations go back to playing their favorite ASCAP tunes. They were wrong. All was quiet among the radio-audience masses. Seemingly satisfied with the music offered, the audience outcry that ASCAP had hoped for never materialized.[92]

The boycott and the battles between ASCAP and the radio industry once again received national attention, including, yet again, the attention of the Department of Justice. As before, there was concern that ASCAP was operating as a monopoly, attempting to engage in price-fixing of music licenses. In addition to being outmaneuvered by BMI, ASCAP was faced with pending criminal charges for price-fixing under the Sherman Act and a civil lawsuit brought by the government.

ASCAP entered into a consent decree with the government in March 1941. In doing so, it avoided a possible negative outcome of a criminal trial and managed to avoid the civil litigation altogether. This time, however, ASCAP had company. BMI, set up by the radio networks as an antidote to ASCAP, was also under suspicion for attempting to operate as a monopoly. BMI had also entered into a consent decree one month earlier.

Both the BMI and ASCAP consent decrees were similar. The decrees placed limitations on the power of the organizations and called for changes to their internal structures. One of the most significant changes was that neither organization could require a member to hand over the exclusive public-performance rights in their copyrights to the organization. Structurally, ASCAP in particular was required to open up membership on its board of directors so that individuals could be placed there by membership vote instead of appointed by current board members, which had been the practice.

The 1941 consent decrees created some calm in the turbulent radio network and ASCAP relationships. Both BMI and ASCAP continued to grow rapidly. Over the next few decades, ASCAP made inroads into the film industry. Several music publishing companies owned by large film studios were members, and they were significant revenue generators for ASCAP. Their purpose was to exploit the music created for and heard in the studio's films.

Warner Bros. Picture Company, for example, owned a large music publishing company that was a member of ASCAP. The Warner publishing catalog accounted for approximately 40 percent of the music played on the radio in the mid-1930s. At one point, in 1935, Warner publishing tried to withdraw from ASCAP but was informed that no right existed for such an action. The publisher tried instead to license its music independently, without ASCAP, but was unsuccessful. This was, in part, because most stations were afraid of being caught up in any potential litigation between ASCAP and Warner Bros. Picture Company. Nor did the stations want to pay fees to both Warner and ASCAP. As a result, the Warner catalog was not played on the air for about seven or eight months. Warner found that the public did not complain about the absence of Warner songs, just as ASCAP would discover with its own repertoire five years later during the radio boycott. Deflated, Warner returned to ASCAP. However, this was just a precursor to the conflict brewing in Hollywood against ASCAP.

ASCAP had benefitted from a creative practice of licensing music for films. It would withhold the public-performance rights of music from movie producers and instead give them synchronization licenses that specifically allowed them to include the music in a film. These "synch" rights gave the producers permission only to put the licensed song in the movie, but the film could not legally be played in theaters without a separate public-performance license. The public-performance rights were separately licensed to theater owners, who were required to purchase the license to show the film.

In 1942, just a year after the consent decrees had been entered into, a collective of approximately 150 theater owners joined together and filed an antitrust lawsuit against ASCAP seeking an injunction of ASCAP's dual-license practice. The lawsuit, *Alden-Rochelle, Inc. v. ASCAP*, lay dormant until 1947, when ASCAP announced changes in the way performance licensing fees given to theater owners were to be calculated.[93] Previously, the fee had been based on a percentage determined by the seating capacity of the theater. The new scheme called for fees to be calculated based on the theater's admission price. This new formula would have meant fee increases across the board, ranging from 200 percent to 1,500 percent.[94] The film exhibitors revolted so aggressively that ASCAP backed down from the proposal.

Nevertheless, ASCAP's withdrawal could not prevent the lawsuit from reemerging. After years of close calls, ASCAP was officially called a monopoly by name. In *Alden-Rochelle* the U.S. District Court for the Southern District of New York held that the exclusive assignment of performance rights of music to ASCAP by its members, and the subsequent requirement by ASCAP that motion picture producers were prevented from negotiating performance licenses with theaters competing with ASCAP, to be a restraint of trade. The court stated:

> That ASCAP is a monopoly, within the language of . . . the anti-trust laws . . . The combination of the members of ASCAP in transferring all their non-dramatic performing rights to ASCAP, is a combination in restraint of interstate trade and commerce, which is prohibited by . . . the anti-trust laws.[95]

The court found ASCAP to be in violation of the Sherman Antitrust Act and granted an injunction preventing it from withholding performance rights from film producers.

The *Alden-Rochelle* decision, along with the battles leading to the 1941 consent decree, brought more concern for the Department of Justice. Between 1941 and 1950, despite attempts to assuage the licensing concerns of broadcasters, filmmakers, and ASCAP, there were still flare-ups. In response, the Department of Justice determined in 1950 that it would be necessary to amend the 1941 consent decrees.

The original terms of the 1941 consent decrees all remained intact. However, the 1950 decrees added a series of new amendments. Some of the most important additions included the following: (1) ASCAP was prohibited from attempting to prevent the withdrawal of a member from the society, provided the member gave three months' notice; (2) ASCAP could no longer base its radio-broadcast licensing fees on a percentage of the income obtained from commercial programs that did not use ASCAP music; (3) radio broadcasters were to have a choice between a blanket license or per-use license; (4) going forward, ASCAP was required to issue a single performing-rights license to film producers; and (5) a rate court was established with the power to set reasonable rates when ASCAP and the license applicant were not able to agree on a fee.[96]

After years of steadily increasing power and the forceful pushback from the radio and film industries, ASCAP, and to some extent BMI, had been reconfigured by the government. The goal of this restructuring was to offer services on a more equitable basis while also allowing the organizations to prosper. ASCAP and BMI had been at the forefront of popular music, serving as both tastemakers and music suppliers. Yet things in the popular music arena were just getting warmed up. It was 1950 and rock 'n' roll would soon make its debut, changing the music industry forever.

The Ripple Effect:
A Silver-Screen Legend Leaves a Lasting Impression on the Music Industry

De Havilland v. Warner Bros. Pictures,
67 Cal. App. 2d 225 (Cal. Ct. App. 1944).

She was one of the queens of the silver screen during the golden age of cinema, in the 1930s and 1940s. In 1935, at just twenty years of age, she began her film career at Warner Bros. studios in the film *A Midsummer Night's Dream*. Studio management was so impressed with her that she was promptly signed to a seven-year contract. Olivia de Havilland, cinema icon, would later file a lawsuit against her film studio that would result in the collapse of an oppressive labor practice employed by film studios during those golden years. Her lawsuit had significant ramifications for the music industry as well.

In the early days of Hollywood, film actors were considered by many film studios to be little more than property. This chattel-like treatment included the then-common practice of film studios lending their actors to other studios for specific movies, often without the actors' input or consent. Actors who were locked into this system had very little say in the selection of their roles. The studio made the majority of the creative decisions. For example, in 1939 Olivia de Havilland was loaned out to MGM for the sweeping epic film *Gone with the Wind*. If an actor resisted the directive to fulfill the loan commitment to a studio or refused to play a role, the studio had the authority, spelled out in the contract, to suspend the actor.

As the saying goes, "time is money," and the studios were determined to maximize any opportunities to make a profit off their actors. Even the period of suspension for a suspended actor was considered fair game for inclusion in the studio's profit calculus. As a result, the practice of slapping on the cumulative time of an actor's suspension period to the end of the actor's studio contract was often employed.

After being nominated for an Academy Award and several other awards, de Havilland no longer wanted the type of role that Warner Bros. designated for her. The studio was insisting that she continue to play sweet, demure, ingénue-like characters. Though de Havilland considered these roles to have been suitable early in her career, she now wanted the opportunity to explore a wider range of roles as she matured. De Havilland's defiant stance against Warner Bros. resulted in her being put on suspension five times in three years. Her last suspension was in August 1943 for refusing to be loaned out by Warner Bros. to Columbia Pictures.

De Havilland wanted out of her contract with Warner Bros., which was originally scheduled to terminate earlier that year, in May 1943. Warner Bros., however, had been keeping track of her suspension periods. The studio then extended the termination date of her contract by adding on the accumulated suspension time. According to Warner Bros., the total extension time from the added suspension periods was 25½ weeks beyond her contract termination date. De Havilland wanted out and responded by filing a lawsuit against Warner Bros. in Los Angeles Superior Court.

She argued that her seven-year contract expired in May 1943 and that California Labor Code Section 2855 prohibited the studio from enforcing contracts beyond seven years.[97]

The trial began in November 1943. Warner Bros. argued that under Section 2855 of the California Labor Code, her contract should be interpreted as being for seven years of *actual* service, not calendar years, and should therefore include the 25½ weeks of suspension. From the studio's perspective, de Havilland's suspension periods were exempt from being considered as time served during the original contract term.

The court disagreed with Warner Bros. and in March 1944, it ruled in de Havilland's favor. The decision also held that personal-services contracts—that is, contracts for the unique talents and abilities, such as acting, of an individual—were limited to seven calendar years, not actual service years. An appeal by Warner Bros. failed, with the California Court of Appeal for the Second District affirming the trial court's decision. Warner Bros. petitioned the U.S. Supreme Court for a hearing but was denied. The studio's final act against de Havilland was a refusal to ever work with her again. However, even with Warner Bros.' threat, de Havilland still went on to have a solid film career.

The verdict, commonly referred to as the "de Havilland decision," was welcome news among the Hollywood thespian community. The effect of the decision was that studios could no longer hold actors to contracts of more than seven years by employing the practice of adding cumulative suspension time. The decision also gave actors more freedom to select roles and guide their own careers, theoretically without fear of retaliation from the studios.

The de Havilland decision has influenced not just the film industry but the music industry as well. Because recording contracts are traditionally based on an artist delivering a certain number of albums, record labels have been concerned with the possibility of steep financial losses if an artist's contract were to expire before the album-delivery obligation had been met. The rationale is generally that the substantial investments made to enable the production and marketing of the albums requires a longer contract. The extended term allows the companies to recoup their investment and earn a return on that investment. Generally, labels have held the view that the artist should be held liable if the album-delivery requirements are not met by the termination date of the contract.

In response to the concerns of several record companies, California Labor Code Section 2855 was amended in 1987. The amendment, Section 2855(b), was directly targeted toward recording artists and created an exception to the seven-year rule.[98] Now record companies were able to sue if an artist left at the end of the seven-year contract period with an unfulfilled album commitment.

A challenge to the language of Section 2855(b) occurred in January 2000, when Geffen Records sued singer/guitarist Courtney Love in Los Angeles Superior Court for breach of contract.[99] Love had notified the label that her contract would be ending very soon. That date would have been the end of seven calendar years under contract with Geffen Records. The label argued that the California Labor Code did not apply in this situation because recording contracts were not personal-services contracts. It also argued that if, in fact, the seven-year rule was applicable at all, then the seven-year period began on the date of the last amendment to Love's contract. The date of the last contract amendment was in 1997, which would have put Love in the third year of her "new" contract, not the seventh year as dated under her original contract. Additionally, the label claimed Love owed five albums or compensation in lieu of the albums. Geffen asked the court to keep Love in her contract and grant an injunction to prevent her from recording with another label. Love counter-sued in February 2001, claiming that Section 2855(b) was unconstitutional.

In June 2002, the Los Angeles Superior Court ruled against Love, finding that Section 2855(b) was not unconstitutional, and removed the claim from her lawsuit. Courtney Love appealed the decision and the California Court of Appeals reinstated her complaint regarding Section 2855(b). This ruling was later overturned. Following a settlement between the parties, the case was dismissed in October 2002.

On the legislative front, a bill had been introduced into the California legislature in 2001 by California State Senator Kevin Murray to repeal Section 2855(b). A top concern among supporters of the bill was the feasibility of artists being able to deliver a large number of albums during a specified contract period while also completing mandatory tours to promote the albums. This issue drew some concern nationally, and Representative Mark Foley (R-Florida), who was the chair of the House Entertainment Industry Task Force, commented that this type of "indentured servitude" practiced by the labels must come to an end.[100] The Recording Industry Association of America (RIAA), a trade organization representing major music companies, lobbied heavily against any amendments to the statute. The bill failed despite lobbying efforts from many entertainers, including Courtney Love and the Recording Artist Coalition.

Some of the artists who have sought protection under the seven-year rule of Section 2855(a), the de Havilland law, include the bands Incubus and 30 Seconds to Mars. When 30 Seconds to Mars, a popular rock band, tried to terminate its contract with Virgin Records in 2008, it was sued for $30 million by Virgin's parent company, EMI. The band had been working under the same contract for nine years and was being sued for nondelivery of three albums.[101] The parties eventually settled out of court. However, during the distressing ordeal, Jared Leto, the band's lead singer, received support from where he least expected it.

Well aware of the history of the de Havilland decision, Leto reached out to de Havilland with the hopes of interviewing her for a documentary he was producing. The documentary followed the making of the band's album *This Is War* as well as their band's trials and tribulations during the EMI lawsuit.[102] Not necessarily expecting to communicate with de Havilland, who has lived in Paris since 1950, Leto was pleasantly surprised one day when he received an envelope in the mail from Paris. It was a note of encouraging support from de Havilland herself.[103]

Rum and Coca-Cola with a Twist of Calypso

Baron v. Leo Feist, Inc., 173 F.2d 288
(2d Cir. 1949).

Kahn v. Leo Feist, Inc., 165 F.2d 188
(2d Cir. 1947).

O n December 8, 1941, President Franklin Delano Roosevelt
stood before Congress and delivered his "Day of Infamy"
speech with fiery passion. He was addressing the nation
about the bombing of Hawaii's Pearl Harbor by Japanese forces,
which had occurred less than twenty-four hours earlier. His speech
announced America's entry into World War II. The country would
join the Allied forces, which among others included the superpow-
ers the United Kingdom and the Soviet Union in the war against
the Axis powers of Germany, Japan, and Italy.

During the war, many songs were written to lift the spirits of
servicemen stationed abroad. The jitterbug was a popular dance
during this period, and several jitterbug-worthy songs, like "Boo-
gie Woogie Bugle Boy" by the Andrews Sisters and "G.I. Jive" by
Johnny Mercer, told entertaining stories about fictional military
personnel while offering relief and distraction from the tragedies
of war. Nowhere was this intersection of popular entertainment

and World War II military life more pronounced than in a song that became one of the biggest hits of that era, "Rum and Coca-Cola." At the height of its popularity, this World War II anthem would become the subject of accusations of blatant copyright infringement.

The United States had created outposts in strategic locations around the world to help shore up allied defenses and provide optimum bases for offensive attacks. One of those strategic locations was the country of Trinidad and Tobago. In 1941, U.S. troops were sent to the country, which at the time was a British colony, to help defend it from attacks by the Nazis, who had stationed several U-boats off the country's coast. There were also rumors circulating that spies posing as locals had infiltrated the country. Strategically, the shores of Trinidad were crucial passageways for British cargo ships. Nazi U-boats were posted offshore in large part to attack British shipping. American soldiers were placed in strategic locations in Trinidad to prevent this.

Although Trinidad never fell under direct attack, there was plenty of work for the American soldiers. A hard day's work was often rewarded by play, and in Trinidad there were plenty of opportunities to have fun. The tropical climate of the country was the perfect setting for relaxing breaks in the sun. Rum was plentiful, as was Coca-Cola. Mixed together, rum and Coca-Cola was a popular drink for off-duty soldiers. Many locals were also willing to join the fun. The soldiers danced, dated, and in some cases simply "enjoyed the company" of some of the local women. During this period in Trinidad, the sight of soldiers with local women became so common that "Rum and Coca-Cola" eventually became a euphemism for the pairing of the white soldiers and the darker-skinned local women.

One aspect of Trinidad that was arguably a perk for the American soldiers was the annual tradition of carnival. Celebrated worldwide in the days leading up to Lent, carnival is an exuberant festival of music, food, and dancing. In Trinidad, the entire country practically stops for carnival and everyone takes part. Among the many festive features of carnival are the music tents. Each year, revelers can look forward to the debut of new carnival music in a party atmosphere under the many music tents.

The 1943 carnival celebrations in Port of Spain, the country's capital, did not disappoint. It was during carnival that a new, catchy song premiered in one of the many music tents. The song, performed by a local singer and musician named Rupert W. Grant, was "Rum and Coca-Cola." Grant, who went by the stage name Lord Invader, debuted his tune to instant success. "Rum and Coca-Cola" had a laid-back tropical beat and clever lyrics sung with energetic phrasing. It was full of sexual innuendo, and the melody was addictive. "Rum and Coca-Cola" was a true calypso hit. By 1943 calypso had become a well-established musical genre in Trinidad.

Calypso, in its modern form, began to be heard in Trinidad in the early 1900s. It evolved from the music brought to Trinidad by African slaves. Over time, the music blended with the musical sounds of the French Creole and Spanish cultures, which were also present during the country's emergence as a Spanish and subsequently British colony.

A well-known musician and Trinidad native by the name of Lionel Belasco was one of the early calypso pioneers. Around 1906, Belasco regularly hosted friends at his home in Trinidad for casual musical jam sessions. At one of those sessions he supposedly performed a tune called "L'Année Passée," French for "last year" or "yesterday." The tune was never performed anywhere outside of Belasco's home gatherings. He eventually left Trinidad and moved to New York City in 1915.

Fast-forward about twenty-five years and Belasco was hard at work in New York City composing original music as well as transcribing and standardizing traditional music from his home country. He applied for copyright protection for each of his original and transcribed songs. In 1941, Massie Patterson, a singer interested in adding some calypso songs to her repertoire, approached Belasco. One year later Belasco and Patterson collaborated with Maurice Baron, a music publisher seeking calypso music for his catalog. Belasco and Patterson played several songs for Baron. Baron was pleased with what he heard. By the end of 1943, the trio had signed a contract between them and Baron published "Calypso Songs of the West Indies," a collection of calypso tunes with both Creole and English lyrics. He was granted a copyright in the collection in January of 1944. The copyright application listed Baron as the "arranger-transcriber" of the collection while Belasco and Patterson were listed as "collectors of the Creole lyrics."[104]

Meanwhile, back in Trinidad, Lord Invader was also very busy riding a wave of local popularity following the debut of his "Rum and Coca-Cola" tune. At nearly every concert, the audience demanded that he play it. The song had debuted in the Victory Calypso Tent, which had been set up and managed by Mohammed Khan, a music entrepreneur. The sharp-dressing Khan wanted to publish a booklet containing the lyrics of the songs performed in the tent. The booklets were sold to carnival revelers. As mentioned earlier, the songs performed in the tents were mostly new songs, and inclusion in the booklet was likely seen as exposure to a broader audience. In March 1943, Lord Invader verbally assigned Khan the right to get a copyright in "Rum and Coca-Cola."

In September of 1943, Morey Amsterdam, a New York City-based comedic entertainer and radio host, traveled with the U.S.O. to Port of Spain to entertain the American troops stationed there. Amsterdam arrived in Trinidad about seven months after Lord Invader had debuted "Rum and Coca-Cola" during carnival. His act, a comedy duo performed with Mabel Todd, his wife at the time, got rave reviews. He remained in Trinidad for about one month.

By the spring of 1944, Amsterdam was back in New York City. He met with a nightclub singer, Jeri Sullavan, who was in search of "novelty" songs to add to her performance set at Versailles, a legendary New York restaurant and nightclub that, in the 1940s, was in its heyday.[105] Sullavan was a well-respected big-band singer and possessed the clout to have her own solo set at the Versailles, which hosted performances by high-caliber entertainers such as Perry Como and French cabaret chanteuse Edith Piaf.

In response to Sullavan's request for a novelty song, Amsterdam offered up the lyrics to a tune he claimed to have written—a novel little ditty called "Rum and Coca-Cola." Sullavan wanted to perform the song but was warned by Amsterdam that because of its sexual innuendo, it might not be appropriate for a young woman to sing.

She wanted to proceed anyway. At this point, Amsterdam's song offering is said to have had lyrics but still needed a solid tune. Sullavan sought composer Paul Baron's assistance in writing music for Amsterdam's lyrics. Amsterdam had supposedly told Sullavan that he had been singing his lyrics to a tune called "It Ain't Gonna Rain No More." Sullavan passed this information on to Baron. The end result was the well-known music of "Rum and Coca-Cola." There was just one major problem. This "new" version of "Rum and Coca-Cola" sounded nearly identical to Lord Invader's "Rum and Coca-Cola" tune that had premiered in Trinidad just one year earlier.

Sullavan sang the new song at the Versailles to a remarkable reception. She said that the audience demanded multiple encores of the song.[106] Spurred on by the overwhelmingly positive response, Sullavan went back to Amsterdam and asked him for more verses. He complied. The updated song was a nightclub hit once again.

Amsterdam applied for a copyright of "Rum and Coca-Cola" in September of 1944, listing only himself as the author of the lyrics and the music. This was significant in part because a song is normally composed of a musical work and a literary work, that is, music and lyrics. Generally, the copyright owner is the composer for the musical work and the lyricist for the lyrics.

The lyrics in Amsterdam's song contained two stanzas that were identical to the song that Lord Invader had granted to Khan in Trinidad. The following month, Amsterdam struck gold. The Andrews Sisters, a female trio and one of the biggest recording acts of the 1940s, recorded "Rum and Coca-Cola." Their version was an astronomical success. The records were pressed with Amsterdam listed as the sole composer. He received a copyright for the song in December.

Sullavan felt cheated when she discovered that Amsterdam had not given her credit on the song. The singer threatened to sue Amsterdam if the copyright credit was not changed. Amsterdam buckled and a deal was struck between himself, Sullavan, and Paul Baron. The deal split the royalties three ways and gave credit to Amsterdam as the lyricist and Sullavan and Baron as co-composers of the music. By January 1945, sales had reached almost 2.5 million copies. It later spent ten weeks at number one on the Billboard charts.

The song was at its peak in the charts. Royalties were flowing to Amsterdam, Sullavan, Baron, and their music publisher, Leo Feist, Inc. The song was also receiving tremendous press coverage. As it turned out, it was a member of the press, a writer for *Time* magazine, who apparently informed Lord Invader, still in Trinidad, about the success of the Andrews Sisters song. Both Invader and Khan decided to travel to New York. Invader arrived first and engaged the services of an intellectual property lawyer. He had decided to sue Sullavan, Amsterdam, and composer Paul Baron as copyright holders of the Andrews Sisters recording. Khan arrived in the city a short while later, and Invader's lawyer helped to negotiate a deal between the two in the event there would be a settlement. It was during this meeting that Invader put into writing a grant to Khan to secure a copyright in his song. Invader had previously granted that right to him verbally.

Lionel Belasco, the calypso pioneer, was also concerned about the Andrews Sisters hit. He believed that the song infringed upon "L'Année Passée," which he claimed to have written in 1906, more than thirty years earlier. There was some evidence to support Belasco's claim, the most glaring being Lord Invader's statement that he had never acquired a copyright in his song "Rum and Coca-Cola" because he believed Belasco was the composer.

Belasco originally became aware of Amsterdam's version of "Rum and Coca-Cola" during a visit to the Leo Feist music publishing offices that occurred prior to the Andrews Sisters release. He had been there to meet with the company's representative responsible for acquiring new material. The meeting agenda did not include a discussion of "Rum and Coca-Cola." While at Feist's office, the publishing representative played Belasco a portion of the demo recording of Amsterdam's version of "Rum and Coca-Cola." After listening to only a part of the song, Belasco said that it was his own. He then proceeded to finish playing it on the piano. The representative asked Belasco to return with proof of his ownership in the song. That was the last meeting between the two; the Leo Feist representative suddenly became unavailable to Belasco.

Belasco, the Trinidadian composer living in New York for almost thirty years; Khan, the Trinidadian music entrepreneur; and Lord Invader, the Trinidadian singer who first performed "Rum and Coca-Cola" all wanted to sue for copyright infringement. They decided that working together would be the key to winning an infringement case against New York music publisher Leo Feist. A plan was cobbled together by the plaintiffs in which Khan would sue Feist for copyright infringement over the lyrics of "Rum and Coca-Cola" and Maurice Baron, the New York music publisher who had collaborated with Belasco and Patterson on "Calypso Songs of the West Indies," would separately sue Feist for infringement of the music. The defendants were Leo Feist, music publisher; Morey Amsterdam, comedian; Jeri Sullavan, singer; and Paul Baron, composer. Maurice Baron, plaintiff, was not related to Paul Baron, defendant.

Both cases were heard in the Southern District of New York in the courtroom of Judge Byers. At the time of the trial, he had served as a judge nearly thirty years and was known for his adeptness with intellectual property matters. The court ruled in favor of Khan and Maurice Baron in both cases.

During the Khan trial, the defendants' first argument against the accusation of infringement was an assertion that the March 1943 assignment of "Rum and Coca-Cola" to Khan by Lord Invader was invalid. They also argued that because Trinidad was officially a British Colony at the time of the assignment, British copyright law and the Trinidad copyright ordinances should apply.[107] Under those laws, they argued, the original verbal assignment was not valid because it was not put into writing at the time of the assignment. Therefore, they argued, Amsterdam held a fair and clear copyright of the song in the United States because by the time the verbal assignment was put into writing in May of 1945, Amsterdam had already acquired a U.S. copyright on the song. Affirming the trial court, the second circuit agreed that British law and the Trinidad ordinances applied but found that even though Lord Invader's assignment to Khan was verbal, the fact that it was put into writing at a later date was acceptable and ultimately satisfied the requirements of both the British law and the Trinidad ordinances.

The defendants also argued, in both the Khan and Baron cases, that neither the music nor the lyrics could have been copyrighted, because the song was in the public domain. A public domain designation means that an artistic or literary work is not under copyright protection, either because the copyright has expired or the window to place the song under copyright protection has closed. Later on appeal in the Baron case, the court would characterize the defendants' use of the public domain argument as desperate, because the origin of the copyrighted song was in question.

Returning to the trial, the defendants argued that Amsterdam's "Rum and Coca-Cola" was merely an arrangement of a Trinidadian folksong that was in the public domain and had been commonly performed in Trinidad. They were referring specifically to Belasco's "L'Année Passée." If they were correct, then Maurice Baron, plaintiff and arranger, would be entitled to a copyright only in his arrangement of "L'Année Passée," published in the book *Calypso Songs of the West Indies*.

Paul Baron, who had written the music for Amsterdam's song and was also a defendant, was questioned extensively about how he came up with the accompanying music for Amsterdam's "Rum and Coca-Cola." Baron said that he based his tune on a calypso song that had been in his head called "King Jaja." He said that the tune was a well-known calypso folksong that was in the public domain. The defense attempted to show that Belasco's "L'Année Passée" was based on "King Jaja." They brought in witnesses to testify that it had been commonly known and sung in the 1930s in Trinidad.

Although a song with the title "King Jaja" did exist, the defendants' witness testimony was sketchy at best. They could not remember which acquaintances had sung it before. Nor could they provide any evidence to demonstrate that "King Jaja" was a known song prior to 1906, the year that Belasco claimed to have written "L'Année Passée." Also, the only written record of "King Jaja" was found in a Trinidadian booklet published in 1944.

Though it is true that many folksongs are in the public domain, several are protected by copyright. Music that is viewed as "cultural," "native," or even "traditional" has often been considered part of a common musical wellspring that is open for the taking. The defendants insisted that it was common practice during carnival for musicians to use commonly known melodies and affix their own lyrics to them.

The court found that the defendants' public domain folksong argument was insufficient. This was largely because of all the evidence that pointed to Belasco having written "L'Année Passée" in 1906 and having shared it with friends and family at his home jam sessions. Therefore, "L'Année Passée" was considered not to have been in the public domain. The court also spoke to the possibility that "L'Année Passée" could have been based on a folksong in the public domain. It stated that even if that was the case, the copying of an unauthorized copy was not a defense in an infringement suit. The court also emphasized that Lord Invader had stated that "Rum and Coca-Cola" was based on Belasco's song.

In the court's view, the "Rum and Coca-Cola" melody had a provable pedigree, and Amsterdam had made a cultural miscalculation by considering a popular tune that he heard during his visit to Trinidad to be a folksong that was free for the taking. The court doubted that Paul Baron, Amsterdam's composer, could have had access to the 1944 book containing "King Jaja." It was pointed out, however, that he *did* have access to copies of the book containing "L'Année Passée," *Calypso Songs of the West Indies*. At least five copies of the book were kept in the library at the CBS offices in New York. Apparently he used the library frequently as a composer and bandleader at CBS. Although it could not be proven that Baron copied directly from the books in the library, it was a sufficient indication of copying, and enough for the trial court to rule that there was "internal evidence of copying even in the absence of proof of access."[108]

In both Khan's and Maurice Baron's cases, the court reviewed and quickly negated another argument brought forth by the defendants, that too much time had elapsed over the nearly thirty-seven-year period between when Belasco composed "L'Année Passée" and when it was copyrighted. The court pointed out that there is no time limit on the duration of a common-law copyright under both U.S. and Trinidadian law. Belasco's common-law copyright, they added, could have been lost only if he had granted it to someone else during the time lapse, which he had not. His common-law copyright became a federal copyright when he joined forces with music publisher Maurice Baron and singer Masie Patterson.

Finally, the defendants brought the morality of the lyrics into question as a last-ditch attempt to defend themselves against copyright infringement. In the Khan case, they argued that Lord Invader's song was "salacious, immoral, and rude."[109] They stated that because of the lyrics' "immoral tendencies," the song should not have been eligible for copyright. The reference was to the sexual innuendo of the "Rum and Coca-Cola" lyrics and how those lyrics described local Trinidadian women and white American servicemen spending time together. An example of this was the double entendre in the line "Both mother and daughter, working for the Yankee dollar." Still, it was an odd choice of defense strategy considering that the double-entendre nature of the defendants' song contributed greatly to its success.

It was true that during this period and for the remainder of the twentieth century, material that was found to be obscene could not receive copyright protection. The test to classify material as obscene, as applied by the New York courts at that time, was whether the overall song had a "libidinous effect."[110] Judge Byers concluded that the lyrics were not libidinous but instead simply reported what was constant and obvious in daily Trinidadian life while the servicemen were stationed there.[111] The appellate court also brushed off the defendants' argument, stating that it was highly unlikely that the lyrics could "promote lust," although the court did consider the lyrics to be "cheap and vulgar."[112]

The defendants appealed their case to the U.S. Court of Appeals for the Second Circuit. Mohammed Khan and Maurice Baron both had their cases against Feist, Amsterdam, and the other defendants affirmed on appeal. Invader and Belasco received payouts as part of the pretrial settlement deals they had negotiated with Khan and Maurice Baron, respectively. However, Morey Amsterdam wound up as an uncontested owner of the copyright for the song "Rum and Coca-Cola." He, along with co-composers and defendants Paul Baron and Jeri Sullavan, purchased the copyright from Mohammed Khan and Maurice Baron in a settlement deal.

"Rum and Coca-Cola" was one of the biggest hits of 1945. Its lyrics illustrated a snapshot of a distinct period in history when the people of Trinidad played host to American servicemen during World War II. The exposure to Trinidadian culture and songs like "Rum and Coca-Cola" helped spread the popularity of calypso music in the United States after the war.

The Emergence of the Teen Idol

Interlude

The theater was filled to capacity with throngs of screaming teen-age girls. With sweaty faces and tear-stained eyes, they jostled one another, trying to get a better view of the stage. The music performed on the stage was difficult to hear over all the commotion in the audience. This is not a description of rabid fans at the latest boy-band show, nor is it an account of a Beatles concert during the height of Beatlemania. Instead, it is a recounting of the scenes taking place when boisterous and devoted fans flocked to concerts in the early 1940s to see a young Frank Sinatra and witness the birth of the "teen idol."

Singer Frank Sinatra had a career that spanned over fifty years. He is well known for song classics such as "New York, New York" and "My Way." At a later point in his life, he was famously associated with friends and fellow singers Dean Martin and Sammy Davis Jr. as a member of the Rat Pack. He was also a regular headliner in Las Vegas concert venues. At every period in his career, Sinatra was fortunate to have a devoted following. That passionate devotion was first revealed largely by the throngs of screaming fans shortly after World War II. Many were teenage girls who grew into lifelong devotees.

Sinatra, originally from Hoboken, New Jersey, received his big break when he began singing with bandleader Harry James and his big-band orchestra in the late 1930s. By 1940, he was singing with Tommy Dorsey's big band and also appeared on Tommy Dorsey's radio program. This was the big-band swing era. Big bands and vocalists shared the stage with relatively equal billing. A vocalist singing with a big band would often be featured on a few numbers, with the majority of numbers performed by the band. Sinatra was different. He was a breakout star. His vocal numbers were so popular that he became more of a draw than the band. In 1940 Sinatra

103

had his first number-one hit record with "I'll Never Smile Again," accompanied by the Tommy Dorsey Orchestra.

By the end of 1942, his popularity had risen to unprecedented heights. In December of that year, he was booked to play his first solo shows at the Paramount Theatre in New York.[113] Celebrated big-band leader Benny Goodman, whose orchestra would be backing Sinatra, introduced the singer. The moment Sinatra walked on stage, the crowd erupted into hysterics. The screams from the crowd were deafening. Goodman, Sinatra, and the rest of the band were stunned. Several female fans had gone into hysterics over the death of actor Rudolf Valentino in the 1920s, but reactions like this, to a living person and during a musical concert, were new to the entertainers. Sinatra had moved into unchartered territory, the realm of the teen idol.

Sinatra's shows at the Paramount were so popular that his run was extended into February 1943. Also, for the first time, advertisers were beginning to recognize the purchasing power of teenagers. Prior to the Sinatra concerts, advertisers had focused on a more mature demographic, completely leaving out teenagers. But teenagers could no longer be ignored as they came out in droves to see Sinatra. His young female fans came clad in typical teen fashion of the day: knee-length skirts and socks rolled down to their ankles. The way they wore their socks led the press to coin the term *bobbysoxers* to describe them. Many bobbysoxers would also attend Sinatra shows wearing bow ties, in homage to their musical crush.

Tall and possessing a frail frame, Sinatra had a boyish charm that was inviting. His youthful looks belied the emotional depth of his soulful and velvety voice. He once described his appeal as a result of his ability to tap into the "loneliness" of the war years, because his fans saw him as "the boy in every corner drugstore, the boy who had gone to war."[114] His expressive and large blue eyes entranced his audiences, and his style of singing had an intimate quality that could speak directly to the listener. Whether expressed through fashion, screams, tears, or all of the above, Sinatra's young fans were under his spell.

The years 1943 and 1944 were big for Sinatra; his time was spent making hit records and performing in film roles. His popularity only continued to soar. On October 12, 1944, Sinatra was preparing to play several back-to-back shows in a steady rotation at the Paramount. That day was a holiday, Columbus Day. Perhaps more people had time off to attend his shows, because more than 30,000 fans came to the Paramount to hear him and swoon before their idol. The capacity of the theater was only 3,500 people.

As Sinatra's sets began, determined and mesmerized bobbysoxers would enter the theater for a show and refuse to leave before the next one began. This caused some fans waiting outside to grow restless.[115] The diehard fans who remained in the theater would stay for show after show. Some would even stand in the theater for nearly eight hours with no food or water, just to see and hear their beloved Frank. That is, until security dragged them out.

That night, the first of its kind at a pop concert, went down in musical infamy as the "Columbus Day Riots."[116] It is also considered the definitive moment when the power of the teen in popular culture was recognized. The teen idol was officially born, with many more to follow.

Payola, Rock 'n' Roll, and the King of the Moondoggers

As the 1950s began, there was reason to be optimistic about the future. One reason was that World War II had ended several years earlier, and the United States was enjoying a postwar period of economic prosperity. The GI Bill was partly responsible for the rapid growth of the middle class. Many veterans of World War II were taking advantage of the bill, which paid for benefits such as higher education and home mortgage loans. The American dream seemed more accessible than ever. Commercial pop culture images at the time suggested that the American ideal was a husband, wife, kids, and a home with a white picket fence. Advertisements featured men looking as though they had just walked off the set of *Mad Men*. The ad imagery also suggested that a stay-at-home mom was best suited to do the housework in a pleated skirt and pearls. Through the lens of several media outlets from that decade, the 1950s was an extra-starched era of conformity . . . that is, until rock 'n' roll came along.

The number-one song in the nation in 1952 was a simple jazz-influenced tune called "Wheel of Fortune" performed by Kay Starr.

But one night in 1952 would usher in a new era of music that transformed popular culture and caused a seismic shift in the tranquil popular-culture status quo of the early 1950s. That groundbreaking event was the Moondog Coronation Ball in Cleveland, Ohio, an event widely considered to be the first rock 'n' roll concert.

The ball, which took place on March 21, 1952, was the brainchild of Alan Freed, a popular DJ who called himself "Moondog." Freed used the name on his popular Cleveland Radio Show, the *Moondog Rock 'n' Roll Party*. His role in the rise of rock 'n' roll's popularity cannot be overstated. An avid fan of R&B music, Freed is recognized for having coined the term *rock 'n' roll*. He used the term to describe the upbeat R&B records he enjoyed listening to and that he played for his radio audience. The music, which had evolved from the jazz, blues, country, and gospel-based traditions that preceded it, was slowly gaining in popularity among a diverse fan base nationwide. Mainstream exposure to the records, however, remained obstructed because many radio stations refused to play the music. Television networks flat-out refused to air rock 'n' roll music because they considered the genre to be inappropriate for the American public. This perceived inappropriateness was due in part to the R&B lyrics, which many critics considered obscene. However, it was also largely because the music was heavily performed by black artists.

In April of 1950, Freed was hosting an afternoon television program that broadcast feature films. About a year earlier, he had met Leo Mintz, owner of Record Rendezvous, a popular Cleveland record store. Declining sales of big-band records and rising sales of R&B records in the record shop caught Mintz's attention. He noticed that when he played the R&B records in the store, teenagers would be bopping their heads and moving to the music. Mintz tried tirelessly to get local radio stations to play the R&B records, but they refused. He found a kindred spirit in Freed. After sharing with Freed his experiences with the teens and the R&B records in his shop, the two joined forces to create a new radio show.

In July 1951, Freed began broadcasting the *Moondog Rock 'n' Roll Party*. Record Rendezvous sponsored the show. It aired late at night, from 11:15 p.m. to 2:00 a.m., and capitalized on the momentum of a musical movement already in progress. R&B had been gaining fans prior to the show, but Freed gave the upbeat R&B genre a radio outlet. By naming the music rock 'n' roll, he gave the musical movement focus. The show was a huge success, and Freed's fans affectionately became known as "Moondoggers." Freed's charisma, enthusiasm, and perfect radio voice, along with the upbeat records he played, were an infectious combination.

The Moondog Coronation Ball was a chance for fans to come together and see Freed live and in person, along with a solid roster of R&B groups. Marketed as "the most terrible ball of them all," it was slated to be the night that Freed crowned himself the "King of the Moondoggers."[117] The Cleveland Arena, where the ball was held, sat 10,000 people. The tickets sold out quickly. On the night of the event, an estimated 10,000 additional people showed up without tickets.

The concert kicked off as planned, but thousands of fans tried to smash through the gates. The police arrived to control the near riot that ensued, and the show was stopped shortly after it began. From the outside looking in, this riotous beginning to rock 'n' roll concerts was proof of the immorality and inappropriate nature that some anti–rock 'n' roll advocates believed was associated with the new genre. For the Moondoggers, it was the mainstream arrival of something that was too exciting to remain underground.

As rock 'n' roll increased in popularity, so did its play on radio stations around the United States. Sponsors like Record Rendezvous helped make the playing of rock 'n' roll records on the radio possible, but rock 'n' roll had another major benefactor—payola.

It may have aided the rise of rock 'n' roll, but it brought about the dramatic fall of Alan Freed.

Payola, or "pay to play," has been in the music industry in some form or another for as long as there has been a business of music. The term comes from the combination of the words *pay* and *Victrola*, which was an early phonograph machine manufactured by the Victor Talking Machine Company.[118] *Payola* refers to the practice of giving a bribe to someone in exchange for the promotion of a product. Specifically applied to the music industry, it is the practice of giving money or gifts to a DJ or radio/television programmer to promote a record. Although the term *payola* itself did not become popular until the 1940s and 1950s, the practice was well established by the late nineteenth century.

Music publishers in the United States and the United Kingdom widely acknowledged in the 1880s and 1890s that payola, known back then as the "payment system," was widely in use. In the days before radio and records, songs became hits if they were performed live and by the right person. The stage and vaudeville stars of the period were the hit makers of the day. Music publishers hired "song pluggers" to move about various music venues, from the dingiest pubs to elegant music stages, to convince singers and bandleaders to sing songs from the catalog of the song plugger's music publisher boss. In exchange for singing such a song, the singer might receive a cash payment, royalties on the sale of the song's sheet music, or both. A renowned singer could command top dollar and special favors from the music publishers.

Even in the 1890s, many music publishers agreed that the practice was questionable. Although several music publishers and the singers with whom they made deals benefitted greatly from the practice, this "payment system" created an unfair advantage for wealthy publishers who could afford the cash and luxury gifts needed to entice singers. Less affluent and smaller publishers, as well as independent composers, were at a serious disadvantage. Recognizing this, several publishers joined together in an attempt to put and end to the practice.[119] Their efforts quickly failed. Instead of getting rid of the practice, it only pushed it underground. Payola continued, but now it was done in secret.

Another attempt at curbing payola was made in 1916. This time, the effort was led by a group of five-and-dime stores that sold records and sheet music. Several of these stores banded together as a sort of "syndicate," agreeing to refuse to sell any songs by a music publisher who was found to be engaging in payola. It seemed like a good idea from the stores' perspective, but the music publishers were perplexed about why the stores even cared about regulating the practice. In the end, the strategy was never implemented.

Payola continued but was increasingly looked upon in a less favorable light. In 1917, John O'Connor, who was the business manager of *Variety* magazine, a trade publication that had reported extensively on the "payment system," helped form the Music Publishers' Protective Association (MPPA), becoming its first chairman. The purpose of the organization was to provide an even playing field for music publishers without the influence of payola. The rules of the organization allowed for music publisher members found engaging in payola to be fined. As the music industry moved forward, these rules were never enforced.

In 1933, the MPPA attempted another strategy to eradicate payola. It did so by taking advantage of the powers available to the newly created National Recovery Administration (NRA). Established by President Franklin D. Roosevelt in the midst of the Great Depression, the purpose of the new agency was to eliminate unfair trade practices as a part of a larger effort to stimulate growth in the economy. The agency would create codes of conduct for trade within various industries. Members of an industry could submit rules for consideration, and that is exactly what the MPPA did.

It submitted a draft code to the NRA that included explicit prohibitions of the practice of payola. The code was approved but did not become effective until March of 1935. However, the Supreme Court ruled on May 27, 1935, that the NRA was unconstitutional and the organization was dissolved, along with any rules it had passed.[120] The efforts of the MPPA, whose code for the music publishing industry was in effect for only two months, were all for naught. It seemed that the old adage "you take two steps forward and three steps back" was the name of the game when it came to trying to eliminate payola.

The only real change in the late 1930s and 1940s with regard to payola was its immense growth in popularity. Once the currency of influence for hit makers singing in pubs and on fine stages, payola had now spread to radio. By the 1950s, record companies had taken the place of music publishers in writing the payola checks.

Back in the early 1950s in Cleveland, things were really heating up for Alan Freed. Musically, the radio had been the haven of big-band performances. Now, teenagers around the world wanted to hear rock 'n' roll just like Leo Mintz had witnessed in his Rendezvous Records store. Established and newly minted record labels rushed to release R&B singles to meet the teenage demand. There were more singles being made than there was time on the air to play them, and with hits determined by record sales, a record had to get on the air. The competition for airtime became extremely important.

To get their singles played over the airwaves, several record companies engaged in the practice of payola. Disc jockeys around the country were given a variety of enticements in exchange for playing a label's records. These enticements included money, luxury cars, and vacations. In some cases, the DJ might be given a writing credit on a song, providing royalties going into the future.

The practice of payola moved ahead full throttle throughout the 1950s, becoming rampant. But by 1958 there were signs that the party was coming to an end. Spurred on by ASCAP, Senator George Smathers, an ardent Southern Democrat representing the state of Florida, introduced a bill in 1958 that would make it illegal for anyone involved in music publishing or the manufacture or distribution of records to hold a license for a broadcasting station.[121] The bill failed to pass. Shortly thereafter, a popular television game show came under suspicion of corruption.

The *$64,000 Question* was a quiz show and one of the most popular shows on television. When an episode aired, it seemed like all of America was tuned in to see if a contestant would walk away with the big prize. In 1958, it was revealed that contestants on the show were being prepped beforehand to answer the quiz-show questions. It was also revealed that the amount of money to be won was prearranged. Further evidence arose of contestants being paid to drop the names of businesses during the course of a show. In one such occurrence, a quiz-show contestant was paid $10,000 by his employer to mention the employer's name.

Much of the scandal over the quiz show seems pretty tame by today's standards. However, in 1958 many viewers truly believed that if a program presented itself on TV as truthful, then it just had to be truthful. Television audiences were shocked by the quiz-show revelations. So much so that the scandal garnered responses from inside the Beltway, with several members of Congress responding with swift moral condemnation.

Reacting to a perceived destruction of the moral fabric of the country, a congressional hearing was held to get to the bottom of the quiz-show scandal. The Subcommittee on Legislative Oversight of the House of Representatives conducted the hearings, which were led by Representative Oren Harris of Arkansas. The hearings opened the door to other questionable practices within the broadcast industry.

Burton Lane, a composer and president of the American Guild of Authors and Composers, put forth a letter in the hearing calling attention to the "deceptive practices" not just in the world of quiz shows but in the music industry as well.[122] As a result, the hearing transitioned to focus on the use of payola in the music industry. Payola was viewed upon by many in Congress as not only an illegal practice but an immoral one. Even President Dwight Eisenhower weighed in on the matter when he referred to it as a "matter of public morality."[123]

During the hearings, several radio DJs were brought forth to testify regarding their knowledge of the use of payola. Many testified, though most were reluctant, that they did engage in the practice of payola. The DJs characterized the money and gifts that they had received not as payment in exchange for playing records but as payment for their services as music consultants.[124]

The payola hearings led to a full-fledged scandal. Broadcasting companies were anxious to clean their ranks and wash their hands of any possible taint from the scandal. In 1959, Alan Freed, who had left Cleveland to host a radio show in New York, was working for ABC radio. ABC required all of its on-air employees and radio programmers to sign an affidavit stating that they had not engaged in the practice of payola. Freed refused to sign the affidavit, considering it to be an indication of a lack of faith in him on the part of ABC.[125] A few months later, ABC fired him.

In April of 1960 another ABC radio host, the legendary television and radio host and music mogul Dick Clark, testified before Congress at the ongoing payola hearings. Clark, who projected a clean-cut image with boyish charm, was also an astute businessman. He held a financial interest in nearly thirty-three music-recording, manufacturing, or distribution companies.[126] Under direction from his employer, ABC, he divested himself of those companies, as well as over 150 songs in which he held a songwriting credit and was earning royalties. During his congressional testimony, he denied any involvement in payola. The committee seemed to take him at his word, commenting on how he was such a "fine young man."[127]

That same month, Freed testified before Congress. Unlike Clark, Freed admitted to having interactions with record companies and distributors and provided a detailed description of those interactions. However, he never explicitly stated that he had engaged in payola. Instead, he said that record labels had paid him as a consultant.

Also, Freed, like many of his contemporaries, took co-writing credits on several songs. Singer and guitarist Chuck Berry, for example, once recalled looking at his copyright notice for his hit song "Maybellene" to discover to his surprise that Freed was listed as a co-writer.[128]

In retrospect, it is clear that there were two sides to payola. On the one hand, it offered unfair advantages to wealthy record labels that could use payola to guarantee airtime for their records while the small labels could only hope for that level of exposure. On the other hand, rock 'n' roll may never have received the wide exposure it did without payola. The music was considered to be risqué and dangerous by many. Its appeal to teenagers seemed threatening to some who viewed it as a catalyst for illicit behavior. It is hard to get around the fact that payola bribes played a large part in getting R&B music over the airwaves to the masses.

After the payola hearings were completed, the subcommittee presented the Federal Communications Commission with recommended amendments to the Communications Act. The amendments explicitly made payola a crime; they became law on September 13, 1960. The new law stated that anyone who had offered or received payment in some form in exchange for the inclusion of material in a broadcast must acknowledge, over the air, that the exchange has taken place. Those not abiding by these laws were subject to a fine or imprisonment.

Although the hearings did produce some tangible results, they actually accomplished very little. As with the previous attempts in the years leading up to the hearings, success was fleeting. For about one year, the hearings brought to the attention of the nation the sketchy and often seedy practice of payola. However, after the hearings and the fallout from the payola scandal subsided, many record companies simply altered their marketing structure and hired independent promoters. These independent workers were free to engage in payola under the direction of a record label. This independent-contractor system enabled the label's hands to stay clean. The 1970s and 1980s saw renewed energy and implementation of payola under this new structure. The gifts continued to flow and included luxury items and sometimes drugs and sexual favors. Though payola has spent a lot of time underground, the practice has never gone away. As recently as 2005, then New York attorney general Elliott Spitzer conducted a series of probes and filed lawsuits against several major record labels and large radio companies, accusing them of engaging in a "sophisticated" form of payola.[129]

After the congressional hearings, Freed's troubles began to snowball. He was indicted by a grand jury in New York on charges of commercial bribery going back over a decade. On May 19, 1960, Freed, along with seven other radio personalities, was arrested and charged with receiving $116,850 in payola.[130] He pleaded guilty to two of the ninety-nine counts of commercial bribery and was assessed a fine.

The payola scandal left him persona non grata in the music business. The cancellation of his show, along with the bribery charges, led him to turn increasingly to alcohol. His streak of misfortune continued when, in 1964, the federal government charged him with income-tax evasion. Suffering from gastrointestinal bleeding brought about from cirrhosis of the liver, most likely the result of heavy drinking, Alan Freed died a broken man on January 20, 1965, from kidney failure. He was forty-three years old.

In March of 2012, several people gathered in Cleveland to celebrate the sixtieth anniversary of the Moondog Coronation Ball. The ball has been an annual event full of nostalgia for many years. Cleveland, the place where Freed coined the term *rock 'n' roll*, is also the site of the Rock and Roll Hall of Fame. On January 23, 1986, twenty-two years after his death, Freed, who claimed he never played a song he did not like, was inducted as a member of the first class of the Rock and Roll Hall of Fame.

PART THREE

1960s–1970s

Playback

1961	• The Marvelettes have a number 1 hit with "Mr. Postman."
1963	• Blues music revival gains steam in the U.S. and the U.K. • Over 250,000 people join the March on Washington in Washington, D.C., in support of civil rights and hear Martin Luther King, Jr., deliver his "I Have a Dream" speech. • U.S. President John F. Kennedy is assassinated.
1965	• Singer Wilson Picket releases "In the Midnight Hour."
1967	• Singer and musician Otis Redding dies in a plane crash in Madison, Wisconsin, en route to a performance.
1968	• Jamaican group The Maytals releases the song "Do the Reggay" and export reggae to the U.K. and the U.S.
1969	• On March 1, singer Jim Morrison is arrested in Miami, Florida, after allegedly exposing himself to the crowd during a Doors concert.
1970	• On September 19, farmer Michael Eavis organizes the first Glastonbury Festival, at the time called the Pilton Festival, on his farm. Tickets are sold for one pound each, and 1,500 people attend. • On October 4, singer Janis Joplin dies of a heroin overdose at the age of twenty-seven.
1972	• Glam rock reaches its zenith with the release of David Bowie's *The Rise and Fall of Ziggy Stardust*. • The Equal Employment Opportunity Act is passed in the U.S., banning workplace discrimination.
1974	• On August 8, President Richard Nixon resigns as a result of the Watergate scandal.
1975	• Rock band Queen releases a video for operatic rock song "Bohemian Rhapsody."

1976	• U.K. punk group the Sex Pistols releases "Anarchy in the U.K."
1977	• Elvis Presley dies at age forty-two. • On December 16, disco film *Saturday Night Fever* is released. • Roland MC-8, the first digital microprocessor sequencer, is released.
1979	• Sony begins selling its portable music player, the Walkman. • On September 16, "Rapper's Delight," recorded by hip-hop trio the Sugar Hill Gang, becomes a hit and brings rap to the mainstream. • On December 14, the British punk rock band The Clash releases its album *London Calling*.

A Dream Girl Deferred:

The Story of a Fallen Supreme

Chapman v. Ross, 209 N.W.2d 288 (1973).

The year was 1964. President Lyndon B. Johnson signed into law the Civil Rights Act of 1964, designed to abolish racial segregation in the United States. *Mary Poppins* debuted in movie theaters and the British Invasion had kicked off with the arrival of the Beatles on American soil. In other news, a group of young women were celebrating their first number-one single, "Where Did Our Love Go?" Originally from Detroit, The Supremes would go on to become one of the top-selling musical acts of all time. At the height of fame, one member of the group, Florence Ballard, would suddenly find herself pushed out of the group by Motown Records. Guided by poor advice and broke, Ballard was determined to fight back and went to court in pursuit of a reversal of her misfortune.

So without further adieu, ladies and gentleman, please welcome to the stage three women from "Motor Town" U.S.A. They are topping the charts with hits like "Baby Love" and "Stop in the Name of Love." Put your hands together for Mary, Diana, and Florence—The Supremes!

Florence Ballard, Mary Wilson, and Diana Ross grew up in Detroit, Michigan. Wilson and Ballard had been friends since meeting at a local talent show when they were teenagers. In 1958, the manager of another Detroit act, the all-male vocal group the Primes, was looking to develop a female act to complement his group. The Primes were an early incarnation of another Motown supergroup, the Temptations. Ballard, who had been friends with Paul Williams and Eddie Kendricks, members of the Primes, was asked to assemble the new group. She recruited Wilson, Diane Ross, and Williams's girlfriend, Betty McGlown, to form the musical group the Primettes.[131]

The Primes and the Primettes toiled away in Detroit seeking to make a name for themselves and to get the attention of a record label. Berry Gordy Jr., an aspiring record executive, former boxer, serviceman, and auto worker, had recently moved into the headquarters of his upstart label, Motown Records. The label was housed in a distinctive white house with blue trim, and the phrase "Hitsville U.S.A." was emblazoned across the front. However, in 1959, "Hitsville U.S.A." was a hitless entity. The label's losing streak quickly ended in 1960 when songwriter and vocalist Smokey Robinson and his group, The Miracles, released Motown's first hit song, "Shop Around." Throughout the 1960s, the hits were flowing out of Motown, infusing mainstream music with a catchy and soulful pop R&B style that became an international sensation.

By 1960, Betty McGlown had left the Primettes. That same year the group met singer and songwriter Smokey Robinson and auditioned for him with the goal of landing a record deal with Motown. Although that audition failed to lead to a contract, Berry Gordy eventually signed the group in 1961. Ballard was seventeen years old at the time. One of Gordy's requirements was that the group change its name. Ballard suggested the name "The Supremes." Diane and Mary initially disliked it, but Gordy liked it and the

Primettes officially became The Supremes. It was during this formative period that Diane changed her professional name to Diana.

The Supremes' early recordings languished at the bottom of the charts, if they charted at all. A strong vocalist, Ballard shared lead vocal duties on their early songs with Ross. She possessed a powerful gospel voice and was considered by some of her contemporaries to have the better voice of the two. Gordy, however, preferred Ross's voice, which was softer and breathier. He believed it had crossover appeal and was better suited for mainstream audiences. After a flat-line start to their careers and three years spent relegated to singing backup for some of Motown's other artists, The Supremes' fortune changed.

The group had its first hit with "Where Did Our Love Go," in 1964. By then, Ross had assumed full-time lead-vocalist duties. Ballard was upset about her permanent relegation to backup singer but continued to sing. The group's success was prolific, with twelve number-one hits from 1964 to 1969. These included timeless numbers like "Baby Love" and "Stop in the Name of Love." At the height of their popularity, The Supremes were one of the biggest acts in music, achieving record sales on a scale closely matching that of the Beatles.

The three young friends, African American women from Detroit, had become global superstars at a time when racial segregation was rife in many parts of the United States and the American civil rights movement was in full swing. The Motown sound was a music sensation, and The Supremes were leading the way. From the outside, their story seemed like a fairy tale come true. Their clothes and hairstyles were influential, and by all outer appearances, Ross, Wilson, and Ballard had finally arrived. Strong record sales, television appearances, and tours such as Dick Clark's Caravan of Stars ensured that The Supremes played for sold-out audiences worldwide. Yet, as is so often the case with fame, the group's friendly images and vestiges of wealth and success masked the turmoil brewing behind the scenes.

The relationships between the women were generally amicable during their ascent to fame and during the first few years following their first number-one hit, but there were problems beneath the surface. There was always an underlying tension between Diana Ross and Ballard during their time in The Supremes. Beginning in 1967, Ballard's relationship with both Ross and Gordy showed signs of deterioration, making her future with The Supremes tenuous. Her relationship with Mary Wilson remained strong despite the surrounding tensions. Ballard felt that Gordy was constantly admonishing her for the quality of her singing, as well as accusing her of making the group's performances less than perfect.

Some of Gordy's accusations stemmed from Ballard's actions as the result of her increasing depression, which caused her to turn to alcohol. Never possessing a high tolerance for alcohol, Ballard could become almost intoxicated after having just one beer. Sensing that Gordy was angling to push her out of the group, Ballard became depressed.

It was common for all the members of The Supremes to have casual drinks before a show. However, by 1967 Ballard appeared to be using alcohol as a way to escape her pain. She claimed that Gordy had been chiding her about her weight, telling her that she was fat. A size 12 and standing 5 feet, 7 inches, Ballard was quite happy with her figure, as were many of her male fans. However, Gordy was thought to insinuate that standing next to Ross, Ballard looked especially large.

The insults and feelings of insecurity over her position in the group caused her to drink on that fateful night in 1967, before a show at the Flamingo Hotel in Las Vegas. After a few drinks, she took the stage with the group. Thinking about Gordy's negative attention toward her weight, she exaggerated her supposed obesity and pushed her stomach out as far as it could go during the performance. The next morning Gordy called Ballard and fired her on the spot. That night was the end of the road for Ballard. She was never to perform with The Supremes again. From that point on, singer Cindy Birdsong would appear in her place.

Ballard was unaware that Birdsong had actually been rehearsing with the other two members of The Supremes and shadowing her performances for weeks. Birdsong had, in fact, stepped in for Ballard on at least two previous occasions when she was ill. When Ballard's career came to an abrupt halt, Birdsong had been conveniently positioned to seamlessly step right in. Gordy has been characterized in many ways over the years, and one thing appears to ring true. When he set his mind to do something, he did it.

Approximately one week after that fateful night in Las Vegas, Motown's vice president met with Ballard. At the time, she was living on a weekly allowance from Motown and was not in control of her assets. The vice president's objective was to have her sign an agreement that would legally remove her from the group in exchange for payments of $2,500 per year for six years, for a total of $15,000. According to Ballard, Motown's lawyer told her that the label was doing her a favor because she was not due any money from the label upon her removal from the group.[132] Ballard, crying, signed the agreement without any legal counsel of her own. After signing the document, she told the vice president from Motown that they "could take it and stick it up their ass."[133]

She later retained the services of a lawyer, Leonard Baun, who agreed to represent her in exchange for 20 percent of any amount she might receive from Motown. Baun convinced her to create a talent management company, Talent Management, Inc., of which he would serve as president and treasurer. Baun was able to obtain $75,689 that Motown held in a joint Motown-Ballard account. Out of those funds, Baun paid himself $5,000 for his services with

Talent Management, Inc., and spent almost $10,000 to purchase 700 shares of stock in Ballard's name. He later paid himself approximately $43,000 in lawyer's fees, well over half the amount given to Ballard by Motown.

Baun worked with Motown for six months with the objective of setting aside its initial agreement and replacing it with one that was more favorable to Ballard. In the new agreement, dated February 1, 1968, Florence Ballard agreed to the following key points in exchange for a lump sum payment of $160,001: (1) that she released Motown from all past, present, and future liability; (2) that she had no right or ownership in the name "The Supremes"; (3) that she had been provided a full and complete accounting from her first day at Motown until the day she was terminated; (4) that she had received a complete accounting for all royalties due her since her first day at Motown until the day she was terminated, and that the accounting was correct; and (5) that she transferred her rights in all future royalties, commissions, and fees to Motown. In addition to the $160,001 payment for forgoing 100 percent of her future royalties, Motown is reported to have given her lawyer a payment of $300,000, which represented Ballard's earnings as a Supreme to date, less amounts recouped as expenses.[134] It is unclear whether Ballard received this additional amount, because the release agreement clearly states that the $160,001 payment was made, in part, for acknowledging the receipt of "a complete accounting for all royalties due her since her first day at Motown until the day she was terminated and that the accounting [was] correct." The payment of $160,001 received by Florence Ballard in 1968 is equivalent to $1.1 million in 2012, adjusted for inflation.

Royalties are traditionally paid to an artist after the record company recoups its costs. These may include recording costs, tour costs, advertising, and so on. Given the magnitude of record sales by The Supremes and the longevity of their hit songs from the

1960s, most of which included Ballard's vocals, it does not take a financial expert to see that Florence Ballard would have been better off with an agreement that did not sign away her rights to future royalties and other payments.

According to Ballard, Motown paid out the $160,001 in three separate checks: $20,196.06 as payment for her time in The Supremes, $5,000 for the release of any rights to the "Diana Ross and The Supremes" name, and a $134,804.94 payment from Motown Record Corporation.[135] In October 1968, Baun, who had received Motown's payments on behalf of Ballard, notified her that the entire $160,001 payment had been spent. Angry and demanding an accounting of what happened to her money, she ultimately fired Baun.

Lacking a steady source of income and believing the terms of her Motown release agreement were unfavorable, Ballard obtained new counsel and filed a lawsuit against the label. The suit was filed on February 1, 1971, in Wayne County Circuit Court in Michigan and sought damages of $8.7 million. In her complaint, Ballard acknowledged that she had signed her original recording agreement with Motown in 1961 at the age of seventeen, still a minor. She further stated that she did not receive counsel other than that provided by Motown when signing the original agreement and her renewal agreement in 1964. Ballard claimed that Gordy told her that he was a "trusted friend" and that Motown would take care of her and act in her best interest.[136]

She claimed that Motown had fraudulently misrepresented the amount of money she was owed. Her assertion was that, according to the original contract, Motown was obligated to pay her royalties on all record sales and to keep an accurate accounting of those sales. She accused Motown of falsely telling her upon her dismissal from the group that she was not entitled to receive a termination payment and that the accounting was up to date. This was difficult for Ballard to accept, given the millions of records sold.

She also claimed that Motown breached its contract with her by not fulfilling a promise to guide her career and finances in her best interest. Specifically, she claimed that the label ignored its duties by not once informing her between 1960 and 1968, the duration of her time with Motown, of the amount of money she was owed, and by spending a significantly greater amount of time promoting and acting in the best interest of the career of Diana Ross.

In total, Ballard sued on eleven counts, including tort claims of misrepresentation and intentional infliction of mental and emotional disturbance, as well as for rescission of the 1968 general release agreement. She wanted the court to rescind the release agreement on the grounds that she had been induced to sign it based on fraudulent misrepresentation by Motown. Conversely, Motown wanted the court to declare that Ballard's lawsuit could not go forward because the general release agreement was fully enforceable. The court ruled in favor of Motown on all counts.

The court briskly swept away Ballard's claims and granted Motown an accelerated judgment. The court held that from the moment Ballard signed the release agreement with Motown, there was no contractual relationship between her and the label, and therefore no liability for Motown for any problems she may have suffered after the date of the release agreement. The court further stated that the payment she had received from Motown was inclusive of any compensation for those injuries occurring during her time under contract with Motown. It also held that Ballard's lawsuit could move forward only if she first rescinded the general release agreement. However, this presented a catch-22 for Ballard because to rescind the agreement, she would first have to return the $160,001 she received from Motown. That would prove difficult because her former lawyer had spent a significant portion of the money.

Ballard appealed the decision to the Michigan Court of Appeals, which upheld, in part, the trial court's ruling.[137] The appellate court found the general release agreement to be valid, which effectively brought Ballard's legal challenges against Motown to a halt, because the indemnification provision of the agreement prohibited Ballard from making any claims against Motown. In other words, Ballard was out of luck.

There was one exception in the appellate-court ruling. Ballard had claimed that Motown's false representation of the money she was due caused periods of extreme stress and bouts of depression after her departure from The Supremes. The appellate court held that her case was to be remanded to the trial court, but only on the issue of emotional distress damages she may have suffered after signing the release. This was a small victory for Ballard, but things were about to get even tougher.

Ballard seemed to have one stroke of bad luck after another. She signed the original release agreement, which paid her $2,500 per year for six years, without legal counsel. Baun, the lawyer she hired to renegotiate that agreement, which resulted ultimately in the February 1, 1968, general release agreement, did not appear to have an understanding of the complexities of the music business. Most importantly, he did not appear to have an appreciation for the royalty schemes of the recording industry. He also failed to recognize that Ballard may have had a right to use the name The Supremes and that the right had a commercial value. To make things worse, he embezzled a large percentage of the money she received from Motown.

After her court battles and her struggles with ineffective counsel, she tried to embark on a solo career, but it never took off. Her struggling career took another turn for the worse when she appointed her new husband as manager. He was a former driver for Motown with no prior entertainment experience, and he made poor and dubious business decisions. They later separated. Eventually, Ballard and her three children were foreclosed upon and forced to leave their house. It was a home that Motown had purchased for her when she was with The Supremes. She believed that Motown had been making the monthly house payments. When the payments went into arrears, she attempted to keep up but was unable to do so. Ballard and her children were forced to move in with her sister.

In 1975, a reporter from the Detroit Free Press wrote a profile story on Ballard that provided a detailed, firsthand account of her experiences with Motown and her life after The Supremes. The article also brought to light that Ballard had been living on welfare. When the article was published, the news of her financial situation spread quickly, and there was a small outcry from the public that Ballard, once a member of one of the biggest musical acts of all time, was living in such dire straits.[138]

The article sparked renewed interest in Ballard. She was invited to sing at a variety of events, including an appearance in 1975 at the Henry and Edsel Ford auditorium in Detroit, backed by the all-female group the Deadly Nightshade. The reception from the crowd was enthusiastic, and her performance received rave reviews. Ballard also received a $72,000 insurance payment for her lawyer's malpractice, which allowed her to buy a small home. It appeared as though things were looking up. But this long-awaited streak of good luck was not to last.

One evening in February 1976, Ballard complained of numbness in her arms and legs and was rushed to the hospital. The next day she passed away. Contrary to urban legend, she did not pass away from a drug or alcohol overdose. It was a stealth coronary thrombosis, a blood clot in the coronary arteries, that ended her life. Florence Ballard, an original member of one of the biggest music groups in history, was dead at the age of thirty-two.

Ballard had experienced moments in her life that were the wonders dreams are made of. Her performances with The Supremes had taken place during the height of the supergroup's popularity. She had been at the forefront of a musical explosion in the 1960s. But along with extreme highs, she also experienced extreme lows in her career. One of those low points occurred when she signed away all her future earning potential from The Supremes in a release agreement that was sorely undervalued.

Looking at Ballard's story, observers may find themselves asking "if only" after every turn. If only she had better legal counsel. If only she had not been pushed out of the group. If only she had not signed the release agreement. It is difficult to avoid thinking that, under different circumstances, Florence Ballard and her heirs could have avoided her post-Supremes hardships and enjoyed the benefits generated by the fruits of her labor of love—singing with The Supremes.

Perhaps Ballard's happy ending can be found on the silver screen. In the movie *Dreamgirls*, the character Effie is loosely based on Ballard. Her character must live on welfare after being forced out of the group. The story ends on a high note, however. As the movie draws to a close, Effie has a hit single and reunites for "one night only" with her former girl group for a sold-out farewell concert. Jennifer Hudson, who plays Effie in the film, won a Golden Globe and an Academy Award for her portrayal. During her acceptance speech, she dedicated the Oscar to "Florence Ballard, who never got a chance."[139] It was a great honor for Ballard, a real-life dream girl, and perhaps a happy ending after all. Then again, that's Hollywood. In the real world, Ballard's story may always beg the question of what could have been.

A Beatle, a Girl Group, and "Subconscious" Copyright Infringement

Bright Tunes Music v. Harrisongs Music,
420 F. Supp. 177 (S.D.N.Y. 1976).

"**H**e's so fine, doo lang, doo lang, doo lang." These are the first few words of the popular song "He's So Fine," made famous by the Chiffons. Recorded in 1962, "He's So Fine" enjoyed five weeks at the number-one spot on the U.S. Billboard charts in 1963. The song also had success in the United Kingdom, reaching the number-twelve spot on the U.K. Singles Chart. Another hit song, "My Sweet Lord," by Beatles guitarist George Harrison, was written and released almost a decade after "He's So Fine." Both songs became the subject of a heated music copyright-infringement lawsuit when Bright Tunes Music, Inc., copyright owners for "He's So Fine," sued Harrison for infringement of their song.

When "He's So Fine" was recorded, Bright Tunes Music, Inc., was one of two small music publishing companies owned by Bright Tunes Productions, located in Brooklyn, New York. The other company they owned was Lionel Music, Inc. The three-person singing group The Tokens, made famous by their hit "The Lion Sleeps Tonight," owned Bright Tunes. Their manager and business consultant Seymour Barash was also a co-owner. After performing and recording in 1961 and 1962, the group decided to produce the music of other artists as well.

After "The Lion Sleeps Tonight" became a hit, Bright Tunes entered into an agreement with Capitol Records, in 1962. The agreement required Bright Tunes to find new talent, select material, and produce and promote the talent. The Capitol Records deal was for a five-year period. During this period, Bright Tunes was required to produce a minimum of twelve singles per year. The songs were to remain the exclusive property of Capitol Records, although Capitol reserved the right to decline any material or artist offered by Bright Tunes.

Within months of the Capitol Records deal, a songwriter by the name of Ronnie Mack penned "He's So Fine" and approached Bright Tunes with the song. They liked it and agreed to produce the song. Mack asked the Chiffons, a female foursome, to sing the tune. Capitol did not receive the song well. The label felt that it did not suit their tastes and turned it down. Bright Tunes was persistent, however, and turned to another label, Laurie Records. The timing could not have been better for Laurie, because the label had lost its top artist, Dion, just two months earlier to Columbia Records.

"He's So Fine" was number one on Billboard's Hot 100 for three weeks in a row. It eventually had sales of more than one million records and reached number one on the pop and R&B charts. Shortly after the song reached number one, Ronnie Mack died. The Chiffons performed several high-profile shows just as the British Invasion of American pop music was about to infiltrate the airwaves. In February 1964, the Chiffons were billed as one of the opening acts for the Beatles' first U.S. concert, held at the

Memorial Coliseum in Washington, D.C. In June 1964, they opened for the Rolling Stones on their first U.S. tour. "He's So Fine" had a lot of fans, and the British rock 'n' roll groups likely benefited somewhat from this wave of excitement during their American debut performances.

While the Chiffons were having success with "He's So Fine," George Harrison was just beginning to try his hand at songwriting. His song "Don't Bother Me" was included on the Beatles' second album, *With the Beatles*. By the mid-1960s he had become exposed to traditional Indian music. This led him to study the sitar, an Indian stringed instrument, and some of his songs were then written with an Indian influence. In 1967, he wrote the score for *Wonderwall*, an instrumental film soundtrack that showcased both his Eastern and Western influences. In 1968, Harrison's song "While My Guitar Gently Weeps," appeared on the Beatles' *White Album*, with Eric Clapton playing lead guitar. In 1969, Harrison wrote two of his most popular songs: "Something" and "Here Comes the Sun." In addition to the Beatles' rendition of "Something," it was also recorded by a wide variety of artists, including Isaac Hayes and Frank Sinatra. "Here Comes the Sun" was also recorded widely by a broad selection of artists, including Richie Havens.

After the Beatles went their separate ways in the spring of 1970, Harrison spent four months in London recording an album, *All Things Must Pass*. Co-produced with Phil Spector, the album included eighteen songs. Sixteen were composed by Harrison, one by Bob Dylan, and the other by Harrison and Dylan together. The musicians on the album were also well known and included Billy Preston, Eric Clapton, and Dave Mason. A reflective and spiritual side of George Harrison came through on the album, with tracks such as "What Is Life," "The Art of Dying," and "My Sweet Lord." Both the album and the single, "My Sweet Lord," moved to the top of the charts.

The immediate reaction of some listeners to "My Sweet Lord" was that it sounded a lot like "Oh Happy Day," a gospel song by the Edwin Hawkins Singers. The "Oh Happy Day" comparisons were not the problem for Harrison, however. The problem was a comparison to "He's So Fine." On February 10, 1971, Bright Tunes filed a lawsuit for copyright infringement against George Harrison on the grounds that "My Sweet Lord" was unlawfully copied from "He's So Fine."[140]

Harrison's manager at the time was Allen Klein, head of ABKCO Music, Inc., a music publishing and management company. He was responsible for managing all of Harrison's business affairs, as well as those of the Beatles. Klein, acting on behalf of Harrison, attempted to thwart the lawsuit by offering to buy Bright Tunes outright. The negotiations for the purchase lasted several years, during which time the lawsuit was put on hold.

Klein's exploits with the Beatles are notorious. The group had originally been in favor of hiring him as manager. That is, everyone except Paul McCartney. When it came time to sign the management agreement, McCartney opted out because he did not trust Klein. McCartney's mistrust of Klein was in part because of stories he had heard from others in the music industry and in part because he wanted the management team of his wife's brother and father to fully handle the group's affairs.[141]

By 1975, the Beatles and Klein had a major falling out. They accused Klein of misrepresenting their finances and breaching his fiduciary duty toward them. This resulted in the severing of the relationship and bitter litigation. Klein's tenure as Harrison's business manager had also ended by this point. In the midst of the collapse of Klein's relationship with Harrison and the Beatles, the negotiations to purchase Bright Tunes continued.

In late 1975, Harrison, no longer working with Klein, made another offer to Bright Tunes. Shortly afterward, Bright Tunes received a third-party offer that was double the amount of the one Harrison had made. It was from someone close to home who possessed firsthand information about the negotiations. The third-party offer had come from Allen Klein.

In a strategic and backhanded move, Klein, who had come up with the idea of purchasing Bright Tunes and initially made offers on Harrison's behalf, had re-emerged and was now bidding against him. With the offers on the table, Bright Tunes thought Klein's offer was, in effect, showing Harrison's hand. Bright Tunes, obviously aware of Klein's former representation of Harrison, believed that Klein possessed insider knowledge regarding the true value of the "He's So Fine" copyright and the amount that Harrison might actually be willing to pay. With this information, Bright Tunes rejected Harrison's offer. Unfortunately for Klein, Bright Tunes rejected his offer as well. Because none of the parties could reach agreeable settlement terms, the Bright Tunes copyright infringement lawsuit went to trial.

The case was presented in the U.S. District Court, Southern District of New York, in February 1976.[142] The objective of the trial was to determine whether Harrison plagiarized "He's So Fine" in his song "My Sweet Lord." Plagiarism, which is the act of stealing and passing off the ideas or words of another as one's own, does not exist by name in law. A copyright owner who believes his or her work has been plagiarized may be able to seek recourse by filing a lawsuit against the alleged offender on a claim of copyright infringement, although it differs somewhat from plagarism. Bright Tunes felt that Harrison had violated its rights by using the musical structure of "He's So Fine" to create "My Sweet Lord" and pass it off as his original work.

The law of copyright contemplates the fact that directly copying another's work is not always the primary concern. It is the copying of elements of another's work and calling it one's own that is

139

generally of more concern and relevance. Provided the accuser owns a valid copyright in the work in question, a court will typically apply a threshold test to analyze whether infringement has occurred in a music infringement case.

Although the infringement analysis varies by jurisdiction, generally speaking the court will first look at whether the alleged infringer had access to the copyrighted work. If the work at issue is found to be similar enough to the copyright holder's original work, but it can be demonstrated that the alleged infringer never had access to the original work, then the infringement claim will likely fail. However, if it can be demonstrated that the alleged infringer had access to the copyrighted work, the court then applies a second test, commonly known as the "substantial similarity" or "striking similarity" test. This test asks whether the new work at issue has substantial similarities to the original copyrighted work.[143] Under this test, the court will analyze whether the alleged copying is "quantitatively and qualitatively sufficient" enough to find that infringement has occurred. In some jurisdictions, exceptions have been allowed if the alleged infringer can show that the level of copying was *de minimis*, meaning the copying was extremely small and insignificant. However, in *Bridgeport Music, Inc. v. Dimension Films*, the Sixth Circuit ruled in 2005 that a *de minimis* use of a song was not a defense to infringement.[144]

A person could be forgiven for thinking that an advanced knowledge of music theory is required for this type of analysis. Conveniently, the judge hearing the case happened to be a composer as well, and displayed sensitivity to the intricacies of music composition. As demonstrated by the court's analysis, two songs that are actually quite simple in sound can create quite a bit of complexity when compared against one another.

The court began its analysis by taking apart the two songs at issue to see if they were both built upon the same, or a substantially similar, music blueprint. First in line for deconstruction was "He's So Fine." The song's musical phrases are grouped into two motifs, Motif A and Motif B. A *motif*, as applied to a song, is a recurring idea or theme. Motif A consisted of the tonal grouping *sol-mi-re*, or translated as a chord progression, G-E-D. This was the pattern of the first line, "He's So Fine," followed by the musical chant "doo lang, doo lang, doo lang." This motif was repeated four times.

Subsequently the song transitioned into Motif B, of which the first two lines are "I don't know how I'm going to do it / But I'm going to make him mine." Motif B was the tonal grouping *sol-la-do-la-do*, or the chords G-A-C-A-C. This motif was also repeated four times. In Motif B's second repetition, the court pointed out that the song contains a grace note.[145] A *grace note* is a musical flourish that is added to a note for ornamental purposes. It is often not actually written into the composition. The grace note in "He's So Fine" distinguishes the second repetition of Motif B from the first to read *sol-la-do-la-re-do*, or G-A-C-A-D-C, with the addition of *re*, or D, as the grace note. The remaining two repetitions are the same as the original Motif B pattern.

Next for deconstruction was "My Sweet Lord," which the court considered to be built upon the structure of motifs A and B in "He's So Fine." In Harrison's song, Motif A is played underneath the first verse, beginning with the lyrics "My Sweet Lord," and repeated four times. Instead of the "doo lang" series, he sings "Hallelujah." The song then transitions into Motif B, which, like in "He's So Fine," is repeated four times. However, the grace note appears in the fourth repetition of Motif B in "My Sweet Lord" instead of the second repetition, as heard in "He's So Fine."

The court then probed deeper into Harrison's testimony about the creation of "My Sweet Lord." Harrison described the creative process as beginning with an idea that sprouted from impromptu vamping on his guitar. He recounted being in Copenhagen,

Denmark, along with his group, which included Billy Preston, a singer and keyboardist, who had played regularly with Harrison and sometimes with the Beatles.

Harrison said he had been playing around on his guitar, alternating between two chords. As he was doing so, he started inserting the words "hallelujah" and "Hare Krishna." He liked what he was developing and went to the rest of his group to share his new work in progress. The group joined in, creating harmonies and singing "hallelujah" and "Hare Krishna" interchangeably. Out of this jam session, "My Sweet Lord" began to take shape. About one week after this initial session, Harrison and his band returned to London and went into the studio. Harrison gave his basic theme, which was Motif A, to Preston as lead musician and asked him to help bring the song into fruition. Harrison supervised the recording takes and was credited as composer when the album was released.

Unfortunately for Harrison, the court found in favor of Bright Tunes. It ruled that Harrison did indeed have access to "He's So Fine." Examples were given, such as the fact that it was number twelve on the charts in Britain on June 1, 1963, while at the same time one of the Beatles' songs was number one. Furthermore, "He's So Fine" was one of the top hits in Britain for seven weeks.

The court also found that "My Sweet Lord" was substantially similar to "He's So Fine" because motifs A and B were very similar. Despite these findings the judge appeared reluctant to make his ruling. In fact, he recognized that Harrison, in his creative process, was probably just drawing upon a "wellspring" of inspiration and choosing which chords and melodies would sound best to listeners. Although Harrison was found to have infringed upon "He's So Fine," the court considered him to have done so subconsciously. Nevertheless, whether the infringement was intentional or not, the net effect was that he was still considered guilty of copyright infringement.

The notion of a "wellspring" from which a songwriter draws inspiration is a poetic way of describing the influence that the sounds and expressions of everyday life have upon the songwriter. For example, blues music is said to be one of the roots of rock 'n' roll. It is distinctive because of its characteristic three-chord progression. Early rock 'n' roll was largely based on the chord progressions of blues music.

Indigenous to the United States, blues music was popular and influential among the bands that would make up the British Invasion during the 1960s. The Beatles, like their American rock 'n' roll and doo-wop counterparts, created music using blues-inspired chord patterns that had become commonplace through popular R&B and rock 'n' roll. Liverpool nightclubs such as the Cavern Club featured a steady stream of young R&B-inspired rock 'n' roll groups. As one of Liverpool's most famous exports, the Beatles were a constant presence in this scene. Their doo-wop, R&B, and rock 'n' roll music influences were everywhere.

It is not surprising that Harrison, who was influenced by the blues and early rock 'n' roll, crafted a song following a chord pattern that was found not only in "He's So Fine" but also in many other popular songs. Perhaps when songs consist of limited chord progressions, created using a finite number of notes and chord permutations based on the Western music scale, it is virtually guaranteed that several songs created by different composers will sound similar.

The damages portion of the trial was delayed significantly after Bright Tunes announced it had sold its copyright in "He's So Fine" on April 13, 1978, to Allen Klein for $587,000. This transaction included a payment of approximately $422,000 to Bright Tunes and $165,000 to the estate of Ronnie Mack, composer of "He's So Fine." As a result, Klein, who had been fired by Harrison and the

Beatles, now, as ABKCO, Inc., assumed Bright Tunes' place as plaintiff against Harrison.

Counsel for Harrison immediately amended its pleading, noting that Klein had been the exclusive business manager for George Harrison from November 1970 to March 1973 and asserted a claim of breach of fiduciary duty by Klein. This was a well-timed strategy as it was subsequently determined that Klein enabled Bright Tunes to demand a higher value by providing information regarding "My Sweet Lord" that only an insider would know. This included estimates of both domestic and foreign royalty income as well as his personal estimate of the value of the "My Sweet Lord" copyright and worldwide future earnings. The court was left to answer not only the question of damages but also whether ABKCO should be disqualified from pursuing the lawsuit. With the delay, the case was not heard for several years.

On April 3, 1980, while damages and counterclaims were under review by the court, Harrison voluntarily settled with subpublishers who held the foreign rights to "He's So Fine." Subpublishers are generally used for overseas sales and have full publishing rights under license from the original copyright owner. According to the license agreement, each subpublisher paid 50 percent of mechanical and performance royalties earned to Bright Tunes. As the new owner of Bright Tunes, ABKCO also settled foreign claims with Harrison. The voluntary settlement by Harrison resulted in each subpublisher of "He's So Fine" receiving 40 percent of past and future earnings of "My Sweet Lord" generated in their respective territories. This agreement was similar in structure to a previous settlement made by Harrison in the High Court of Britain in 1977. It resulted from a charge of copyright infringement brought by the Peter Maurice Company, Ltd., in 1973. Since 1963, the company had been a subpublisher of "He's So Fine" worldwide, except for the United States and Canada. The British litigation was against the wishes of the management of Bright Tunes.

On February 19, 1981, the trial court handed down an opinion regarding the award of damages. Though the court viewed ABKCO's actions in the deals as troublesome enough to render it potentially ineligible for recovery, the court opted to rule on what the damages would have been if there had not been any underhanded behavior from ABKCO. After several calculations, it determined that $1.6 million of earnings from "My Sweet Lord" were attributable to "He's So Fine." The money would be paid to Bright Tunes and ultimately ABKCO, as the owner of Bright Tunes.

The next step was to make a determination on the issue of Allen Klein's fiduciary responsibility. Klein's "covert intrusion" into the settlement negotiations between Harrison and Bright Tunes was troubling to the court.[146] Even though he no longer represented Harrison, his fiduciary duty toward him remained in issues relating to Bright Tunes. Harrison had been unaware of Klein's secret activities. The court found that Klein's offer made Bright Tunes less willing to settle with Harrison during negotiations because of the information received from Klein and his status as Harrison's former business manager.

Klein's conduct over the previous few years, leading to his breach of fiduciary duty, led the court to limit his $1.6 million dollar award to $587,000, which was the price he had paid for Bright Tunes. The rationale was that ABKCO should not profit from the purchase of Bright Tunes' only asset, the copyright in "He's So Fine." At the same time, the court did not want ABKCO to forego its acquisition cost of $587,000 for the song's copyright. Therefore, it directed ABKCO to hold the Bright Tunes copyright in a constructive trust and to transfer it to Harrison upon his payment of $587,000 to ABKCO. The purpose of a constructive trust is to prevent one party from benefitting unjustly at the expense

145

of another. Although it is not a trust in the traditional sense, the court orders the party being unjustly enriched to secure the property and transfer it to the proper owner.

In November 1983, ABKCO appealed to the Second Circuit Court of Appeals.[147] It argued that no breach of fiduciary duty to Harrison occurred because confidential information was not passed to Bright Tunes. ABKCO also argued that the scope of the constructive trust directed by the lower court was too broad. The rationale was that it over-reached by including the settlement value of foreign rights previously concluded with Harrison on April 3, 1980. The appellate court affirmed the district court's decision, agreeing that ABKCO had breached its fiduciary duty. However, it saw a need for more work on the trust and remanded that issue back to the district court. The issue on remand was how much of the $587,000 purchase price paid by ABKCO for Bright Tunes was attributable to the value of foreign rights previously settled with Harrison in 1980. This amount was to be deducted from the $587,000 and held in a constructive trust for the benefit of Harrison. Upon remand, the district court attributed $316,980 of the $587,000 to foreign rights involved in the 1980 settlement. The final amount Harrison was required to pay ABKCO was $270,020, plus interest.

ABKCO's final appeal was before the Second Circuit, which delivered a decision on September 5, 1991.[148] ABKCO contended that the district court made an error in its calculation of the amount required for Harrison to pay for the Bright Tunes copyright. It argued that the court's internal calculations showed that Harrison should pay $459,034 instead of $270,020. The difference was due largely to the earnings assumptions regarding foreign royalties. Harrison made a cross-appeal, asserting, among other issues, that the court should not allow ABKCO to receive a 20 percent management fee for administering the trust. After weighing the evidence, the court affirmed the findings of the trial court.

ABKCO's appeal was denied, leaving Harrison to pay just $270,020, plus interest, to acquire the "He's So Fine" copyright from the trust and own it free and clear.

The years of legal wrangling might seem out of character for Harrison, the Beatles member sometimes referred to as "the quiet one." Perhaps "the quiet fighter" is a more fitting nickname when one considers that his estate now owns the copyright to both "He's So Fine" and "My Sweet Lord." Harrison passed away in 2001 of cancer, at the age of fifty-eight.

Proving Infringement Note by Note

We often hear songs that remind us of familiar tunes. Most people have only a passing interest in this similarity. However, when a songwriter has a similar experience, the belief is often that someone has copied his or her work without permission. The next action may be to sue the composer of the similar-sounding tune for copyright infringement.

Two of the essential elements for proving music copyright infringement are (1) that an artist had access to the original work and (2) similarity. With respect to similarity, courts have required that the plaintiff show that the allegedly infringing work is "strikingly similar" or "substantially similar" to the original work.[149] The plaintiff must demonstrate that the allegedly infringing work has constituent elements of the original work. Although experts do weigh in, the ultimate requirement for establishing similarity is not an analysis of the music but rather the ears of ordinary lay observers. A jury must decide whether an ordinary, reasonable lay listener, the average person, would find substantial similarity in the work of the plaintiff and the defendant.

Most music experts acknowledge that it is quite common to find a similarity between popular compositions because of the limited number of notes available to composers in certain music genres. Some types of music, such as pop and rock, are acknowledged to use common rhythms and harmony. In *Gaste v. Kaiserman*, the Second Circuit warned that a court must be "mindful of the limited number of notes and chords available to composers and the resulting fact that common themes frequently appear in various compositions, especially in popular music."[150] This phenomenon has been observed in various types of music. In the classical music genre, for example, the first chord in Wagner's *Tristan und Isolde* is built upon the notes F, B, D-sharp, and G-sharp. This chord pattern has been the subject of much debate among classical music scholars, who have observed the same pattern in other classical compositions. Commonly used chords and patterns make it extremely difficult to prove a case of infringement, because establishing that multiple works contain common themes is insufficient. Bolstered by this line of thinking, defendants often attempt to defeat a claim by showing that their allegedly infringing chords or riffs are in fact commonly used in a number of other prior works.

The Ninth Circuit Court of Appeals developed two tests to help with this process, the extrinsic test and the intrinsic test.[151] First, the *extrinsic test* requires the court to consider objective evidence of the similarity of expression in the two works. The analytical and expert dissection of the works is critical because the plaintiff's case will never reach the jury if it does not survive this stage. If the plaintiff survives the extrinsic test in the summary judgment stage, then the plaintiff must satisfy the jury on the objective factors and also meet the *intrinsic test*, which asks the jury to decide whether an ordinary, reasonable observer would find a substantial similarity.

In the Ninth Circuit, proof of infringement under the extrinsic test involves a balancing test referred to as the "Inverse Ratio Rule." Under this test, the greater degree of access proved, the lower the standard of proof for objective similarity. Defendants can defeat the extrinsic test by showing that the allegedly offending notes are simply stock musical phrases that do not have copyright protection. In such situations, an expert musicologist is often required.

If the stock musical phrase argument is unavailable or fails, the extrinsic test requires a detailed examination of chord progressions and harmonic analysis in both works to see how they relate to each other. The plaintiff may show the same chord progression in both works, but the issue here is not just the chord progression. Even if the same chord progression exists, the defendant can defeat a claim by demonstrating the differences in melody,

149

Interlude (cont.)

rhythm, and rhythmic phrasing combined. For example, some major chords, such as D, C, and G, may appear in both works being compared, but the addition of a different melody, tonality, rhythm, and lyrics can sometimes qualify a work as original. The court will determine, with the aid of expert testimony, among other things, whether notes are played with the same pitch, words are placed in the same position, or tempos are similar. For example, an expert might perform a chord-by-chord analysis and opine that choruses of songs demonstrate substantial similarity because they both "emphasize the second scale degree, C, over an A in the bass, resolving to the third scale degree, D, over a D in the bass in the last half of the measure."[152] This was the opinion of an expert in *Swirsky v. Carey*, where it was alleged in a lawsuit filed in 2000 by Seth Swirsky that Mariah Carey infringed upon his work with her song "Thank God I Found You." The Ninth Circuit reversed the California district court's dismissal of the lawsuit, which was based in part on the court's criticism of the expert's methodology. The lawsuit was subsequently settled in 2006.

There is still some uncertainty among the courts as to the best method to approach the substantially similar issue. Some courts, including the First, Second, and Eleventh Circuit, have adopted the term *probative similarity* to apply to the initial determination of substantial similarity. There is also uncertainty among fans and musicians about the determination of substantial similarity. This was evident from the Internet discussions generated by a lawsuit filed in 2008 by Joe Satriani against the band Coldplay.

In *Joe Satriani v. Christopher Martin*, Satriani alleged that Coldplay's hit song "Viva la Vida" "copied and incorporated substantial, original portions" of his musical composition, "If I Could Fly."[153] Demonstrations by musicians and samples of the songs posted on the Internet resulted in a flurry of comments ranging from those saying they could hear no similarities to those saying only a few notes were similar to others saying they were obviously the same song. So although there are several methods in place to test for copyright infringement, the methods themselves continue to be reevaluated. A conclusive, failproof, all-encompassing analysis will likely never be implemented. Although each test looks for the similarities between two musical works, each analysis is itself a unique framework of external and internal information.

When the Manager Takes All:

You Can't Always Get What You Want

Michael Philip Jagger and Keith Richards, Claimants-Petitioners, and ABKCO INDUSTRIES, INC., and ABKCO MUSIC, INC., Respondents (Case No. 1310 1000 73), arbitration award, May 11, 1976.

S ome say that behind every successful band stands a great manager. A great band manager will help a band stay organized and provide guidance for some of its most important career decisions. A top-flight manager always operates with the band's best interest in mind. For every great manager, however, there are many tales describing the unscrupulous acts of bad managers. Those tales include scandalous acts such as swindling the band, using inside information against the best interest of the band, and other acts of impropriety. The Rolling Stones, one of the most successful bands in history, were not immune to the industrious machinations of a bad manager. During the late 1960s they had a manager who, at the end of their relationship with him, walked away with ownership of practically the entire Rolling Stones song catalog as it existed at the time.

On September 2, 1971, the Stones filed a $29 million lawsuit in New York State Supreme Court against their former business manager, Allen Klein. The Rolling Stones' band members at the time were parties to the suit. They were singer Mick Jagger, guitarist Keith Richards, bassist William "Bill" Wyman, and drummer Charles "Charlie" Watts. The complaint alleged that Klein, as the Rolling Stones' business manager, tax consultant, and accountant, exercised his authority in a manner that benefitted himself more than his client. It was also alleged that Klein's actions were malicious and damaging to the Stones.

At the band's inception in 1962, Mick Jagger and Keith Richards were nineteen years old. The band's first gig was in July 1962 at the Marquee Jazz Club in London. In its early days, the band performed in various pubs, hotels, and clubs, primarily in London and the surrounding area. Brian Jones, a founding member, performed the dual tasks of band member and business manager. He was approximately twenty years old and responsible for promoting the band and negotiating with venue owners.

The first big break came when they began playing the large and fashionable Crawdaddy Club in London. In attendance one evening, specifically to see the Stones, were Andrew Loog Oldham and Eric Easton. Oldham, just nineteen years of age, had worked as a publicist for various British rock 'n' roll acts. Easton was an agent who had experience promoting musical acts. The meeting between Oldham, Easton, and the Stones eventually resulted in Oldham and Easton becoming co-managers of the Stones in April 1963. Oldham and Easton established a production company, Impact Sounds, to produce the group's recordings. Brian Jones, although unhappy about losing his managerial duties, played on as a band member.

Shortly afterward, the Stones entered into an agreement with Decca Records. The agreement was signed by Oldham. According to Oldham, a key feature of the agreement was that the group would retain artistic control and own the recording masters, which would then be leased to Decca.[154] The group received an advance payment that had to be recouped by Decca before any royalty payments were paid out. The band's upward trajectory was now set in motion, and the Stones began to perform constantly. After performing from late September 1963 to early November 1963 with the Everly Brothers, Bo Diddley, and Little Richard at various venues in London, they continuously worked twenty-nine of thirty-one days in January 1964.

The real catalyst for the rise of their careers appears to have been their first U.S. tour in June 1964. This was followed by television interviews in the United States and appearances on variety shows such as the *Ed Sullivan Show*, the *Red Skelton Show*, and the *Les Crane Show*. The Stones were releasing a continuous stream of music to the public in 1964.

After playing a significant number of cover songs, Mick Jagger and Keith Richards began writing songs in 1964. The Stones went on to earn gold records for their original songs, including "(I Can't Get No) Satisfaction," "Jumpin' Jack Flash," "The Last Time," and "It's All Over Now." "The Last Time" was the first Jagger/Richards song to reach number one in the United Kingdom. It also reached number nine on U.S. charts.

Despite the band's success, changes were made to the management team in 1965. Easton was terminated and Oldham relinquished his managerial duties, but he continued to produce records for the band until 1967. Court documents from the Chancery Division of the High Court in London show allegations that Oldham had been a heavy user of drugs and alcohol and that he was frequently drugged or drunk or both. In addition, it seems that although he was an effective record producer, he had poor business skills. He is reported to have said that there were occasions when he would carry no money and that he thought of the company's money as his own.[155]

Allen Klein, introduced to the band by Oldham, took over as manager. He was president of Allen Klein & Company, later to be changed to ABKCO Music, Inc., in 1968. The Stones were generally happy to see Klein take over the role of manager. He was an aggressive and tough negotiator who had no qualms about court battles. Most of the group thought he could provide the guidance they needed to fully exploit their career potential. However, Bill Wyman has said that, in retrospect, he was always troubled by Klein.[156]

In 1965 one of Klein's first acts as manager was to review contracts that the Stones may have entered into while they were under twenty-one years of age, which at the time was the age of capacity in the United Kingdom. In some cases, the Stones and Klein were able to disaffirm agreements based on the fact that the band members were minors when they entered into the contracts. In 1966, while Klein was managing the band's business affairs and Oldham was focusing only on music production, Klein purchased Oldham's ownership rights in the Stones' music. Oldham continued to produce until late 1967, when he moved to Latin America. Klein also renegotiated the Stones' contract with Decca in 1966 for a five-year period.

Bolstered by these changes, the Stones continued their output of recorded music in 1966. However, 1967 was a different story, beginning with the infamous Redlands drug bust, which occurred on February 12 at Richards's home in Sussex, England. About twenty police officers raided the home, resulting in the arrests of Richards and Jagger. The group began having public confrontations with authorities over drug-use offenses. Each confrontation raised a red flag for local authorities in potential touring destinations. The substance problems for Richards and Jones, in particular, were serious enough that it sometimes made acquiring visas difficult, hampering where the group could play. Another serious problem was that the group, although selling millions of records and bringing in millions of dollars, had little cash of its own. The band members were put into the position of having to request money from Klein to cover their expenses on occasion. After developing serious drug and alcohol problems, Jones left the band in 1969. He passed away that same year, having drowned in the swimming pool at his home.

The Stones' financial situation grew dire, causing them to believe management changes were necessary. They terminated the services of Allen Klein on July 30, 1970. The band also left Decca Records for Atlantic Records in August 1970. With Klein out of the picture, outside advisers examined the band's financial situation and discovered that in addition to the financial problems they expected to see, the band also owed large tax bills in Britain. They were advised to move to France to avoid the high tax rates in Britain. By doing so, they could also receive favorable tax treatment in Britain, under then-current British tax law, for living outside of the country for a certain number of days during the year.

The Stones took the advice of their advisers and in the spring of 1971 moved to the South of France following a "farewell" tour of the United Kingdom.[157] Although they continued to produce music while in France, they reportedly existed in a hazy world of drug use. The upside of this turbulent time, however, was the production of *Exile on Main Street*. Recorded in the basement of Richards's villa in the South of France, the gritty and raw album is considered by some critics to be one of the greatest albums of all time. Yet, the creation of timeless albums aside, their financial problems remained.

In August 1971, the Stones, along with Brian Jones's father, filed a lawsuit in Britain's High Court against Andrew Loog Oldham and

Eric Easton, former managers of the group. It was alleged that the two had made a secret deal in 1963 with Decca Records, the Stones' former record label, to deprive the group of royalties. It was also alleged that Oldham persuaded Brian Jones, who was a performing member but also the band's business manager in the early years, to accept a 6 percent royalty on the wholesale record price on behalf of the band, hiding from Jones the fact that Decca was willing to pay the band a 15 percent royalty. On top of this, the band alleged that Oldham had cut a secret deal in which Decca paid a 14 percent royalty to Oldham and Easton. Additionally, Oldham's contract with the Stones gave him a 25 percent management fee.[158] One month later, in September 1971, the Stones filed their $29 million lawsuit against Allen Klein and his associated corporations to recover money the Stones believed Klein had withheld from them. A settlement agreement was reached in May 1972.

Although a settlement agreement had been reached, the case was far from over. The parties agreed to arbitration. The arbitrator's decision was finalized on May 11, 1976. As a result of the decision, Klein became the sole owner of all the Rolling Stones songs written by Mick Jagger and Keith Richards through 1970.

Although it is not exactly clear why Jagger and Richards agreed to these terms, the state of the Decca contracts likely played a role. The first thing that Oldham did when he became manager in 1963 was to secure a contract for the Stones with Decca. The contract was between Decca and Oldham's production company, Impact Sound. In 1966, Klein purchased Oldham's interest in the Rolling Stones. He also renegotiated the contract with Decca at approximately the same time. Decca had entered into the contract with Oldham's company, and Klein assumed the contract after purchasing Oldham's interest. Klein already owned the rights to the band's original music through 1965 as the result of his purchase from Oldham. The renegotiated Decca Records contract expired in 1970, with the rights to the songs produced during the contract term likely reverting to Klein because Decca's original agreement was to lease the master recordings from the Stones, through Oldham, during their contract with them.

Then there was the matter of the group's publishing company. The Stones had set up their own publishing company, a U.K. company called Nanker Phelge Music. The name had been a "pen name" the Stones used for their early songwriting.[159] "Nanker" was a word the band had used to describe a contorted look on a person's face. "Phelge" was the surname of an eccentric flatmate that Jagger, Jones, and Richards had while they were living in a dingy apartment in London during the band's early days. Klein set up Nanker Phelge U.S.A. and convinced the band to direct all of its income from the U.K. company to the American operation. Believing that Nanker Phelge U.S.A. was just the American version of the U.K. company, the Stones willingly complied with Klein's wishes. It was later discovered that Klein "wholly owned" Nanker Phelge U.S.A. and that the company had nothing to do with Nanker Phelge U.K.[160]

When all was said and done, the Stones had sued Klein a total of seven times in seventeen years. The Rolling Stones' music catalog, now owned by ABKCO, is vast. The songs include "(I Can't Get No) Satisfaction," "Jumpin' Jack Flash," "You Can't Always Get What You Want," "Play With Fire," "The Last Time," and "Gimme Shelter." The Rolling Stones still receive royalties on the pre-1971 songs, but Klein's company holds all of the publishing rights. He also took control of the master recordings from that period.

In his autobiography, Keith Richards explained that his experience with Klein was an "education." For all of the lowball tactics employed by Klein, he did help the Stones achieve astounding success. Richards succinctly summed up the band's experience with Klein, the smooth-talking manager, by saying that "Allen Klein made us and screwed us at the same time."[161]

PART FOUR

1980s–1990s

Playback

1980	• John Lennon is murdered at age 40 in New York City. • Kurtis Blow becomes the first rapper to sign with a major label.
1981	• MTV debuts on cable television. The first video played is "Video Killed the Radio Star" by The Buggles. • The AIDS virus is first identified.
1982	• Michael Jackson releases his *Thriller* album.
1983	• Herbie Hancock releases the single "Rockit."
1984	• Madonna's *Like a Virgin* album is released.
1985	• Live Aid concert debuts in U.S. and U.K. to promote Ethiopian famine relief. • New Coke is unveiled; people revolt.
1986	• Aerosmith and Run DMC release "Walk This Way."
1987	• Guns N' Roses release album *Appetite for Destruction*.
1989	• The Berlin Wall falls. • Protesting students are killed in Tiananmen Square in China.
1991	• On September 10, Nirvana releases "Smells Like Teen Spirit." • On December 17, the United States District Court for the Southern District of New York rules in *Grand Upright Music, Ltd. v. Warner Bros. Records Inc.* that the use of a music sample without permission amounts to copyright infringement. The effect on the music industry, especially hip-hop, is a move to use only "precleared" samples. • Miles Davis dies at age sixty-five.
1992	• The Cold War officially ends. • MP3s are invented.
1993	• Polygram Records purchases Motown Records. • "This new thing called *the Internet*" takes off with the release of the Mosaic Web browser.
1994	• Kurt Cobain commits suicide at age twenty-seven.

1995	• The Rock and Roll Hall of Fame museum opens in Cleveland.
1996/97	• Rappers Tupac Shakur and Biggie Smalls are murdered in separate incidents.
1997	• Elton John's "Candle in the Wind" surpasses Bing Crosby's "White Christmas" to become the best-selling single of all time.
1998	• Britney Spears releases "Baby One More Time."
1999	• Napster, a file-sharing and first-generation peer-to-peer service, becomes operational. • Y2K-bug jitters run rampant.

"Don't Turn Your Back on Me":

Mutiny at Motown

Motown Record Corp. v. Brockert,
160 Cal. App. 3d 123 (1984).

Since the early days of rock 'n' roll, major record labels have often come under fire for engaging in unfair and oppressive practices against their recording artists. The proverbial story involves a starry-eyed unknown artist who is offered a record deal and signs a contract with the label. The young unknown artist becomes a big success only to discover that the initial contract was written to heavily favor the label. The outcome of the story typically follows that the label reaps the benefits of success while the artist is left to struggle financially, possibly going bankrupt and unable to sign with another label.

In the early 1980s, this proverbial cautionary tale became a reality for Tina Marie Brockert, known professionally as Teena Marie. She was a soulful songstress known as "Lady T" to some of her fans. She chose to challenge her label when it tried to block her departure. Teena Marie had grown unhappy with her recording artist contract with Motown Records and informed the label that she wanted to be released from her contracts. In this variation of the proverbial story, the artist wants to escape her oppressive contract with the label but faces dire consequences and legal action if she tries to leave. Though the law generally disfavors the enforcement of performance in personal-services contracts, it is allowed in the recording industry under certain circumstances by statute in California.

In 1984, Marie appealed a decision against her stemming from a lawsuit filed by Motown for breach of contract. Teena Marie's desire to end her contracts with Motown provided the California Court of Appeal the opportunity to answer the question of whether a California law allowing an employer to obtain injunctive relief, sometimes referred to as a "negative injunction," from breach of contract for personal services was applicable to a contract that provided the employer with the option of paying an artist the statutory minimum. In this case, the employer was a record label and the employee a recording artist. The California statute permitted injunctive relief for a breach of contract only if the contract was in writing for personal services and the minimum compensation was not less than $6,000 per year.

Teena Marie appealed a trial-court decision that granted Motown's request for an injunction, preventing her from ending her contract with Motown so that she could enter a contract with another record label. In its lawsuit against Marie, Motown claimed that when she informed the label she wanted to leave, it exercised an option in the contract to pay her at least $6,000 per year and that Teena Marie would be in breach of the contract if she signed with another label. The trial court agreed that Motown was entitled to injunctive relief under the statute.

The statute limited the availability of injunctive relief to personal-services contracts that included a clause guaranteeing the employee a minimum of $6,000 a year. The California Court of Appeal reversed the trial court's grant of the injunction, based upon a finding that the employer *option* to pay an amount equivalent to the statutory minimum did not satisfy the *required* statutory minimum compensation for keeping the employee under the contract.[162] In reaching this decision, the court noted that its decision might be viewed as a response to her song "Don't Turn Your Back on Me" because the court was answering her plea.[163] Teena Marie's appeal resulted in clarification of a law that had been used in lawsuits involving other recording artists, including Redd Foxx and Olivia Newton-John. This clarification helped many recording artists obtain control over their careers.

Teena Marie was born Mary Christine Brockert and grew up in Santa Monica, California. She was raised in a predominantly black neighborhood and was heavily influenced by black culture. This culturally diverse exposure provided a subtext to her soulful expressiveness. Before becoming a well-known artist, Marie, a singer and guitarist, performed in school plays, shopping malls, and pretty much anywhere she was allowed. She was an R&B artist whose voice possessed the evocative emotional qualities found in top R&B soul singers. Marie initially stood out in the R&B world, in part because many people, after hearing her for the first time, were surprised to discover that she was white. Marie was able to stand solidly on her talent, and her first taste of success was being welcomed into the R&B fold by legions of predominantly black audiences. As she became better known, her fan base expanded and her talents struck a chord across all demographics.

In 1976, Teena Marie signed her first record deal with Motown Records. Her contract was a personal-services contract. A personal-services contract is between an employer and employee for the unique and special talents of the employee. Still a largely unknown artist at the time, she was offered and signed a one-year contract.

Using a strategy familiar to the recording industry, Motown gave Teena Marie a one-year contract that also granted the label six options for renewal for one-year periods. The contract was renewed on the same terms—that is, royalty rate, number of albums required, and so on—over a six-year period. The contract gave Motown an exclusivity clause that prevented her from recording for another label while under contract. According to the contract, Motown could exercise its option to renew up to a maximum of six times. The options in the contract could be exercised provided Motown paid her $6,000 per year.

While under contract with Motown, she recorded primarily as a solo artist but also worked as a songwriter and sometimes as a producer for other artists on the label. Marie became friends with funk and soul legend Rick James, who produced her debut album, *Wild and Peaceful.* The two would later record a duet, a successful ballad called "Fire and Desire." Their close friendship lasted until James's death in 2004.

In the late 1970s and early 1980s, Motown was in a relative slump compared to its heyday in the 1960s and early to mid-1970s. Marie, on the other hand, skyrocketed from unknown artist to undeniable success with the potential for continued success during the label's slump period. Her growing unhappiness at Motown was due largely to the structure of her contract. She had evolved from being in the shadows during her first three years with Motown to releasing four albums during the second half of her six-year tenure. Her 1980 album release *Irons in the Fire* reached number thirty-eight on the Billboard 200, and its top single, "I Need Your Lovin'," reached number thirty-seven on the Billboard Hot 100. Her 1981 album, *It Must Be Magic,* earned a gold certification and reached number twenty-three on the Billboard 200. Teena Marie produced and wrote or co-wrote every song on the album. Despite her success, she felt that Motown's efforts in releasing her music were not sufficient for the music prolificacy and stature she had achieved. Another concern was that, even after six years and demonstrated success, she was still working under the same contract terms as the day she joined Motown.

One possible reason for the presumed lack of artist attention may have been Motown's apparent diversion of corporate funds to finance movies instead of allocating such funds solely to the production of music, as in previous years. Motown, having moved from Detroit to Los Angeles in the early 1970s, was extremely successful with its first movie, *Lady Sings the Blues*. However, its subsequent films had difficulty achieving both critical and financial success. The 1978 movie *The Wiz*, for example, was considered both a critical and commercial failure. Motown lost a reported $10 million on the project.

In California, a personal-services contract cannot be enforced for more than seven years.[164] In May 1982, during her sixth year with Motown, Marie notified the label in writing that she would no longer continue to perform under her contract. The contract was set to expire in April 1983. The label was incensed over Marie's plans to depart. In August 1982, Motown demonstrated its displeasure by filing a $1 million breach of contract lawsuit against her in Los Angeles County Superior Court. The label based its claim upon their supposed satisfaction of minimum compensation requirement codified in California Civil Code Section 3423 and sought injunctive relief to prevent her from leaving.[165]

In September, one month after the lawsuit was filed, Motown exercised its option to pay Marie at a rate of $6,000 per year, the statutory minimum compensation amount. In November of that same year, Marie informed Motown that she had signed with Epic Records and would be recording for the label going forward. The trial court made its decision just in time for Motown, granting them a preliminary injunction in December 1982, which prevented Marie from leaving Motown. She appealed to the California Court of Appeal for the Second District. The issue on appeal was whether the option clause to pay her not less than $6,000 per year satisfied the minimum compensation requirement listed in California Civil Code Section 3423.

The statute provided that a court could issue an injunction to prevent breach of a personal-services contract only if the employer has satisfied the statutory minimum compensation requirement of California with a minimum guarantee of $6,000 per year. Section 3423 is sometimes called the anti-injunction statute because its goal is to limit the rights of employers who would attempt to prevent performers from working for a new employer.

Personal-services contracts—that is, those contracting for unique talents—are important to many businesses in California. These include entertainment, sports, and any venture requiring employees who have special skills. The law regarding personal-services contracts generally provided that although damages can be sought for breach of contract, the employee cannot be compelled to perform. Over time, an exception to this rule has developed that provides that although an employee under a personal-services contract cannot be compelled to perform, he or she can be enjoined from performing for another employer under certain circumstances. The rationale for this type of injunctive relief is rooted in the English courts.

In *Lumley v. Wagner*, the English courts held that Johanna Wagner, a well-known opera singer, could not be compelled to sing at Benjamin Lumley's theater even though she had contracted to do so.[166] Wagner was seen as having unique and exceptional talent. She had agreed to sing at Lumley's theater twice a week for three months in exchange for compensation. While under contractual obligation to Lumley, she agreed to perform at a competitor's venue. Lumley sued for an injunction to prevent Wagner from performing at the competitor's venue. The court was concerned that preventing an artist from performing elsewhere while requiring the artist to specifically perform the original obligation could lead to an unsatisfactory performance by the artist. Additionally, Lumley had specifically contracted with Wagner for her special talent. As such, monetary damages would not compensate for the loss of the performance at Lumley's venue while Wagner performed elsewhere. The court held that the grant of an injunction preventing Lumley from performing for Wagner's competitor, instead of compelling her to perform for Wagner, was appropriate.

Lumley is typically interpreted as applying to performers of "high distinction" in their field, as Wagner was when Lumley hired her. The court in Marie's appeal noted that *Lumley* had influenced the California legislature's enactment of Section 3423. In balancing the rights of the artist with those of the employer, the legislature had concluded that a measure of high distinction would be the willingness of the employer to pay the artist the $6,000 per year minimum as a prerequisite to having the right to seek an injunction against an artist who sought to breach a contract. The court noted Marie's unknown status at the time of her initial signing with Motown and the fact that Motown had initially contracted to pay her the "union scale for ten masters per year," which amounted to a "guarantee of $600 to $900 per year." Clearly, when she was signed based on that amount, she was not a star in Motown's eyes. The court emphasized that even if she had become a star during her time under contract with Motown, the fact that she was not a star when she initially signed was significant. Motown and some other record labels had been strategically including the option clauses in their contracts in case the performer became one of "high distinction." This sort of option clause had been a frequently used contract device in the entertainment industry to give an advantage to the employer. As such, the court noted that the statutory-minimum-compensation issue had public-interest implications for the entertainment industry and beyond.

At the time of the Motown lawsuit, in 1982, Section 3423 had been in effect for a little over a century. The original language of the statute prohibited injunctions against performers for breach of a personal-services contract. It was amended in 1919 to incorporate the holding in *Lumley*, thereby allowing an exception for performers of high distinction. This made it permissible for California courts to grant injunctions for breach of a personal-services contract but conditioned this right on the payment of the $6,000 minimum compensation. In 1919, $6,000 per year was a significant sum—it was five times the average annual income of consumers. This was indicative of the intent to have the minimum statutory compensation amount in Section 3423 reflect the magnitude of the "high-distinction performer" label. As the court noted, this amount in 1919 was equivalent to a minimum compensation figure of $100,000 in 1984.

Prior to Marie's case, the only cases by the California Court of Appeal interpreting the $6,000 minimum compensation requirement were *Foxx v. Williams* and *MCA Records Inc. v. Newton-John*. In *Foxx v. Williams*, the California Court of Appeal reversed the trial court's holding that comedian Redd Foxx could not leave the recording company that distributed his comedy albums for another.[167] Contrary to the trial court, the appellate court concluded that the $3,000 royalty payments Foxx received each six-month royalty-payment period did not satisfy the $6,000 per year minimum compensation requirement. The appellate court explained that Section 3423 required that the $6,000 payment be a guaranteed amount, and that the royalty payments to Foxx were not guaranteed because they were based on prospective sales of his albums and therefore did not provide a guarantee of any set amount.

In *MCA Records Inc. v. Newton-John*, the court held that the required $6,000 minimum compensation was satisfied under singer

Olivia Newton-John's contract and therefore sufficient to grant an injunction against her.[168] During the first two years of her contract with MCA, Newton-John would receive payment for the on-time delivery of albums. After the initial two-year period, MCA had the option of extending the contract for up to three additional one-year periods. Her argument was that she received less than the minimum $6,000 for albums produced for MCA. She claimed this was the result of the production costs of those albums, for which she was responsible.

The court explained that MCA had paid her royalties and a nonrefundable advance of $250,000 for each album recorded in the first two years of the contract. She was also given $100,000 for each album recorded during her option years. The nonrefundable advances of $250,000 and $100,000 per record were paid by MCA whether the albums were successes or failures. The court ruled in favor of MCA Records Inc. and granted an injunction against Newton-John. It stated that MCA's option-year payments were guaranteed payments that would result in the $6,000 minimum payments, as long as she kept her album production costs below $94,000. This case contributed to the decision of several California-based record labels to include these kinds of option clauses in their artist contracts. It was basically a low-cost insurance policy for the labels because it could be exercised at the very last moment, when it appeared an artist's departure was imminent.

In Marie's case, the court rejected Motown's argument that a new contract was created every time it exercised the contract option clause. The label argued that upon exercising the option they were effectively agreeing to pay Marie $6,000 for that year and therefore guaranteeing the payments. The court disagreed and stated that Motown's exercise of the option clause did not create a new contract. Instead, the court stated that Motown was simply using the option as a valuable "insurance policy" and getting it cheaply. Furthermore, the court noted that the exclusivity of her services was contemplated in a separate term of her original contract with Motown and was not a part of the option contract terms.

The court stated that the enforcement of Marie's exclusivity clause by way of an option clause violated "fundamental fairness." Motown had filed its lawsuit in August but did not exercise the option clause until September. The court considered this to be a "novel litigation strategy to sue for injunctive relief to enforce a contract not yet in existence." The court noted that the option clauses allowed the employer, in this case Motown, to threaten the artist with an injunction if he or she tries to leave. Secondly, in the case of an artist earning at least $6,000 in royalties per year, for example, exercising the option clause would effectively obligate the labels to pay the artists only what the label would have paid them anyway in royalties. The court opined that as a result "these cagily drafted option clauses might not guarantee a cent."[169]

Section 3423 was eventually amended a few years later, in 1993, to a minimum guarantee of $9,000 for the first year, $12,000 for the second, and $15,000 for the third through seventh years of a personal-services contract.[170] This represented the first amendment to the statute since 1919.

Teena Marie's case had a lasting effect on the music industry, at least in California. Some people refer to the decision and its benefit to other recording artists as the "Brockert Initiative." Labels were no longer able to use an option clause to provide compensation to an artist through a static and low minimum annual payment. This provided a path for some artists to change record labels without the threat of an injunction.

Sadly, Teena Marie passed away in her sleep in December 2010. She was only fifty-four years old. An inspiration to many artists and a soulful songstress to her fans, she was once asked her opinion about her challenge against Motown and the effect of the Brockert

Initiative. Her reply was, "It wasn't something I set out to do. I just wanted to get away from Motown and have a good life. But it helped a lot people, like Luther Vandross, the Mary Jane Girls and a lot of different artists, [who] were able to get out of their contracts."[171]

PARENTAL ADVISORY EXPLICIT CONTENT

The Filthy Fifteen and the Censorship Files:

Music Censorship in the 1980s and 1990s

President Jimmy Carter, a liberal-minded man from humble beginnings in the deep Georgian South, rose to hold one of the most powerful offices in the world. He ran for re-election to the U.S. presidency in 1980. Though Carter had accomplished several good works programs during his first term, including the creation of the Federal Emergency Management System (FEMA), the U.S. economy was lackluster. Gas prices were high, and many Americans were anxious to move in a different direction. Internationally, the Berlin Wall still stood and the Cold War with the Soviet Union persisted.

When Carter sought re-election, his opponent, Ronald Reagan, ran on a platform that was in direct opposition to Carter's. Reagan promoted a new brand of conservatism that promised to enrich all economic classes. His proposed model of supply-side economics was promoted as encouraging unregulated growth for most Americans, which would, in theory, "trickle down" to all economic classes. His campaign cleverly employed optimistic branding full of lofty promises. Reagan won the election in a bruising landslide over Carter, carrying forty-four states to Carter's six.

Reagan's win marked the beginning of an era that would later be characterized by some as a decade of economic growth coupled with incredible selfishness and excess. A large swath of the American population had become both economic and social conservatives, and they were emboldened to express their conservative viewpoints in this conservative-friendly environment. During this time, in the realm of the creative arts, popular music continued to flourish and often pushed the envelope through the use of increasingly explicit lyrics. This explicitness ignited protests by some against the music industry. The protests, in turn, fueled fears that the right of freedom of speech through music would be extinguished. The 1980s became the era of music censorship.

Since its birth in the 1950s, rock 'n' roll music had cleverly incorporated metaphors to describe sexual themes in lyrics. For example, the lyric "roll with me Henry," from the song "Wallflower," made famous by Etta James, is said to refer to a romp in the hay. In the 1980s several artists demonstrated increasing lyrical freedom and explicitness in their lyrics, especially when it came to sex, violence, and other adult-oriented themes. This rise in creative explicitness contrasted the strong wave of conservatism concurrently rolling across America. There were many individuals and groups who were determined to prohibit, if not ban, the sale of music with seemingly explicit lyrics. This period would witness a historic music-censorship showdown between creative artists, the music industry, parental advocacy groups, and the government.

One of the top films in 1984 was Prince's *Purple Rain*. Filmed in Prince's native Minneapolis, the movie told the story of a struggling musician, a character loosely based on Prince and played by Prince. The character found success in his pursuit of music after overcoming personal tribulations and embracing a need to be true to his art.

His music was accepted at the end of the film by a large fan base and his future seemed bright. The irony of it all is that it was the film's soundtrack, the iconic and bestselling album *Purple Rain*, that sparked the music censorship battles of the 1980s.

In the mid-1980s, then-senator Al Gore and his wife, Tipper, like millions of other Americans, purchased a copy of *Purple Rain*. Ms. Gore was not pleased after listening to the track "Darling Nikki." She found the song to be incredibly explicit and inappropriate, and was especially concerned about its appropriateness for her children. Outraged, she sent out a rallying cry to many of her Washington friends in an attempt to find a way to keep explicit songs like "Darling Nikki" out of the hands of children.

"Darling Nikki" is a song about a casual encounter with a female "sex fiend" named Nikki. In the lyrics Prince meets her while she is "masturbating" in a "hotel lobby," and eventually they have "head spinning" sex, complete with references to devices and extreme physical prowess. So, nursery rhyme or nice little ditty, the song is not. Nor was it trying to be.

Horrified by the lyrics, Ms. Gore found it to be absolutely unacceptable that her children could have access to a song like this simply by going down to the record store and purchasing it. Furthermore, she was concerned that as a parent she had no say in whether her children would be sold the explicit album. Even worse, she thought, that because there were no warnings listed on the album, she would not know if an album contained explicit lyrics unless she actually listened to it. Ms. Gore was determined to change this and decided that the best thing to do was to get organized.

She reached out to the wives of several other congressmen who agreed with her call to action. These influential women formed the Parent's Music Resource Center (PMRC) in May 1985. The PMRC's mission was to create a rating system for albums that would be similar to the rating system employed by the Motion Picture Association of America (MPAA). The primary concern among critics of the PMRC's mission was that labeling an album with a rating would be the first step in ultimately censoring an album altogether.

The "Washington Wives," as the PMRC were colloquially known, were not the originators of the album-rating-system idea. About six months prior to the PMRC's formation, the National Parent Teachers Association (National PTA), at their annual meeting in October 1984, discussed promoting a rating system for music. Over the following months, the National PTA attempted to convince the music industry to employ a ratings system. By and large the industry balked at the suggestions. The National PTA's rating-system efforts barely made a ripple and went largely unnoticed in the media. When the PMRC took up the cause, the organization was able to bring the issue to the forefront of the news media, and the music industry began to take notice of the activism of the Washington Wives.

The PMRC quickly began to place songs under an umbrella of those they deemed as unsuitable for children. They released a list of songs that they considered to be the most contemptible. The list, known as the "Filthy Fifteen," was a collection of fifteen songs that epitomized the themes and explicitness the PMRC was attempting to keep away from children. In addition to sex and violence, the group targeted songs that it believed encouraged behaviors it deemed undesirable, such as suicide, drug and alcohol use, and homosexuality.[172] The list included "filthy" songs such as Madonna's "Dress You Up" and Cyndi Lauper's "She-Bop." Heavy metal tunes like Judas Priest's "Eat Me Alive" and Twisted Sister's "We're Not Gonna Take it" were also included. At the top of the list was the song that started it all, Prince's "Darling Nikki."

The PMRC targeted a variety of music genres but focused a lot of its attention on heavy metal music. The heavy metal genre, which was in the midst of a popularity explosion in the 1980s, did produce a slew of songs that were of an explicit nature. MTV did not play any heavy metal music in its first few years of existence. However, as the genre's popularity grew, MTV began to play heavy metal videos late at night on dedicated programs like *Headbanger's Ball*.

In the days before YouTube, *Headbanger's Ball* became *the* source for metal videos, like those featuring the wild costumes of Twisted Sister or the latest from Iron Maiden. *Headbanger's Ball* was also the show that would help catapult Guns N' Roses into the music stratosphere when they began to air Guns N' Roses' breakthrough video, "Welcome to the Jungle."

With a rapid rise in the popularity of heavy metal creating more demand than ever for the genre, the PMRC began working overtime to limit its sale. The organization was particularly concerned with sales to minors. The group approached the Recording Industry Association of America (RIAA), a trade organization that represented a large percentage of record labels, to create a ratings system. The RIAA did not balk at the idea, as it had done to the National PTA's proposal. But the RIAA believed that creating a uniform rating system and providing printed lyrics for the benefit of parents would not be practical. The RIAA offered instead to place a generic warning on albums that read "Parental Guidance: Explicit Lyrics." The PMRC did not think the RIAA's proposal adequately met its concerns and rejected the offer. With negotiations stalled, the battle moved to the Senate.

On September 19, 1985, the Senate Committee on Commerce, Science, and Transportation commenced an open hearing on the accessibility of explicit music, which was referred to as "porn rock" during the hearing. The PMRC apparently had claimed not to want any government, regulatory, or legislative action to accomplish its rating system goals, but it was hardly a surprise that the hearings were held. As it turned out, five members of the Senate committee conducting the hearings were husbands of PMRC members, including Senator Al Gore.

Testimony was delivered at the hearing from people on both sides of the aisle in the album rating-system debate. Musicians Frank Zappa, John Denver, and Twisted Sister front-man Dee Snyder testified on behalf of recording artists. They believed that censorship was at the heart of the PMRC proposals. They expressed concerns that the rating system could lead to the elimination of access to music across the board, and not just for children. Further, they maintained that it was the job of the parents and not the government or the music industry to regulate children's access to music.

In the end, the hearings accomplished very little in terms of immediate legislation. But it was somewhat entertaining for the public to be treated to displays such as Snider's hulking figure testifying on Capitol Hill in a sleeveless shirt, with his tattooed arms and wild mane of curly blond hair, amid a sea of politicians in blue and gray business suits and polished loafers. The real effect of the hearings, however, was the national attention they brought to the issue of censorship and music. Reverberations from the hearings were felt at the major labels and in state legislatures across the country.

In early October 1985, while the hearings were still taking place, many major labels declared that they would not be placing warning labels on their albums. However, succumbing to the prospect of potentially threatening music-censorship legislation, the RIAA reached a compromise agreement with the PMRC and the National PTA. The PMRC and the National PTA would agree not to pursue legislation requiring a formal rating system in exchange for the placement of warning stickers on records, provided that the record labels reserved the right to determine which albums the warning labels were placed upon. Additionally, several record labels began trying to persuade their artists to modify any potentially explicit songs to prevent having warning labels placed on their albums. Some record labels also started to review the song lyrics actively before an album was released, and in some cases they would drop a potentially offending song from an album before releasing it for sale.

While the album-rating system was gaining steam, courts, for the first time, were beginning to hear cases connecting song lyrics to harmful behavior. In 1985, the family of John Daniel McCollum brought a lawsuit against CBS Records and Ozzy Osbourne in the Superior Court of California.[173] The family's civil action was an attempt to hold CBS and Ozzy Osbourne liable for the suicide of their son, John. This was the first time a case was brought before a court linking song lyrics and the violent acts of a listener through a theory of proximate cause, that is, an unbroken chain of events stemming from an initial event that results in an injury that would not have taken place had the initial event not occurred.

Nineteen-year-old McCollum was an avid Ozzy Osbourne fan. He used to spend a lot of time listening to his Osbourne albums on the turntable in his living room because he enjoyed the intensity of the turntable's sound. On the night of October 26, 1984, McCollum spent the evening listening to two different Osbourne albums in his living room, *Blizzard of Oz* and *Diary of a Madman*. He later moved into his bedroom, where he listened to another Osbourne album, *Speak of the Devil*. With his headphones on and the music playing, he placed a .22-caliber handgun to his temple and pulled the trigger, killing himself. When he was discovered the next morning, the needle was still scratching against the turning record.

Unfortunately, McCollum's life appears to have been very tumultuous. He suffered from "severe emotional problems," in addition to alcohol abuse. McCollum's suicide was no doubt a tragedy for his family and a terrible loss of a young life. Through their devastation, the family sought recourse in the courts, claiming that CBS and Osbourne should be held accountable for the death of their son. They maintained that Osbourne's music was not worthy of protection under the First Amendment.

The family put forth three theories of liability against CBS. The first theory was that CBS had "negligently disseminated" Osbourne's music. Secondly, they argued that CBS "disseminated the music knowing" that it would result in an "irrepressible impulse" causing the listener to commit suicide. The last theory put forth was that CBS had "intentionally aided" in McCollum's death.

Regarding Osbourne, the McCollum family argued that he had a "special relationship" with his listeners because, as they asserted, many of his fans believed he was talking directly to them when they listened to his music. As such, through the alleged special relationship, the McCollum family argued that Osbourne had a duty not to encourage and promote suicide as a means of escaping the difficulties of life. The family believed Osbourne's song "Suicide Solution" promoted suicide.

The family appealed the California Superior Court's ruling that, in addition to the fact the family had not alleged facts sufficient to satisfy a valid tort claim or violation of a criminal statute, the First Amendment was an "absolute bar" to all of the McCollum family's claims. In 1988, the California Court of Appeals for the Second Appellate District, Division Three, affirmed the lower court's dismissal of the lawsuit. The court concluded that in this case, there was no applicable exception to the First Amendment's protection, which is generally applicable to artistic expressions that include music and lyrics. The court rejected the plaintiffs' argument that the "imminent lawless action" exception to First Amendment protection applied in this case.

The imminent lawless action test was established by the Supreme Court in *Brandenburg v. Ohio*.[174] The *Brandenburg* test is used to determine whether speech is "directed to inciting imminent" illegal acts and therefore not worthy of First Amendment protection. The test, expanded by the court in *Hess v. Indiana*, requires that the speech in question be directed toward the goal of producing lawless conduct and be likely to result in imminent lawless conduct.[175] The court in *Hess* further refined the test to define the imminent-conduct requirement as not being satisfied by speech directing action to occur at some indefinite time in the future.

The McCollum family's claims failed to meet this test. The appellate court held that Osbourne's lyrics did not incite McCollum's suicide, nor was his death an imminent consequence of the lyrics. It held that speech "could not be restricted if it merely led to a penchant for violence." Finally, the appellate court found that Osbourne and CBS were not liable for McCollum's death because a proximate cause between Osbourne's music and McCollum's suicide did not exist. The possibility of McCollum's suicide was not a foreseeable risk of Osbourne's creative work.

In 1990, a similar case went to trial in a Nevada district court involving two friends, James Vance and Raymond Belknap, who were both fans of the heavy metal band Judas Priest. Like McCollum, they also suffered from emotional problems. Their problems seemed to stem in part from unstable homes. However, there also appeared to be loving mothers present in both families. Both young men were frequent drug users.

One evening, the boys were listening to the song "Better By You, Better Than Me" from Judas Priest's *Stained Class* album. While listening to the song, the boys were allegedly heard shouting, "Do it! Do it!" while getting riled up. They went outside to a nearby playground, where they both sat down on the merry-go-round. Belknap held a rifle in his hand. He placed the rifle under his chin and pulled the trigger, killing himself. Vance, who had just witnessed his friend's violent death, took the rifle and, like Belknap, placed it under his chin and pulled the trigger. He survived but was left with severely disfiguring injuries. Vance would later claim that although he did not want to die, he felt as though he had been compelled to pull the trigger.[176] Vance passed away three years later, after checking himself into a hospital to be treated for depression. He died from an overdose while under treatment.

The families of Vance and Belknap brought a wrongful death suit against Judas Priest. As in *McCollum*, they attempted to show a causal link between the shootings and the Judas Priest song. However, in this case, the First Amendment was not available to bar the claims. The families' claim was essentially an invasion of privacy claim. They suggested that Judas Priest had invaded the boys' privacy through subliminal messaging in their music, and that the boys' predisposition to suicide caused them to act upon that messaging. They argued that Judas Priest had placed subliminal commands in the form of the words "do it" in the song "Better By You, Better Than Me." Arguing that the boys were predisposed to suicide because of their emotional nature, the families believed that Judas Priest should be held liable for Belknap's death and Vance's injuries because the two friends were more susceptible to subliminal messages.

Noting that this was a matter of first impression, the court in an unpublished opinion stated that subliminal messages, if any existed in the music, did not amount to speech and as such were not protected by the First Amendment, or subject to the *Brandenburg* test.[177] After reviewing the Judas Priest song and the technology used to produce the recording, the court found that the words "do it" did exist subliminally on the recording. However, the court determined that the band did not intentionally put the words on the recording. Instead, according to the court, the placement was most likely the result of the way the song was recorded, which involved the use of a twenty-four-track tape. The multi-track tape was condensed into two tracks, from which the album recording was made. Through expert testimony, the court determined that "do it" was not actually on any of the twenty-four-track tapes. Instead, "do it" was a sound that was the unintentional result of Rob Halford, the band's lead singer, exhaling on one track combined with the sound of a "Leslie guitar"— an electric guitar played through a Leslie brand guitar amp, which is capable of adding a series of effects to the guitar—on another track.

The court ultimately ruled in favor of Judas Priest, stating that for the families to be victorious, they needed to demonstrate that the band had "intentionally intruded" upon the boys' privacy. The court held that because the subliminal message of "do it" was not intentional, the band, if it had invaded the boys' privacy through its music, had done so negligently. Nor did the court find a proximate-cause link between the band's music and the boys' acts. The court stated that the expert testimony in the case convincingly demonstrated that although subliminal messaging may exist, there was not enough evidence to indicate that it could lead to this level of violent behavior. The court added that it was likely that other outside factors led to the violent behavior. Based on the court's findings, Judas Priest was not held liable for Vance and Belknap's death.

The absolute protection of the First Amendment has constantly been challenged in the courts when it comes to the creative arts. The Supreme Court created an obscenity exception to this protection when it held by a 5–4 vote in *Miller v. California* that obscene speech is not protected by the First Amendment.[178] As a result, there have been numerous attempts to censor music artists on the basis that their music is obscene. The difficulty, of course, is deciding when an artist's work is actually obscene. The Court held that a work is obscene if it "appeal[s] to the prurient interest in sex, which portray[s] sexual conduct in a patently offensive way, and which, taken as a whole, do[es] not have serious literary, artistic, political, or scientific value." This decision was significant because it gave, for the first time, a definition of obscenity that established parameters for determining whether an item is in fact obscene. The Court set the parameters as follows:

(a) whether "the average person, applying contemporary community standards" would find that the work, taken as a whole, appeals to the prurient interest; (b) whether the work depicts or describes, in a patently offensive way, sexual conduct specifically defined by the applicable state law; and (c) whether the work, taken as a whole, lacks serious literary, artistic, political, or scientific value.[179]

Prior to the efforts of the PMRC, no attempt at music censorship since the dawn of popular music, and there have been several, had been capable of drawing the attention that the PMRC actions drew. Even though the Senate hearings failed to produce any legislative action, many states began to take it upon themselves to regulate the sale of music to minors. By 1989 there were at least twelve state legislatures that had introduced bills containing mechanisms to classify recorded music as obscene and regulate its sale to minors.

Washington state, for example, made news in March of 1992 by becoming the first state to pass a law that restricted the sale of recorded music. Commonly known in the music industry as the "erotic law," those caught selling music deemed "erotic" to minors could be fined $500 or sent to jail for violating the law.[180] Under the Washington law, a music selection could be deemed erotic only by a judge. Furthermore, all records deemed erotic had to carry an "adults only" label. Although the Washington state legislature was optimistic about the passage of the law, some members conceded that it would be very difficult to regulate "erotic music," so they hoped that retailers would voluntarily take it upon themselves to segregate adults-only records as newsstands had done with adult magazines and other adult-themed media.

The passage of the Washington state statute occurred at a time when the world was tuned into the rise of grunge music coming out of Seattle. In 1992, when the statute was passed, Seattle-based bands had virtually wiped the 1980s heavy metal bands off the music map and were beginning a domination of the music industry that would last for the next couple of years. It was no surprise then that the passage of the statute prompted strong reactions from bands like Nirvana, Pearl Jam, and other Seattle bands. For example, Soundgarden, another Seattle band, along with the ACLU, challenged the statute by filing a lawsuit in King County Superior Court.[181] In October 1992, the statute was held to be unconstitutional because it was too vague in its drafting and violated the due process rights of music consumers. The statute was permanently enjoined. Other states, however, succeeded in including recorded music as a category in "harmful to minors" statutes.

With the heavy metal "threat" waning in the transition into the 1990s, the obscenity spotlight turned even more to the burgeoning gangster rap scene and previously underground hardcore rap styles. In 1988 NWA released its seminal album, *Straight Outta Compton*. One release from the album, "Fuck Tha Police," was a graphic commentary on racial profiling and brutality at the hands of police. The song became an anthem for many. Not surprisingly, it attracted deep resentment from law enforcement. In 1989, Priority Records, NWA's label, received a letter from Milt Alheric, the assistant director of the FBI. In his letter, which he said was an official statement from the FBI, he expressed his concern and "strong disapproval" of the song. This was also the first time that the FBI had "taken an official position" on a creative work.[182]

There was just as much concern from law enforcement when rapper Ice-T released "Cop Killer," by his rap-metal group Body Count. Time Warner, the parent company of Ice-T's label, Sire Records, received a deluge of protests. Time Warner executives had allegedly received bomb threats as well. Ice-T yielded to public pressure and declared that the song would be left off of future album copies.

The rap group 2 Live Crew, not to be outdone in the censorship debate, was busy making its mark as well. In 1987, a record-store clerk was arrested for selling a copy of the group's album *2 Live Is What We Are* to a fourteen-year-old boy. Although the case against the clerk was eventually dropped, the owner closed the store. The album also soon received a warning sticker under the new PMRC-RIAA arrangement, and several major chains refused to sell it. Getting a reputation for its sexually explicit songs and bad-boy-meets-goofball personas, demand for 2 Live Crew's music was strong, although selling the records was becoming an ever-riskier activity.

On June 30, 1988, Tommy Hammond, a co-owner of a record store in Alexandria City, Alabama, was arrested for selling *2 Live Is What We Are* not to a minor but to a police officer. Curiously, the police officer was not posing as a minor, and the album had been kept away in a special container behind the counter and only sold to an adult by request. It would seem that the act of carrying the controversial album outweighed the fact that the storeowner was following the legal procedure for selling it. Hammond was initially convicted of selling obscene music and was given a $500 fine, but his conviction was later overturned when in a subsequent trial, which resulted after he appealed the conviction, the jury decided that the album did not meet the community's obscenity standard.

There were several attempts across the country to ban or curb the sale of 2 Live Crew's music. By the spring of 1990, county prosecutors in six states had classified the group's music as obscene. However, nothing matched the efforts taken by prosecutors in a few Florida counties and a very determined sheriff. Before Broward County, Florida, made headlines as the county of long voting lines and the "hanging chad," the sheriff's department there was committed to keeping "obscene" music out of the county with the full force of the law.

In February of 1990, a request was made by the deputy sheriff asking Broward County Circuit Judge Mel Grossman to rule that probable cause existed to deem 2 Live Crew's album *As Nasty As They Wanna Be* obscene under the state's "sale of harmful matter statute." The probable cause ruling was issued on March 9, 1990. The Sheriff's Office subsequently warned retailers through a mailer that outlined the probable cause ruling and informed them that they could be arrested and prosecuted if they sold the album. The retailer response was immediate, and most withdrew the album from sale.

In response to the ruling, 2 Live Crew filed a lawsuit against the Sheriff's Office on March 16, 1990, on the grounds that its actions were a violation of the First Amendment. Sheriff Nicholas Navarro in turn sought to put the album on trial to have it officially classified as obscene under state law, and a trial was subsequently held before U.S. District Court Judge Jose Gonzales on May 14 and 15, 1990, to determine whether *As Nasty As They Wanna Be* was obscene. On June 6 Judge Gonzales ruled in *Skyywalker Records, Inc. v. Navarro* that the album was in fact obscene.[183] He also ruled against the Sheriff's Department, finding its actions toward the record retailers to be in violation of the First and Fourteenth amendments because they were a prior restraint, or acts of censorship, occurring before an obscenity trial had been held.

Just two days later, Charles Freeman, a record-store owner, was arrested by Sheriff Navarro for selling the album. Then, only two days after Freeman's arrest, 2 Live Crew was arrested following a performance at an adults-only show in Hollywood, Florida, for allegedly violating state obscenity laws. The following day the group appealed Judge Gonzales's obscenity ruling. The group was concerned that although it had been victorious in the ruling against the Sheriff's Department, the fact that the court had also found the album obscene opened up the possibility for criminal prosecutions under county obscenity laws. Considering the group's arrest and that of Freeman, they were wise to be concerned. On October 3, 1990, Freeman was found guilty. The members of 2 Live Crew were subsequently acquitted on October 20, 1990, of the charges stemming from their arrest in Fort Lauderdale, Florida. The jury found that the album was not obscene. However, it was not until 1992 that Judge Gonzales's obscenity ruling was overturned by the U.S. Court of Appeals for the Eleventh Circuit in *Luke Records, Inc. v. Navarro*.[184]

The censorship-in-music fervor began to wane as the 1990s pressed on. Although tensions remained between those in favor of music censorship and those against it, the national spotlight began to move on. Yet the placement of parental advisory stickers on records continued and is still employed today. Additionally, across the board, the courts were reluctant to connect music with behavior out of fear of creating a chilling effect upon free speech.

The music industry was changing. The channels of distribution through which music could be obtained were growing rapidly. Brick and mortar record stores were losing ground as the point place for record sales, and people were beginning to opt out of purchasing whole albums and buying singles instead. As the twentieth century drew to a close, the music censorship issue remained, but was relegated to the back burner. The digital revolution was approaching, and the record industry would soon find itself struggling to survive.

A Bittersweet Symphony:

A Bitter Side of Sampling

ABKCO Music, Inc. v. The Verve (settled).

The story of "Bittersweet Symphony," a seminal song by the band The Verve, is the tale of a journey through the creative process of songwriting and the enormous success that a hit song can bring. It is also a tale of the harsh realities that can descend upon creative artists at the pinnacle of their success. The "Bittersweet Symphony" saga is a well-known story among many fans of The Verve. Those who possess even a casual knowledge of the band are typically shocked to hear the story behind the music. Due in part to the out-of-court settlement, a complete record of the proceedings is not available. However, this story has developed its own urban myths and there are several retellings of it in the blogosphere that appear based more on rumor than on fact. This account is an attempt to accurately piece together a controversial matter that elicits strong feelings from all sides. Like most stories about public figures, the facts often get distorted as they are passed from one person to the next. However, amid the distortion, one thing is certain. The Verve lost 100 percent of the publishing rights to their biggest hit, "Bittersweet Symphony."

The original members of The Verve were Richard Ashcroft (vocals), Simon Jones (bass), Nick McCabe (guitar), and Peter Salisbury (drums). The band's early days were spent in a dark, mildewed rehearsal space in Wigan, a mid-size working-class town in Northeast England that was famous in the 1970s as one of the hot spots for the Northern Soul dance scene. The rehearsal space, paid for by the band's unemployment checks, was a place for their dusk-'til-dawn jam sessions. Rehearsals were free-flowing music sessions. The naturally charismatic Ashcroft referred to the Wigan jam sessions as the band's own Hamburg period, alluding to the legendary and prolific days that the Beatles had spent in Hamburg, Germany, honing their craft.[185]

Influenced by bands like the Manchester-based Stone Roses, The Verve began to form a sound of its own. The early sound was part alternative, part psychedelic, and part rock 'n' roll. The Verve's live shows featured displays of energetic bursts from Ashcroft, who would lose himself in the music. His performances caused some to give him the nickname "Mad Richard." Guitarist Nick McCabe stood out for his sharp and expressive guitar playing.

The Verve emerged onto the musical landscape of the early 1990s. At the time, the popular guitar-rock music flowing through major media outlets consisted heavily of songs by "hair bands" that had become a fixture on MTV and radio. Bands like Mötley Crüe, Poison, and Warrant topped the charts. As the 1980s drew to a close, many of those bands continued to create quality music. However, a bloated staleness had begun to creep into the genre that was in direct contrast to the raw, explosive energy that had ushered it into popularity in the 1980s.

Seattle's grunge-music scene jolted the mainstream and displaced the 1980s rock bands almost overnight. Spandex and hairspray were replaced by disheveled hair and flannel. Bands like Nirvana, Pearl Jam, and Alice in Chains led the way. A stark contrast to the glittery hair-band scene, this Seattle sound, popularly known as grunge music, became a sensation in the United States and dominated the rock scene from the early to mid-1990s.

Grunge was making its way across the pond to the United Kingdom. Its heavy presence on the British airwaves sparked a creative backlash from some in the U.K. indie music scene. *Britpop*, a term used very loosely here, was born in part out of a reaction to this perceived infiltration from grunge. The scene quickly grew to become a collective of indie bands focused on British themes, lyrics, and sounds that were distinctly not grunge-like. Groups like Suede wanted to separate themselves from what they perceived as the darkness of the grunge sound and provide a more upbeat and sometimes colorful take on modern music.[186] These groups served as a self-styled antithesis to Seattle grunge. Their movement was fueled by a desire to recapture a sense of British musical influence that these groups believed was beginning to fade from television and radio in favor of grunge. Eventually several Britpop bands, including several from the Manchester, England, music scene of the 1990s, would dominate the charts.

This first wave of Britpop began to lose steam after about five years. However, its influence could be seen in the bands springing forth in the mainstream during its decline. With the press focused on the likes of Blur and Oasis, the media often overlooked many talented bands. The Verve, one of these overlooked bands, would soon emerge into the mainstream to find both critical and commercial success.

In 1991, the Verve signed a deal with Hut Records, a division of Virgin Records. Their first studio release included three singles that each reached the top of the indie charts in the United Kingdom. The first album, *A Storm in Heaven*, released in 1993, was modestly successful. However, it was not until the group's second album, 1995's *A Northern Soul*, was released that expectations began to grow. Each member of the band received composition credit for most of the songs on the first two albums. After a harsh breakup, primarily between Nick McCabe and Richard Ashcroft, the band reconstituted itself and began work on songs that had been composed primarily by Ashcroft. Those songs included "Bittersweet Symphony," which was released on June 16, 1997. The song would later be included on the highly popular and critically acclaimed album *Urban Hymns*, which was released on September 29, 1997.

By the time of the release, the band had moved away from its "neo-psychedelic" sound to an experimentally soulful and introspective sound. One of the early releases from the album, a track titled "Drugs Don't Work," hit number one on the U.K. charts. In the United States, the Verve's fan base grew dramatically. In Great Britain, the album entered the charts at number two, selling 250,000 copies during the first week. That was the fifth-highest first-week total in British record retail history at that time. Worldwide, five million copies were sold.

Ashcroft's motivation for writing "Bittersweet Symphony" came largely from his discovery of an orchestral version of "The Last Time" that was recorded by the Andrew Oldham orchestra. He thought the music would be the perfect building block for a new song. The band sampled a portion of the orchestral piece to create "Bittersweet Symphony." The sample became the recognizable looping symphonic riff that has become the song's signature feature. Additional layers of melody, harmony, original lyrics, and other flourishes were added on top of the sample.

The orchestral piece was an instrumental version of "The Last Time," which Oldham recorded along with a group of studio musicians. The song had been originally recorded and made famous by the Rolling Stones. Oldham had been the Rolling Stones' manager and producer at the time the Stones' version was recorded. The orchestral version had very little commercial success, selling only 200 copies on its first release.

The use of copyrighted music as a sample requires separate permission for the sound recording and the composition. The copyright owner of the sound recording, or master recording, is often either a record company or the record's producer. However, that ownership can be assigned, sold, or transferred. The copyright owner of the composition is generally the songwriter. It is common, however, for songwriters to assign a portion, or in some cases all, of their rights to a music publisher. With the rights in hand, the publisher can pursue strategies to grow the song's popularity as well as handle administrative duties such as distribution and accounting of royalties. ABKCO Music and Records, Inc., owned the composition copyright as a result of a settlement deal with the Rolling Stones. Decca Records was thought to own the copyright to the Oldham sound recording.

The band received permission from Decca to use the sound recording of Oldham's version of "The Last Time." Permission to use the composition was also required. The person with the power to grant permission was Allen Klein, the founder and president of ABKCO Music and Records, Inc., a music publishing and management company. Allen Klein, an accountant by training, was an inexhaustible scrutinizer of details. He made his name in the music business by going through the details of contracts and squeezing out large amounts of cash from labels and publishers for clients such as Sam Cooke and Bobby Darin. The Verve approached Klein to request permission to sample a portion of "The Last Time" prior to the release of "Bittersweet Symphony." He turned down the request, stating, "I don't care if everyone else in the world allows it, I don't agree with sampling as a matter of principle and certainly not on a Stones song."[187]

Under pressure to obtain permission in time for the June release of "Bittersweet Symphony," Jazz Summers, the Verve's manager, thought Klein might be willing to discuss his position further. However, Summers also knew that Klein was a skillful and tough negotiator, and would likely demand a steep price for the license. Like Klein, Summers was the head of a music publishing company and an experienced artist manager, having worked with the likes of George Michael and Lisa Stansfield. He is reported to have warned the group of the risk of releasing "Bittersweet Symphony" without permission from Klein and gave the band the choice of moving forward, with the caveat that it could very well lose the publishing rights to the song.[188] If the group chose to release "Bittersweet Symphony" without clearance, litigation was a near certainty, especially dealing with Allen Klein. Based largely on the Verve's belief in the commercial potential of "Bittersweet Symphony," the consensus was that any offer made by Klein should be accepted.

After some prodding from Ken Berry, the president of EMI Recorded Music, Klein finally agreed to hear the song and eventually approved the license. As it turned out, the man who once said in an interview that "we're not in the business of sampling" surprisingly said that he liked the Verve's song.[189]

The details of the license agreement between the band and Klein have not been made public. However, such documents generally include terms that define (1) whether the license is exclusive or nonexclusive; (2) the term of the agreement—the wording of many take the agreement into perpetuity; (3) payment method—that is, flat fee, royalty, or both; (4) rights of the licensee, including how much of the song can be sampled; (5) a courtesy credit to the owner, if desired by the owner; and (6) rights of the owner, for example, the right to terminate upon breach of the agreement. Summers was delighted when Klein said that the financial split on the publishing would be "50–50."[190] He reportedly thought this meant 50 percent of the publishing royalties would go to the Stones through ABKCO and 50 percent to the Verve.

With permission to use the sample of "The Last Time" in hand, the Verve looked forward to the release of both the single and album later that year. Things began to fall apart shortly after *Urban Hymns* was released. "Bittersweet Symphony" had become a genuine success. The Verve reportedly said that once the song became popular, Klein began to claim that the band had infringed upon his copyright by sampling more of "The Last Time" than had been agreed upon. Klein then demanded 100 percent of the publishing rights for "Bittersweet Symphony."

After more than thirty years in the music business at the time, Klein had the reputation of being a fierce protector of his music catalog. His company, ABKCO, has been a frequent party to small and large court cases. In 1965 he had assumed the role of manager of the Rolling Stones after Andrew Oldham stepped down to focus solely on producing. Upon Oldham's departure as manager, Klein purchased Oldham's interest in the Rolling Stones. He was terminated after a falling out with the Stones.

The Verve likely considered the financial implications of drawn-out litigation, as well as Klein's excellent and aggressive track record in the courts. The choice to accept his demand of 100 percent of the publishing rights may have seemed like the lesser of two evils. The band reluctantly agreed to Klein's demands.

ABKCO music publishing now owned the publishing rights to "Bittersweet Symphony." As composers of "The Last Time," Mick Jagger and Keith Richards were given credit as songwriters of "Bittersweet Symphony, along with Ashcroft."[191] Generally, music publishers receive royalties on behalf of the songwriter and share them with the songwriter in an arranged split amount. Often that split is 50 percent for the publisher and 50 percent for the songwriter(s). However, Ashcroft's payment arrangement is unclear. One article suggests that Ashcroft may have received only a one-time $1,000 payment as the lyricist.[192] Ashcroft is officially listed as a songwriter for the song, but Jagger and Richards are now officially listed as songwriters as well with ABKCO as its publisher.[193]

The success of "Bittersweet Symphony" generated several business opportunities for Klein, and he seized upon them by licensing the song for use in various commercials, much to the band's dismay. One of the most visible was its use in a Nike commercial that first aired in the United States and Canada during the Super Bowl in January 1998. The Verve's share is supposed to have been $175,000 for the use, which was subsequently donated to charity.[194] The amount that Klein received is unclear, although well-known songs used in commercials can often bring in $1 million or more.[195] A statement released by the band's management shortly after the commercial aired stated that the group consented to Nike's use of their song in an effort to thwart further commercial use of the song. Although Klein held the publishing rights to the song, the band still had the right to approve the use of their actual recording of the song.

After the commercial, "Bittersweet Symphony" and other songs by the Verve became even more popular and catapulted sales well into the millions. The *Irish Times* reported in March 1998 that the Verve was the biggest rock band in Britain, with *Urban Hymns* staying near number one since its release six months earlier. In the United States, The Verve was nominated in 1998 for Video of the Year at the MTV Music Awards. The group was also playing sold-out shows. Yet even though the commercial placements generated significant sales and publicity for the song, the idea of commercial placement is something that still "sicken[s]" Ashcroft.[196]

With the ABKCO negotiations behind it, The Verve were excited about their prospects, until Andrew Oldham came knocking in 1999 with a lawsuit of his own.[197] The former manager and producer of the Rolling Stones had been living in Columbia since 1967 and was anxious about the prospect of reaching a settlement with The Verve after "Bittersweet Symphony" had proven so successful. He insisted that he, not Decca, owned the rights to the song. Further, in an interview, he said that legal action was taken because he felt that his contributions had not been appreciated when he was associated with the Stones. Oldham and The Verve settled for an undisclosed amount.

The "Bittersweet Symphony" experience has created a significant amount of debate over the years. On the one hand, some express the view that The Verve received a raw deal and were taken advantage of by Klein. Others are more skeptical and question whether The Verve did indeed use more of the sample than provided for in the agreement. Some critics questioned Richard Ashcroft's use of the phrase "barely audible" when describing the level of his use of "The Last Time" in "Bittersweet Symphony."[198] Such commentators suggest that a comparison of the two songs shows that the sample is "not quite as minimal as Ashcroft made it out to be."[199] Ashcroft explained the situation to MTV News, saying "that the sample was only a small part of the background, but could not be easily removed. I was in a position (where) if I took it out, even though it's subliminal, this subliminal can be important, so I was in a no-win situation."[200] The degree of sampling by The Verve, whether too much or as negotiated, remains subjective. However, the song remains for many, as Ashcroft once described it, "a perfect piece of pop art with the sentiment that 'you're a slave to money then you die.'"[201]

"Bittersweet Symphony" was nominated for a Grammy for Best Rock Song in 1999. The nomination went to Ashcroft along with Jagger and Richards as the songwriters. The Verve split up in 1999, reuniting in 2007 for a tour promoting their album, *Forth*. The band once again split up after the tour. Ashcroft has continued to perform as a solo artist and most recently with his newest group, United Nations of Sound. Whether one believes the use of sampling in "Bittersweet Symphony" was too much or just right, the experience of losing the rights to the song is one the band apparently and understandably chooses not to revisit. However, in a rare moment of public reflection on the matter, Ashcroft declared that in his opinion, "Bittersweet Symphony" is "the best song Jagger and Richards have written in twenty years."[202]

Reimagining Copyright—
A Moral Rights Opportunity

A caveat regularly given to aspiring musical artists is to always remember that the music business is in fact just that, a *business*. The cases discussed in this book certainly support that statement. It follows that the income generated by music is an important part of the commercial aspects of being a professional musician. However, there is another side that is equally important, if not more so. That is the nonmonetary value of the creative work as determined by the work's creator. This intrinsic value is not so easily measured in economic terms.

Unfortunately, that intrinsic value that an artist finds in his or her work does not translate well under the current U.S. legal structure. Although there are state and federal laws that attempt to protect musicians' rights, the general legal approach in the United States is based on economic injury. For those artists who measure the value of their work in terms other than economic, there is another set of rights designed to protect the noneconomic value—moral rights, based on the French term *droit morale*. Although there has been some recognition of the concept in the United States, it is currently not available to musicians.

In July 2010, Peter Yarrow and Noel Paul Stookey, the surviving members of the folk group Peter, Paul & Mary, sent a cease and desist letter to the National Organization for Marriage (NOM), a group supporting California's 2008 Proposition 8 ballot, which eliminated the right of same-sex couples to marry.[203] The letter stated that Mr. Yarrow and Mr. Stookey supported same-sex marriage and objected to NOM playing Peter, Paul & Mary's recording of "This Land Is Your Land" at its rallies, because NOM's philosophy is contrary to their advocacy positions. They further stated

205

that if the organization continued using their music, legal action may be pursued. If Yarrow and Stookey pursued legal action, what would it be? Suppose they did not hold a copyright in the song and had even given away rights to the recording? Are they out of luck? The answer is generally yes under state and federal copyright laws. However, under the concept of moral rights, they might have a claim.

The concept of moral rights requires more of an engagement of the intuitive right brain over the linear and logical left brain in this exercise of creative inquiry. Moral rights have implications that go beyond financial value. The concept is based on the idea that a creator of a work has a natural right to that work. That is, the work naturally possesses some traits of identity and personal expression that relate to the creator of the work.[204] Although the breadth of moral rights is vague, the types of moral rights that have been recognized to some extent in the United States include (1) attribution, which ensures the artist has been given credit and the power to deny credit if the work is changed without his or her consent and (2) integrity, which prevents the work from being changed without the artist's consent. Other moral rights that have been recognized in Europe for example include (1) publication, which is the right not to release a work before the artist is satisfied with it; and (2) retraction, which gives the artist the right to renounce a work and withdraw it from sale or display.[205]

The Berne Convention for the Protection of Literary and Artistic Works is an international treaty governing intellectual property.[206] It attempts to integrate both economic considerations and moral rights in relation to creative works. The United States became a signatory to the convention in 1988 but has taken the position that U.S. law is sufficient to provide protection to artists. The treaty requires that member nations recognize moral rights of attribution and the right to object to a work that is damaging to an artist's reputation.[207] Congress has not found it necessary to legislate specific moral rights protection, because sufficient protections are believed to be available in various areas of the law, such as unfair competition, privacy, defamation, and under the Lanham Act. In fact, the Copyright Act specifically prohibits any person in the United States, who is eligible for copyright protection under the Act, from relying on the protection of any right or interest specified in the Berne Convention while in the United States.[208] Therefore, it remains that only the copyright owner or owner of a trademark has the power to file a lawsuit against an alleged infringing party, and only that owner will benefit from any favorable decision.

When moral rights are available, an artist who, for example, does not own the copyright in a work would still be able to deny its use by others if that use fails to meet his or her approval. Even with the common practice of a songwriter-artist assigning copyright ownership in exchange for a record deal, moral rights would provide a means for the artist to continue to have approval rights over the use of his or her music.

In response to moral rights concerns, Congress did eventually enact the Visual Artists Rights Act of 1990 (VARA), which amended the Copyright Act and provided a limited version of moral rights protection. VARA protects only a "work of visual art."[209] Several states have also passed laws establishing moral rights protection. However, at both the federal and state levels, this protection applies exclusively to authors of visual arts. Musicians cannot seek relief.

In determining whether, under VARA, intentional distortion, mutilation, or modification of a work of visual art would be prejudicial to artists' honor or reputation, *honor* means good name or public esteem. For example, let's say a sculptor created a work of art and sold it to a collector, and the collector decided to modify the sculpture slightly by eliminating a portion and then displayed it in a public place. Let's also say that the portion removed happened to be a signature feature on all the sculptor's creations. Under VARA, the sculptor could potentially complain that his or her work had been intentionally distorted and that his or her reputation would suffer because the work was being displayed without its signature feature. Similarly, an author can object to an attribution to him or her in a work that does not accurately reflect his or her contribution. The law has not extended analogous protections to musicians.

In a 1949 case, *Shostakovich v. 20th Century Fox*, some composers from the Soviet Union objected to the use of their music in a movie that reflected a view opposed to their political ideology.[210] Because they held no copyright, the claim was based on a civil rights law, which the court characterized as a moral rights claim. The court found it difficult to articulate the injury and thus rejected the claim. It concluded that the composers had no right under the civil rights law to restrict the use of their names to indicate authorship of works. Their claims were, however, recognized in France, where a strong tradition of recognizing moral rights exists.

The availability of moral rights in the United States could be a positive step for the rights of musicians. It would provide a level of protection for their work even if they did not retain the copyright. As mentioned earlier, moral rights are based upon the idea of a natural right or purpose in a work. Some commentators point out that recognition of a natural right does not have to be a "zero-sum game."[211] They explain that one person's gain does not necessarily mean another person's loss. Philosophically speaking, a person does not suffer from honoring another person's rights, and could actually benefit from doing so.

The adage is true that the music business is a business, but it is equally true that the root of the business is creative musical expression. The debate over whether to incorporate moral rights into U.S. law in a manner that benefits musicians will most likely continue for some time, as the balance between the often-conflicting worlds of commercialism and creativity continues to seek equilibrium.

2 Live Crew Goes to Washington

Campbell v. Acuff-Rose Music,
510 U.S. 569 (1994).

"Oh, Pretty Woman" is a song that is deeply embedded in the American music songbook. You could probably walk up to just about anyone and sing the first line, "Pretty woman, walking down the street," and that person would probably know the lyrics well enough to join you through to the chorus. Or if you are the listening and not the singing type, and you are in the mood to hear this classic tune, you can easily find and download the song. While you're at it, you might consider taking a trip down rap's memory lane and listen to the *other* version. The infamous rap version is a song by the same name performed by 2 Live Crew.

In 1989, the popular and controversial hip-hop group recorded their "colorful" take on the song written by Roy Orbison. The fallout from doing so resulted in a lawsuit by Acuff-Rose, the publishers of "Oh, Pretty Woman," who accused the rap group of copyright infringement. In music law, there are a few landmark cases that everyone knows. *Campbell v. Acuff-Rose Music* is one of those cases.

Co-written by Orbison and Bill Dees, "Oh, Pretty Woman" was released in 1964 and has become a classic. It continues to receive airplay and has been included on several film soundtracks. Before releasing "Oh, Pretty Woman," Orbison had become well known for several songs, including "Only the Lonely" and the hauntingly soulful ballad "Crying." Audiences were struck by the uniqueness of Orbison's sound, exemplified by his distinctive songwriting and the expansive range of his bel canto tenor voice. He became known for his powerful live performances and his blend of blues, bluegrass, country, and rock 'n' roll.

Orbison and Dees assigned their rights in "Oh, Pretty Woman" to Acuff-Rose Music, Inc., in 1964, a music publishing company founded by country star Roy Acuff and songwriter Fred Rose. Acuff-Rose's extensive catalog included hits from Marty Robbins, Hank Williams, and the Everly Brothers. By the latter half of the 1960s, Orbison struggled to match the success of his earlier releases. During the 1970s, his popularity waned, although he continued to be revered by many. Almost twenty-five years after releasing "Oh, Pretty Woman," Orbison's popularity was beginning to surge once more. He was riding the wave of a comeback brought about, in part, by his collaborations with artists like K. D. Lang and his involvement with the Traveling Wilburys, a group featuring Tom Petty, George Harrison, Jeff Lynne, and Bob Dylan. As Orbison's renewed popularity surged, a hip-hop hurricane was brewing in Miami. Chaos, controversy, and multiplatinum albums were left in its wake. The name of the storm was 2 Live Crew.

A rap group formed by rappers DJ Mr. Mixx (David Hobbs), Fresh Kid Ice (Chris Wong Won), and Amazing (Yuri Vielot), 2 Live Crew was gaining momentum through word of mouth within the state of Florida.[212] They caught the attention of record-label owner and fellow rapper Luke Skyywalker (Luther Campbell). Campbell gave the group a record deal, signed on as manager, and eventually became lead MC. The group was very popular in the underground rap scene and quickly became known for its sexually explicit lyrics and imagery.

2 Live Crew seemed to court controversy with every release, while at the same time becoming immensely popular with mainstream audiences. The group's popularity was driven in large part by the success of the song "Me So Horny." In addition to the sexually suggestive title, the beat lit up the dance floor. When "Me So Horny" was released in 1989, rap and hip-hop had already swept through pop culture with staying power. "Me So Horny" was featured on 2 Live Crew's album *As Nasty As They Wanna Be*. The song and album titles seem relatively tame by today's standards, but in the late 1980s they drew the ire of groups such as the Parents' Music Resource Center. 2 Live Crew became a poster child for music censorship, and the backlash against the group contributed to the implementation of the album advisory labeling system that remains in place today.

The majority of 2 Live Crew's songs were banned from airplay. Nevertheless, Luther Campbell, demonstrating his clever business acumen, was responsible for the release of clean versions of several of 2 Live Crew's songs, which were acceptable for radio. However, most of the songs remained banned and circulated in the underground. Despite the lack of mainstream airplay, the group sold millions of records.

In addition to his music impresario duties, Campbell crafted a rap entitled "Pretty Woman." He claimed he wrote it with the intent to "satirize" the original "Oh, Pretty Woman" tune. The rap song used a bass riff, a short musical phrase, and some lyrics from the original Orbison song. Before its release, 2 Live Crew's management notified Acuff-Rose that the group had written a parody of "Oh, Pretty Woman." They informed the publisher that all credit as owners and composers of the original song would go to Acuff-Rose,

Orbison, and Dees, and that they would pay a fee for the ability to use the song. As copyright owners of the "Oh, Pretty Woman" composition, Acuff-Rose had the right to grant licenses for the creation of derivative works based on the song. The publisher politely responded that although it was aware of the popularity of 2 Live Crew, the company could not possibly license the original song as such. Perhaps *As Nasty As They Wanna Be* was a bit too explicit for Acuff-Rose's tastes.

The group shrugged off the refusal and released "Pretty Woman" on an album entitled *As Clean As They Wanna Be*. Acuff-Rose watched as the album sold more than 250,000 copies. Acuff-Rose sued 2 Live Crew, its individual members, and its record company, Luke Skyywalker Records, for copyright infringement.

The suit was filed on June 18, 1990, in the U.S. District Court in Nashville, Tennessee. During the pretrial discovery phase, Campbell asserted in an affidavit that his intention for the song was to have comical lyrics that would satirize Orbison's original work. In early January 1991, the court granted a summary judgment in favor of Campbell and dismissed the lawsuit. The court found that there was no material dispute of the facts, and that the legal application of the law to the facts supported a conclusion that 2 Live Crew had not infringed on the rights of Acuff-Rose. The rationale was that Campbell's version of "Pretty Woman" was, in fact, a parody that constituted a fair use of copyrighted material under Section 107 of the Copyright Act.[213]

The case was appealed to the Sixth Circuit. Two of the judges on the three-judge panel had significant disagreements with the lower court. Whereas the lower court did not view the commercial nature of Campbell's use of the copyrighted song as an impediment to availing of the protection of fair use, the appellate court thought otherwise. The court was also concerned about the substantial amount of Orbison's song that Campbell used. In its opinion, Campbell had used too much of the original, and the portions he used were considered important elements of the original song. The most important issue, in the court's opinion, was the risk of future harm to the potential market for Orbison's song. It disagreed with the district court that the difference in audiences between the two songs would mitigate that risk. It was in agreement with the lower court's conclusion that Campbell's song was a parody of the original but concluded that that the parody designation alone did not qualify Campbell's use as a "fair use." The appellate court delivered a victory for Acuff-Rose in reversing the opinion of the trial court, based on its conclusion that Campbell's song caused market harm to Acuff-Rose.[214]

The U.S. Supreme Court granted Campbell's petition for certiorari because it considered the resolution of whether a parody was a fair use of another's copyrighted work to be of significant public interest. Oral arguments were held on November 9, 1993, with a decision issued on March 7, 1994. Justice Souter wrote the opinion for a unanimous court, with Justice Kennedy adding a concurring opinion. The issue for the Court was whether 2 Live Crew's parody of Roy Orbison's song was protected against claims of infringement, based on the fair-use defense, within the meaning of Section 107 of the Copyright Act of 1976. The Supreme Court had not previously resolved the issue, and there was a lack of agreement among the lower courts. The Supreme Court had considered whether a parody could be a fair use only once. On that occasion, a divided court affirmed the lower court's opinion without issuing one of its own.[215]

The doctrine of fair use is an exception within federal copyright law that permits the use of another's copyrighted work without permission and serves as a defense against liability for copyright infringement. The unauthorized use must be determined on a case-by-case basis, using the four factors specifically listed in Section

107 of the 1976 Copyright Act: (1) the *purpose and character* of the work, including whether it is commercial or for nonprofit educational purposes; (2) the *nature* of the copyrighted work; (3) the *amount and substantiality* of the portion used in relation to the copyrighted work as a whole; and (4) the *effect of the use upon the potential market* for, or value of, the copyrighted work.

The Court began the four-factor test by examining the first factor, looking at the purpose and character of Campbell's "Pretty Woman." This factor required an assessment of whether the song "merely 'supersedes the objects' of the original creation or added something new with a further purpose or different character." The objective was "to see whether the new creation . . . ha[d] developed into something that ha[d] its own meaning . . . distinct from the original work."[216] That is, was the new creation "transformative"? Transformative is a defining characteristic. Justice Souter went on to explain that although a transformative classification is important, it is not absolutely necessary in the case of parody because the classification alone does not resolve any issues. It is just one of the considerations in the overall four-factor test.

In the discussion of the ingredients of parody, Justice Souter wrote that parody "needs to mimic an original to make its point, and so has some claim to use the creation of its victim's (or collective victims') imagination, whereas satire can stand on its own two feet and so requires justification for the very act of borrowing." He quoted from a 1903 opinion by Justice Oliver Wendell Holmes, discussing whether a consideration should be made of the work's good or bad taste when considering parody. "[I]t would be a dangerous undertaking for persons trained only in the law to constitute themselves final judges of the worth of (a work), outside of the narrowest and most obvious limits. At the one extreme some works of genius would be sure to miss appreciation. Their very novelty would make them repulsive until the public had learned the new language in which their author spoke."[217]

The very nature of parody is to criticize something that is already in existence. Justice Kennedy reinforced this point in his concurring opinion. To parody, he offered, means truly targeting the copyrighted work and making a statement that goes beyond just adding some humorous elements to it. It is the recognition of the original work that provides the context through which the parody is understood. For example, the half-hour, episodic, and parody-filled cartoon hit *Family Guy* would probably be a ten-minute cartoon for children if it could not reference the likenesses, images, and voices of its many pop-culture targets. Where is the fun in that?

The Court considered 2 Live Crew's "Pretty Woman" to be "reasonably" commenting on or criticizing Orbison's song through its references to the original. It is probably fair to say that lyrics like "Big hairy woman, all that hair ain't legit / Cause you look like Cousin It" definitely make a statement of some sort. The Court pointed out that a value judgment on 2 Live Crew's commentary, and any commentary or critique of a parody, was inappropriate.

The Court also emphasized that the court of appeals had incorrectly denied the fair-use defense on the grounds that the parody was of a commercial nature. The appellate court held that because copyrighted material was being used for commercial purposes, it was presumptively unfair and an infringement. The Supreme Court concluded that this approach was incorrect. It explained that the use as commercial or not for profit did not automatically indicate that the use was fair or unfair. Consistent with the other considerations in the four-factor test, the commercial or not-for-profit nature of the use had to be balanced against all of the evidence.

With respect to the second factor, the "nature of the copyrighted work," Souter illustrated that although it is important to know whether the original work falls within the protective purposes of copyright law, it is "not much help in this case, or ever likely to help much in separating the fair use sheep from the infringing goats in a parody case, since parodies almost invariably copy publicly known, expressive works."[218] Thus, this second factor typically weighs the expressiveness of the work against its utilitarian value. Those works ranking high on the expressive end, such as a creative literary work, are typically valued as more protected than a utilitarian work such as an instruction manual. In the case of parody, this expressive-versus-utilitarian valuation is not helpful because it is typically necessary for the writer of a parody to use "the heart" of an expressive work to conjure up enough recognition of the original for the parody to be effective.

Building upon the notion of the heart of an expressive work, the Court next looked at the third factor, the amount and substantiality of the portion used in relation to the copyrighted work as a whole. This factor looks at whether the quantity and value of the material used is reasonable in relation to the purpose of the copying. The Court once again pointed out the challenge of parody. The challenge is that parody, by definition, is born of an original work. It is this connection that forms the tension between the original work and the parody. The question of how much of the original is reasonable to use in a parody depends on whether the reason for using it is in fact to parody the original or instead to create a substitute of the original that threatens the original's share in the marketplace.

The Sixth Circuit had concluded that 2 Live Crew copied excessively from Orbison's song. The Supreme Court explained that in regard to the amount of the copying that has occurred, it is important to recognize that a parody of a particular original work must, by design, be able to "conjure up" enough of the original to make it recognizable during the criticism or satire. The Court viewed

Campbell's use of the first line of lyrics and bass riff of the original Orbison tune as using the heart of the original, and therefore a substantial amount of the work was used for the purpose of conjuring recognition of the original tune.

The Court also noted that 2 Live Crew produced "distinctive sounds" in addition to mimicry. Therefore, though 2 Live Crew had used some original elements of "Oh, Pretty Woman," its parody was not based on a verbatim copy of the original song. As such, 2 Live Crew did not take more than was necessary to create the parody.

Finally, the Court analyzed the fourth factor, the effect of the use upon the potential market for or value of the copyrighted work. This factor measures the depth of potential harm to the consumer market of the copyright holder's work as a result of the dissemination of the alleged infringer's work. The Supreme Court reversed the ruling of the Sixth Circuit, which, citing *Sony Corp. of America v. Universal City Studios, Inc.*, held that there was a presumption of market harm because 2 Live Crew's use of Orbison's song was a commercial use.[219]

In *Sony*, the Supreme Court held that the copying of a television program for commercial use would serve as a market substitute for the original program and harm the original's market share. The Court distinguished *Sony* from 2 Live Crew's actions by explaining that *Sony* dealt with the duplication of an original work and a verbatim copy of a copyrighted work for commercial use, which would carry with it a presumption of market harm. However, 2 Live Crew had not made a verbatim copy of Orbison's song. Instead, the song, a parody and transformative, likely had a different market appeal and did not compete with the market for Orbison's song.

The copyright holder of an original work has the right to grant permission for the creation of any derivative of the work. Considering that any income earned from the derivative work is shared with the copyright holder, there is a strong incentive to preserve the integrity of the derivative market. As such, the market analysis must include an examination of the harm to the potential derivative markets of the original work.

Although a parody may negatively affect demand for the original, the court's duty is to distinguish between "[b]iting criticism [that merely] suppresses demand [and] copyright infringement[, which] usurps it."[220] Because 2 Live Crew was a rap group, the derivative market for rap music was an appropriate place to look for potential harm. The Supreme Court ultimately found in favor of Campbell by concluding that a parody could constitute fair use, but remanded on the fourth factor to the lower court, holding that an evidentiary matter existed that needed to be resolved before concluding that "Pretty Woman" was fair use through parody. This required a determination of whether Campbell's use of "Oh, Pretty Woman" was excessive and a market analysis of whether Campbell's use harmed the market for the original song. Ultimately, Acuff-Rose and 2 Live Crew settled the case. Acuff-Rose dismissed the lawsuit, and 2 Live Crew agreed to license its use.

Following the decision, 2 Live Crew continued to release singles until disbanding in 1995. It is unlikely that the group had any idea that its parody of "Oh, Pretty Woman" would lead to a journey all the way to the Supreme Court. Perhaps this journey through the legal system, along with an earlier court battle in which the group prevailed against a claim that 2 Live Crew's album *As Nasty As They Wanna Be* was obscene, gave Campbell a taste for jurisprudence and the function of government. For in the spring of 2011, he ran for mayor of Miami-Dade County. He lost the race but won a solid 11 percent of the vote.[221] If the past is in any indication, Campbell is just getting warmed up.

The Rise and Fall of a Boy-Band Impresario

No matter how you measure it, Lou Pearlman was a wealthy man. He lived in a multimillion-dollar mansion, drove expensive cars, and wore a Rolex valued at $250,000 along with a set of cuff links and matching ring valued at $175,000. Bursting with confidence, good negotiating skills, and a way with words, he fit the description of a music mogul perfectly. At one point, Pearlman managed two of the most successful boy bands of all time: the Backstreet Boys and 'N Sync. Each group sold millions of records and generated millions of dollars in revenue. While Pearlman was raking in the money, the band members received comparatively little of the wealth.

After managing various businesses, Pearlman sought a change in direction and entered the entertainment industry during the 1990s. Having little experience, he hedged his bets by borrowing the boy-band concept and style from the singing group New Kids on the Block. He applied that concept to the first act he signed, in 1993, the Backstreet Boys. After a brief period, it was apparent that his boy-band formula worked. The group went on to sell more than 100 million albums worldwide. His second group, 'N Sync, was signed in 1995 and went on to sell over 60 million albums.

The success of New Kids on the Block showed Pearlman that there was a strong market for a group of young, clean-cut white men who could sing and dance. Pearlman's timing with the Backstreet Boys was perfect.[222] Their popularity soared among a new generation of screaming 'tweens. 'N Sync followed right behind with similar momentum and success.

Back in the early 1980s, New Edition, a group of teenage black men managed by Maurice Starr, was entertaining audiences around the world. All the group members could sing and had synchronized dance moves, both of which are boy-band necessities. New Edition had several hit songs, but record sales never reached the height achieved by other boy bands that arrived on the music scene in the late 1980s and 1990s. When New Edition was popular, the term *boy band* was not yet a commonly used pop culture term.

Starr and New Edition parted ways in the mid-80s and he set out specifically to find a talented group of young men who were white and could perform in a similar manner.[223] He believed that a white group would have even greater mass appeal than New Edition. After hundreds of auditions, Starr found his boy-band performers, and New Kids on the Block was formed in 1984. The group was immensely successful and went on to sell more than 100 million albums and hundreds of millions of dollars worth of merchandise. The merchandise included everything from T-shirts to lunch boxes. After Maurice Starr left as manager, the group disbanded, in 1994.

With the huge success of his two groups, Pearlman was growing richer by the day, and discontent was brewing among the members of 'N Sync and the Backstreet Boys. In 1997, Brian Littrell, a member of the Backstreet Boys, sought a detailed picture of just how much money his group was making and how that money was being spent. In response to Pearlman's reluctance to provide the requested information, Littrell initiated a lawsuit against Pearlman alleging concealment and misappropriation of revenues.[224] A review of the group's contract by Littrell's lawyers showed that Pearlman had legally made himself a sixth member of the group. By doing so, he was not only able to receive his commission as a manager but was also able to receive a share of the profits set aside for the band members.

Pearlman had allegedly made $10 million from the recent European summer tour, compared with the group's receipt of $300,000.[225] The remaining Backstreet Boys joined Littrell's lawsuit in 1998. Pearlman countered that he had made large investments in the group that had to be recouped. Though it is true that managers of new groups often provide capital up front with the expectation of a later payoff, the revenue imbalance between the parties was significant. Pearlman and the Backstreet Boys reached a settlement deal, the terms of which remain sealed.

In September 1999, following an announcement by 'N Sync that it was leaving RCA Records to join Jive Records, Pearlman, along with BMG Entertainment, RCA's parent company, filed a $150 million breach-of-contract lawsuit against the group.[226] Pearlman also requested an injunction to prevent the group from recording with Jive Records, home of Britney Spears and the Backstreet Boys, who had recently changed labels. 'N Sync countersued, alleging fraud, breach of contract, and breach of fiduciary duty. The injunction was denied, and the judge directed the parties to work toward a settlement.

'N Sync moved to Jive Records, where its highly successful second album, *No Strings Attached*, was released. The song and album were named in honor of the group's liberation from Pearlman. Although terms of the settlement were not disclosed, *Billboard* magazine reported on the amount of money accruing to Pearlman and his companies at the time of the lawsuit. It reported that "Pearlman or his entities received 55 percent of all gross touring revenue, plus 37.5 percent of the net; 75 percent of all record royalties and 100 percent of any advances; 80 percent of the merchandising; 100 percent of the music publishing; and 55 percent of gross celebrity endorsement monies, plus 37.5 percent of the net from such deals."[227]

Pearlman claimed that he was in the business of discovering, evaluating, training, financing, and equipping young singers, musicians, and performers. His formulaic approach involved maintaining complete control over his groups, as evidenced in his signed agreements with them. The agreements show that among other things, Pearlman selected the music and had sole rights on the trademark and copyrights, sole ownership of the merchandising rights, and right of publicity to use the groups' image in any manner he chose.

Pearlman, the alleged boy-band puppet master, was guided by greed. He was making a lot of money but also spending it as fast as he made it. His charisma took him far in the music industry, but his high-rolling life in the fast lane crashed and burned. In 2007, Pearlman was found hiding in Indonesia and federal authorities charged him with securing more than $20 million in personal and business loans using fake documents from an accounting firm that did not exist. He also made two fraudulent loans in 2004 for $19 million and two in 2006 for slightly less than $1 million. In addition, he was convicted of defrauding more than 1,000 investors out of more than $315 million in a Ponzi scheme that had lasted for years. Pearlman is currently serving a twenty-five-year sentence. Two of the lawyers who represented him in the cases against the Backstreet Boys and 'N Sync filed suit against him for nonpayment of legal fees. Also, shortly before his conviction, an exposé by *Vanity Fair*, published in 2007, alleged that Pearlman was a sexual predator who targeted some of the teen boys he had been grooming for stardom.[228]

The Backstreet Boys, for example, have been moving on from their time with Pearlman. Free from his questionable management and accounting practices, the group has been able to look toward a positive future. Some members of the Backstreet Boys and 'N Sync have continued to perform as a group. Former members, like 'N Sync's Justin Timberlake, have achieved immense success as solo artists in their post-boy-band days. In contrast, Pearlman has plenty of time to reflect on the past while he sits in jail, knowing that his days as a high-flying music mogul are over.

PART FIVE

Twenty-First Century

Playback

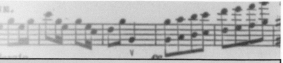

2000	• Metallica sues Napster for copyright infringement, marking the first time an artist filed a lawsuit against a peer-to-peer software organization.
2001	• In March, the dot.com bubble bursts.
2003	• On April 28, the iTunes store is launched by Apple, selling close to 25 million songs by December.
2004	• Ray Charles dies. • In February, Facebook is launched by Mark Zuckerberg.
2005	• YouTube debuts.
2006	• After several court battles and a costly settlement, peer-to-peer service Kazaa switches to providing legal music downloads. • Twitter launches.
2007	• Radiohead, after declaring that the music business is dead, sells its new album, *In Rainbows*, as an online download according to a "pay what you like" scheme.
2008	• Online music-listening service Spotify debuts in Europe. • On September 15, investment bank Lehman Brothers declares bankruptcy, ushering in the Great Recession. • On November 4, Barack Obama is elected president of the United States.
2009	• On June 25, singer Michael Jackson dies at age fifty.
2011	• Napster merges with online music-subscription service Rhapsody.
2012	• E.U. and U.S. regulators approve the sale of EMI to Sony/ATV and Universal. • *Billboard* names Adele Artist of the Year for the second year in a row.

Game Over:
A Club Queen, a Video Game, and Right of Publicity

Kirby v. Sega of America, Inc.,
144 Cal. App. 4th 47 (2006).

R ecording artist are often touted as much for their style and persona as they are for their musical talents. In addition to the flamboyant costumes of artists such as Lady Gaga, these colorful aspects of style have included Michael Jackson's shiny, single white glove and red jacket, David Bowie's Ziggy Stardust costume, and Elvis Presley's jewel-studded white jumpsuit and cape. While there are many examples it's difficult to leave out Kiss's black outfits and white-faced masks and Madonna's characteristic hair bow, short skirts, and colorful outfits, which were imitated by millions of young girls in the 1980s. Many would say that imitation is the sincerest form of flattery—that is, until the imitation has the potential to cause economic harm to the artist. This was the issue in *Kirby v. Sega of America, Inc.*

In the early 1990s, the charts were filled with dance-pop anthems that pulled people out of their seats and onto the dance floor. Near the top of the techno-soul pack was a motley threesome of scenesters straight out of the clubs of New York. The group, Deee-Lite, was fronted by a nouveau psychedelic siren. She had a

233

unique style and flair, becoming a popular fixture on TV and radio by virtue of Deee-Lite's mega-hit single, "Groove Is in the Heart." Before Lady Gaga, there was Lady Miss Kier.

Kier, born Kierin Kirby and a native of Pittsburgh, was Deee-Lite's lead vocalist. She had a passion for fashion. Kier moved to New York in the 1980s to study at the Fashion Institute of Technology. She discontinued her studies after just one year but continued to design clothes, holding a variety of jobs to support herself. One of those jobs was as a go-go dancer. Spending time in the New York club scene, she met a man named Dmitry Brill, known as Super DJ Dmitry.[229] The two formed a friendship after Kier designed a pair of silver boots for him. Soon after, the pair began to experiment with music, and a short while later they were introduced to Dong-Hwa Chung, otherwise known as DJ Towa Tei. The three eventually joined forces, and Deee-Lite was born.

Deee-Lite had a strong following on the dance-club circuit. That popularity led to a multi-record deal with Elektra Records. The group's debut album, entitled *World Clique*, was released in 1990 and went gold, as did its breakout song and biggest hit, "Groove Is in the Heart." The video for the song, which also included rapper Q-Tip, bass player Bootsy Collins, and former James Brown band members Maceo Parker and Fred Wesley, received constant airplay on MTV. The psychedelic-styled video opens with a close-up of Kier speaking into the camera, saying "How do you say Dee-Gorgeous?" She continues to rhythmically speak her song intro, and one of the last things we hear before Bootsy Collins kicks in with the bass line is Kier purring the phrase, "Oooh-la-la la-la-la-la-la-la." For the remainder of the video, she dances and sings dressed in a multicolored cat suit with her bright auburn hair flipped out in the back.

The band released two more albums after *World Clique* to disappointing sales. Deee-Lite did, however, go on to have a few hits on the U.S. dance charts. By the mid-1990s, the group had disbanded, with Kier later spending a significant amount of time living and performing in London, England.

In another corner of the entertainment industry, the 1990s saw an expansion of the video-game market, with Sega Corporation at the forefront. Sega, a developer of gaming software and hardware, is a Japanese company that was founded by three Americans in the 1950s. As gaming systems became faster in the video-game hardware market, Sega was unable to develop a leading product in the 4-bit and 8-bit gaming-console markets. A solution was found with the introduction of its 16-bit Genesis game console, which allowed it to compete more directly with Nintendo, the market leader. Things began to fall apart when Sony entered the market with PlayStation, a 32-bit console.[230] In addition to marketing and manufacturing problems, Sega's 32-bit offering, the Sega Saturn, had significantly fewer games. Although it was the preferred system among some gamers, it failed commercially. Licking its wounds, the company looked to the future and began working on its next-generation console, Dreamcast, a comparatively large 128-bit system.

Even with the company reporting five consecutive years of losses as product development continued, Sega sought to guarantee a high level of market competitiveness for itself. One strategy was to develop a game that focused on a female hero. PlayStation's *Tomb Raider*, featuring Lara Croft, had become successful beyond expectations, and Sega wanted such a game for its Dreamcast console. One game selected for development was *Space Channel 5*.

Sega released the Dreamcast console in Japan in 1998. The *Space Channel 5* video game, designed for the console, was released to a favorable reception in 1999 and 2000 in Japan and the United States, respectively. However, just as things were starting to look up, Microsoft entered the console market with the wildly successful Xbox. This, along with the strong marketing and financial positions of Nintendo and Sony, led Sega to announce in 2001 that it was leaving the console business and would focus only on video games. Despite a good design, Sega had been unable to create enough demand for the console. The problem was made worse when Sony's PlayStation outsold the Dreamcast by a demoralizing ratio of approximately ten to one.[231]

Space Channel 5 represented an opportunity for Sega to have a top-selling video game. After leaving the console market and putting its focus entirely on software development, Sega released *Space Channel 5* on Sony's PlayStation 2 in Europe in March 2002 and in the United States in November 2003. *Space Channel 5: Part 2* was released for PlayStation 2 in Europe in February 2003 and in North America in November 2003. *Space Channel 5: Ulala's Cosmic Attack* was released in 2003 for the Nintendo Game Boy Advance, a hand-held device.

The main character of *Space Channel 5* is Ulala (pronounced "ooh-la-la"). She is a twenty-fifth-century rookie news reporter who has been placed on assignment to cover an invasion of aliens. The aliens threaten the future of planet Earth by shooting humans with ray guns that force them to dance uncontrollably. Saving the planet from space monsters is an arduous task for any would-be hero; however, Ulala is well prepared in her battle-worthy outfit, consisting of a miniskirt, go-go boots, and, of course, a jet pack.

Her reporting skills are not the only things put to the test in the game. She is forced to save Earth by giving the aliens a taste of their own medicine and making them dance. The object of the game is to make Ulala dance the same steps as the aliens. Points are awarded for accuracy in copying the dance moves, and the accumulation of points then causes the aliens to be destroyed or humans to be rescued. The player then moves to the next level of play. One human rescued by Ulala is the moonwalker himself,

Michael Jackson, or as he is called in the game, "Space Michael." Superstar performer Michael Jackson lent his voice to the character that had been designed in his likeness.

Sega contacted Kier in July 2000, during the release of the first *Space Channel 5* game. She was asked if she would be interested in promoting the game in England and possibly Europe. Kier declined the offer. She had been out of the spotlight for a few years by this point.

As Deee-Lite's frontwoman, Kier had constructed a colorful image that was part art-school fashion, part go-go girl, and part club queen. A review of *Space Channel 5* in the June 27, 2000, edition of the *Washington Times* describes Ulala as having "a Deborah Norville appeal and Lady Miss Kier's dance moves."[232] It was an interesting combination to say the least. However, the *Times* was not alone in linking Kier to Ulala. Kier also saw the connection.

Believing that the video-game company had misappropriated her identity, she accused Sega of designing Ulala in her likeness. She filed a lawsuit against Sega in the California Superior Court in April 2003.[233] Her claims included violations under California's right of publicity statute and common law, as well as a claim of false endorsement under the federal Lanham Act. The court accepted Sega's argument that the First Amendment provided a complete defense to Kier's claims and thus granted Sega's motion for summary judgment, dismissing all of Kier's claims. Kier appealed to the California Court of Appeal for the Second District. The court affirmed the trial court's decision that Kier's claims of misappropriation of her likeness and identity by Sega failed because the First Amendment provided a complete defense.

Kier's claims were related to the common-law right of publicity that provides remedies to a celebrity if his or her identity is misappropriated for commercial purposes. Slightly more than half of the states have passed right of publicity statutes. Both the statutes and common law vary by state. For example, New York has a limited statutory right of publicity but does not recognize a common-law right.[234] California's right of publicity statute allows a celebrity to sue for damages against someone who has knowingly used his or her identity for commercial purposes without consent. Someone who is outside of the public eye and has a claim for misappropriation of identity would typically sue under a claim of invasion of privacy in California.

In California, the right of publicity statute is nearly identical to the common-law right of publicity. One of the main differences between the two is the additional element in the statute that requires the defendant to have *knowingly* used the plaintiff's likeness without permission.[235] As such, the statute was not created to replace the common-law right of publicity but to complement it.

Kier also sought federal relief under the Lanham Act.[236] The Lanham Act is often invoked alongside state right-of-publicity claims. The act itself does not specifically recognize the right of publicity. It does, however, offer individuals protection from false and misleading statements delivered by another that effectively suggest that the aggrieved individual has endorsed or affiliated with the other person's product or service.

Kier had attempted to show that Ulala's character design could be construed to indicate her endorsement of the game. As the court explained, she needed to demonstrate that she had in fact not provided such endorsement and that there was a likelihood that an ordinary consumer would reasonably believe that she had endorsed the game. Proving this can be extremely difficult. Kier believed that Sega's prior contact with her during the release of *Space Channel 5* was strong evidence to prove, in part, that Ulala was in fact a likeness of Kier. Therefore, she hoped to prove that Takashi Yuda, the game's creator, and Sega had knowingly made Ulala in Kier's likeness. As such, because Ulala was based on

Kier, consumers would likely be deceived into thinking that Kier endorsed the game.

The difficult task of determining whether Kier's right of publicity had been violated required the appellate court, in its review of the trial court, to analyze images of Kier dressed as her stage persona in comparison with images of Ulala. This comparison was necessary to sort out the similarities and differences between Kier and Ulala. The court recognized several similarities. Both had red lips and similarly shaped eyes and faces, and they both wore their hair in shades of pink. The court also acknowledged that both wore brightly colored clothes, short skirts, and platform shoes. Additionally, the name *Ulala* sounds like a derivation of "Ooh-la-la," the catchphrase used often by Kier.

The appellate court also pointed out several differences between Ulala and Kier. Ulala's hair was in pigtails and her costume consisted of an orange-cropped top with the numeral 5 printed on the front, an orange miniskirt, orange gloves, boots with stiletto heels, a blue ray-gun holster strapped to her thigh, a blue headset, and a jet-pack. Kier insisted that, like Ulala, she also regularly wore short skirts, crop tops with numbers, elbow-length gloves, pigtails, and space helmets as part of her stage persona. The court was not persuaded by Kier's insistence and decided that based on the evidence, it appeared that Kier was more often seen in form-fitting bodysuits with her hair in a page-boy flip held back with a headband as her signature look. In a spectacularly detailed observation, the court also noted that even when Kier does wear her hair in pigtails, the length of her pigtails is longer than Ulala's, and Kier "has tendrils of hair draping over her forehead which she holds back with clips."[237]

The court equated these differences in appearance to a "lack of stasis" in Kier's persona. That is, they viewed her as an artist who was continually changing her style and therefore lacked a branded, singular visual identity. Kier described herself as an artist who enjoys changing her appearance, often making as many as five changes of costume during a show.

The court also examined Ulala's dance choreography for elements of Kier's influence. Ulala's movements were described by the court as "limited, short, choppy dance movements and styles (that) differ markedly from Kier's." In contrast, Kier's movements were considered to be varied, fluid, and rhythmic. The court determined that the choppy nature of Ulala's movements was too dissimilar to Kier's fluid dancing, and that therefore Ulala's choreography was likely developed by someone who knew very little of Kier's dancing. Sega's choreographer for *Space Channel 5* had denied knowing of Kier prior to choreographing Ulala's dance routine.

In his testimony, Takashi Yuda, the creator of *Space Channel 5*, claimed that Kier was not used as a reference for Ulala. He stated that the character was originally going to be male but was changed to a female to make the video game appealing to girls. He also claimed that the name Ulala was a variation of the Japanese name Urara (pronounced "Ooh-ra-ra") that had been changed in order to make it easier for English speakers. Nevertheless, Sega's solicitation of Kier prior to the release of the game was interpreted by the court as evidence that the company was aware of the Lady Miss Kier persona and believed that Kier's celebrity association would benefit the release of the game.

A single artist filing a claim against a major corporation can be a truly daunting notion, but it seems Kier was initially optimistic that the scales of justice might tip in her favor. When evaluating her odds of success, she probably counted in her favor a video-game character who even the court would acknowledge had a similar appearance and whose name sounded like a derivation of Kier's "Ooh-la-la" catchphrase, in addition to a solicitation from Sega. All these things probably boosted Kier's confidence and willingness to go forward with the lawsuit. Sega's response, however, was to invoke the First Amendment as a defense.

Free-speech protection under the First Amendment is a fiercely guarded right in the United States. Courts weigh in with caution on matters brought before them that potentially challenge the breadth of free speech. They are hesitant to make any judgments that could have a chilling effect. The underlying reason behind such fierce protection is to ensure the free flow of ideas and individual self-expression.

The creative product of an idea is an "expressive work." Video games, for example, are considered expressive works. Though the right of expression is protected under the First Amendment, an expressive work may not have that same protection. Whether the expressive work, or speech, is for commercial purposes does not determine whether it can be protected. Instead, protection turns on whether the speech is false or misleading.

There is a delicate balance between a person's right of publicity and free speech. The creator of an expressive work can use another's identity without permission, provided the new work has "transformative elements." Elements of a transformative nature are those that add something new to the original expression (that is, the celebrity image). Transformative elements alter the original expression to a point where a new expression is created that possesses a different meaning and purpose from the original.

The court applied the transformative test established by the California Supreme Court in *Comedy III Productions, Inc. v. Gary Saderup, Inc.*[238] In that case, the owner of the Three Stooges' publicity rights sued an artist who was selling lithographs and T-shirts containing an image of the Three Stooges that the artist had designed. The California Supreme Court held that the artist's drawings were not protected under the First Amendment because they added very little to the literal depictions of the Three

Stooges and the resulting product did not therefore amount to a new expression of the original work. To reach its conclusion, the court formulated the transformative test as a means of balancing right of publicity claims and First Amendment interests. The test asks "whether a product containing a celebrity's likeness is so transformed that it has become primarily the defendant's own expression rather than the celebrity's likeness."[239]

Unfortunately for Kier, the California Court of Appeal found that Ulala was not a "mere likeness or literal depiction of Kier." In its eyes, Ulala was a transformative work composed of transformative elements that produced a character possessing a new meaning and purpose. According to the court, Sega had created a character that was so transformed it reflected Sega's vision of a character and was not a likeness of Kier. This was held to be true despite an acknowledgement by the court that Kier may have been an inspiration for the character. The differences noted, such as hairstyle and clothing, were the basis for the court's reasoning. Furthermore, it reasoned that Ulala's twenty-fifth-century futuristic space setting differed from any previously seen depiction of Kier. Lastly, Ulala's dance moves were seen as being unlike any performed by Kier in her videos. With these findings, Sega's character was considered to be entirely separate from Kier and protected under the First Amendment. As such, Kier's Lanham Act claim that Ulala's design would serve as a false product endorsement by Kier failed as well.

The loss to Sega was surely painful for Kier, but the court added insult to injury when it awarded legal fees to Sega. The court noted that it was bound by a mandatory provision in the right of publicity statute that required the court to award legal fees to the prevailing party.[240] Sega was awarded $608,000 in legal fees, and Kier was ordered to foot the bill. In response to Kier's argument that the lawyer's-fees provision was a disincentive for artists to enforce their rights of publicity, the court simply stated that it was up to the legislature to change the law.

The balance between a celebrity's right of publicity and free speech continues to be debated. Uniqueness and variety are qualities Kier possesses in abundance, but it could be argued that those qualities contributed to her losing the case against Sega. Ulala may not have been a literal depiction of Kier's stage persona, but even the court acknowledged the design similarity. In the end, substance prevailed over style. However, in the entertainment industry, style can be just as important as substance.

The Romantics Take On Guitar Hero

The Romantics v. Activision Publ'g, Inc.,
532 F. Supp. 2d 884 (E.D. Mich. 2008).

Aspiring rock stars and air-guitar enthusiasts celebrated the 2005 release of *Guitar Hero*. Those who have been compelled to jam out to Deep Purple's "Smoke on the Water" or stumble through Led Zeppelin's "Stairway to Heaven" (and let's face it, I'm talking about a lot of us) understand the stroke of genius in the creation of this game. The clever integration of music into the game was a welcome feature for many music publishers and some recording artists. It provided a wealth of opportunities to exploit their catalogs because each version of the game has about thirty songs either performed by or made famous by a wide variety of artists.

By 2010 there were more than twenty versions of the game, including versions featuring music from just one epic rock group, such as *Guitar Hero Aerosmith*. But sometimes it is possible to have too much of a good thing. In February 2011, Activision, the game's publisher, announced an end to the franchise. A few months later, an Activision spokesperson sought to ease the lament of some fans by stating that the game was not dead, just going on hiatus.[241] Whether it is destined for the video-game graveyard or a gaming resurrection, *Guitar Hero*'s journey was speculated to have oversaturated the video-game market with too many versions. Nevertheless, the game had a pretty good run.

In its heyday, despite the jamming masses, all was not well with the game. One of the songs contained in the *Guitar Hero* music catalog was "What I Like about You," a song made famous by new wave group the Romantics. The version used in the game is a "sound-alike" cover version, which is a song recorded by someone other than the original performer and recorded for the purposes of sounding like the original. The Romantics believed the use of a sound-alike version was an improper use of their song. On November 20, 2007, the band filed a lawsuit against Activision, the distributor of *Guitar Hero*.[242]

The Romantics originated in the neighborhoods of East Detroit. The band's name stems from its formation on Valentine's Day in 1977. They were a collective of tough and hardworking young men. Musically, their style infused the signature three-chord pattern of punk music with a catchy pop appeal. Their mission was to create music that would be an antidote to the "nihilism" they thought existed in punk music coming from the United Kindgdom.[243] Short hair and red leather suits soon became their signature look. The original members of the band were Wally Palmar, Jimmy Marinos, Mike Skill, and Rich Cole.

The band drew its influences from a variety of bands from the 1960s, including some from the British Invasion and from Detroit's music scene, like MC5, Bob Seeger, and the Stooges. They are often labeled as being new wave, but the members have remarked that the label comes from a deluded misunderstanding of the punk music scene in the United States, used to make selling punk music more "palatable." Their biggest hit, "What I Like about You," was originally recorded in 1979 and published in 1980. It features a memorable guitar riff at the beginning followed by distinctive handclaps keeping time with the beat. The song is tight, simple, and upbeat. Its popularity has lasted for over twenty-five years, and it is regularly played in movies, television shows, and now *Guitar Hero*.

Activision received a nonexclusive synchronization license to use the song from EMI Entertainment Worldwide, EMI's music publishing arm, which held the copyright in the song. A synch license grants permission to the licensee to use the music and lyrics of a copyright holder's song in timed synchronization with visual images, such as in a television program, film, or video game. This is of particular concern when a cover version of the song will be used.

A cover version of the song "What I Like about You" was recorded by WaveGroup Sound, an audio production company that has produced several recordings for use in *Guitar Hero*. This version was synched to the graphics in the game *Guitar Hero Encore: Rocks the 80s*. In that game, the song appears when a player has demonstrated the skills needed to reach the song through gameplay. The words "as made famous by the Romantics" then appear on the screen next to the title. To the casual observer, the *Guitar Hero* placement probably seemed like a good deal for the band because it generated publicity for the song. Some of the band members thought otherwise.

The band claimed the sound-alike version was nearly identical to its original recording. Red Octane, the publisher of *Guitar Hero* and also a subsidiary of Activision, was named as a defendant along with Harmonix Music Systems and WaveGroup Sound. The band lineup at the time of the lawsuit consisted of Wally Palmar, Mike Skill, and Coz Canler. Only two of the original band members were involved in the lawsuit. One original member, Jimmy Marinos, declined to participate. The suit accused the defendants of unjust

Wall Street Sees Green in Music Publishing

One of the best-known music publishing catalogs in the music industry is the Sony/ATV catalog. Co-owned by the estate of the late singer Michael Jackson and Sony Corporation, the catalog owns publishing rights to approximately 750,000 songs.[248] Jackson acquired ATV Music in 1985 for $47.5 million, at the time reported to be the most expensive purchase by an individual of a music publishing catalog. Yoko Ono and Paul McCartney considered bidding a reported 20 million British pounds ($40 million), but declined due to valuation concerns. Michael Jackson closed the deal. Although expensive, 250 Beatles tunes came with the deal. The Michael Jackson–ATV deal opened some eyes to the value of music publishing as an investment. Over the past two decades, demand for music catalogs has increased as music publishing has grown into a multibillion-dollar business. Wall Street has certainly taken notice.

The goal on Wall Street is to make money. A money manager on Wall Street or elsewhere, diversifies the assets of an investment portfolio to maximize returns while avoiding the loss of value. Institutional investors, such as pension funds, typically diversify their stock- and bond-laden portfolios with alternative assets such as private equity, real estate, and commodities. The objective of a private equity firm is to take over a troubled company and make the changes required so that its value will increase, then sell it for a profit. Limited partners, primarily institutional investors such as pension funds, provide the financing by investing a portion of their fund in private equity. If the private equity fund is successful and generates gains, the limited partners benefit along with the fund's general partners who make the decisions. The presence of numerous billionaires in this industry attests to the level of fees earned.

Typically, the acquisition of a company by a private equity firm requires large amounts of debt to be incurred. Deals are generally structured so that the company being acquired becomes responsible for repaying the debt. Often, the private equity firm will make personnel changes to increase the probability of greater cash flows. One of the first actions may be to reduce labor costs by laying off employees, reducing salaries and benefits, and in some cases changing the workforce from union to nonunion.

Until the Internet bubble burst in the late 1990s, annual returns for private equity funds frequently exceeded those of stocks and bonds by a wide margin. At the time, there was limited public discussion of music publishing as an investment for a private equity fund. This changed after the bubble burst and new investment ideas were sought.

The recorded-music business had begun a long-term downtrend by the late 1990s, and the problem was primarily in retail. That sector generates revenues from the sale of CDs and DVDs, digital downloads, ringtones, and sound-recording licensing. Revenue declines showed no end in sight, in part because of the effects of changes in consumer taste regarding compact discs (CDs), the availability of single downloads, and illegal downloads.

A look at the music publishing side of the business showed signs of opportunity for the private equity firms. While revenues generated by music publishing operations were stable for periods comparable to those for recorded music, music publishing offered diversification and minimal exposure to illegal downloading. The sources of revenue are mechanical royalties as payment for use of the musical composition in any physical format and sometimes digital royalties for permanent downloads, performance royalties as payment for the public performance of the composition, synchronization royalties as payment for use with visual images such as advertisements on television and in film, and other royalties for uses such as sampling.

The business of publishing music has been around for centuries. In Europe, for example, publishing revolved around the trade of sheet music containing classical music compositions. Publishers were focused solely on the printing and selling of sheet music from this genre. It was not until the late nineteenth century that the music publishing business began to operate in the multifunctional form that is its foundation today.

In the mid-nineteenth century, during and after the Civil War, popular entertainment forms like minstrel shows and traveling circuses produced music with mass appeal. As music began to be marketed for mass entertainment, sheet-music sales soared along with the songwriters' desire for greater copyright protection. The music publishing industry was in a perfect position to meet and develop the increasing popular music demand as well as assist with the concerns of composers. By the beginning of the twentieth century, music publishing had become a lucrative industry that over the next century would maintain its luster.

A music publisher often owns the copyright in a song's composition. The record label usually holds the copyright in the sound recording of that same song. In a typical music publishing relationship, the songwriter transfers the copyright in the song to the music publisher. The publisher will then own the copyright for at least thirty-five years, if the song was written after 1977, or in some instances, for the life of the copyright.[249] The publisher will collect royalties and share them with the songwriter.

The allocation to each party is determined by the music publishing agreement. There are no "one size fits all" agreements, because there are a variety of considerations in determining the share percentage. These considerations include the type of agreement, such as whether it is for an individual song or an album, or whether the publisher serves as an administrator and performs duties such as collecting royalties and exploiting licensing opportunities. Other considerations include the celebrity and leverage of the songwriter.

The conditions that led to the acquisition of the Beatles' catalog were set in motion nearly two decades prior to Michael Jackson's purchase. In 1962, the Beatles' music publisher, Dick James, suggested that the band establish its own separate music publishing company to publish Lennon-McCartney songs.[250] Royalties from the catalog would be evenly divided, with 50 percent for James as administrator and 50 percent for the Beatles. The name of the new company was Northern Songs. Its first item of business was to purchase Lenmac Enterprises, a holding company set up by the Beatles' manager, Brian Epstein, which owned fifty-nine Lennon-McCartney songs. The company went public in 1965. James and his partner, Charles Silver, held onto a controlling interest.

In March 1969, while participating in his famous bed-in at an Amsterdam hotel, John Lennon opened a newspaper to find a story about Dick James selling his majority stake in Northern Songs to ATV, a British television company, for approximately 1.2 million pounds.[251] The entire band was upset by this discovery. They felt angered and slighted, believing that James had taken advantage of their trust. The group felt that James should have offered his controlling interest to them instead of ATV.[252] After undertaking a few valiant efforts to purchase the shares, including a novel strategy that involved an attempt to have the Beatles' songbook designated a national treasure in the United Kingdom, the sale to ATV ultimately went through. Paul McCartney and John Lennon retained their interests, which combined amounted to 30 percent.

Lennon and McCartney's Northern Songs publishing contract required the duo to continue writing songs until 1973. Out of frustration and a desire to get out from under the publishing contract, they both sold their interests in Northern Songs to ATV. They would still receive a share of royalties as songwriters. However, their control over publishing was lost forever.

In 1981, McCartney attempted to buy back Northern Songs from ATV after being offered the catalog for 20 million pounds (approximately $40 million). He did not want to appear greedy and asked Lennon's widow, Yoko Ono, to split the purchase. Ono apparently believed ATV's price was too high and thought the catalog could be purchased for less. The offer was allowed to lapse after Ono and McCartney were unable to reach a joint decision.

In 1983, Michael Jackson and Paul McCartney released two duets. One was "Say, Say, Say" from McCartney's *Tug of War* album, and the other was "The Girl Is Mine," which appeared on Jackson's mega-selling album, *Thriller*. While working together on the song, McCartney gave Jackson some helpful advice: invest in music publishing.[253] This advice would prove to be prophetic.

In the mid-1980s, ATV was in the middle of financial woes, and the company sought to divest its holdings. ATV Music Publishing was soon purchased by an Australian entrepreneur who, in 1985, sold the business to Michael Jackson, along with Northern Songs, which held all the Beatles songs written before 1971. Jackson purchased ATV for $47.5 million.

"That's just business, Paul," were the words apparently used by Jackson in response to McCartney's questions about the purchase.[254] However, McCartney has stated that there was never any "bust-up" between the two over the sale.[255] In 2009, the same year of Jackson's death, McCartney appeared on *The David Letterman Show* and responded to the host's questions about the sale. McCartney answered, "We've never kind of got to it, and I thought 'hmmm,' so we kind of drifted apart . . . [Jackson] was a lovely man, massively talented, and we miss him."[256]

Michael Jackson's death in the summer of 2009 sent shock waves around the world, crashing Twitter and the Internet with the news.[257] His many fans could not believe that the artist who had performed on the world stage since the age of five was now gone. Amid the grief, questions over the status of his ATV catalog rose to the surface. Queries from frenzied investors sought to find out if the catalog would be offered for sale. Jackson had sold half his stake in ATV to Sony in 1995. His 50 percent interest was then estimated to be worth nearly $750 million. Shortly after his death, it became clear that his interest was not for sale.

The Sony/ATV catalog may not have been on the auction block, but Jackson's death caused several investment groups seeking investment opportunities to look more closely at the world of music publishing. Although investment organizations such as pension funds and private equity funds have dabbled in the entertainment industry for years, the death of Michael Jackson and the existence of the Sony/ATV catalog contributed to a renewed interest in music publishing as an investment.

In 2009, several pension funds and private equity groups snapped up music catalogs. Some of the most notable purchases included the acquisition of the Rodgers and Hammerstein catalog by Imagem Music Group, a music publishing company owned by ABP, a Dutch pension fund and the third largest state pension fund in the world.[258] The Imagem purchase came on the heels of private-equity fund manager Pegasus Capital's purchase of music publisher Spirit Music Group for $55 million just two weeks earlier.[259] The Spirit Music Group catalog holds songs that include many made famous by Frank Sinatra and Madonna.[260] In early 2012, Pegasus, through Spirit Music Group, purchased the catalog of Pete Townshend, guitarist, vocalist, and songwriter for the British rock group the Who. The deal included Townshend's copyright interests in nearly 350 songs.

The rise of private equity ownership in the music industry is a trend that has shown no signs of slowing. Music publishing catalogs are generally viewed as low-risk acquisitions with the potential for high returns. However, whether the private equity realm is the best home for a music catalog remains questionable.

The acquisition of the EMI Group by private equity firm Terra Firma in 2007 was proof that private equity and the music business do not always mix. The deal was once described as an example of "the worst excesses of the boom era private equity world."[261] Guy Hands, head of Terra Firma, purchased the storied British music label for just over $6 billion. He was not the first private equity investor to purchase a major label.

In 2005, for example, Edgar Bronfman Jr., chief executive of Warner Music Group, took the label public using financing provided, in part, by private equity firms including Bain Capital, a fund started by former governor Mitt Romney.[262] It lost over 50 percent of its initial share price within its first four years on the market, was privatized in 2011, and was delisted from the New York Stock Exchange. Despite the massive drop in share value, the private equity investors saw full returns on their investments through dividend payments and other cash flows.[263] Similar to some private equity acquisitions, the workforce at Warner Music Group was reduced in the first few years of ownership, the investors saw a return of capital of approximately $1 billion within one year of acquisition, and the company's financial position became more fragile as outstanding debt grew to more than $1 billion. Warner Music Group reported in its financial statements that, due in part to the debt load and the debt service required, it could not guarantee that it would always be able to pay its obligations. Those included the payment of artists' royalties, the acquisition of new artist contracts, and the funding of operating costs to produce and distribute music.

In 2007 when EMI was acquired, its music publishing catalogs included popular songs from the Beatles written after 1971, along with music by Queen and Pink Floyd. EMI music publishing represented approximately 20 percent of the music publishing market. This was second only to Universal Music Group's 23 percent. The company maintained its music publishing market share despite the rough times and remained at approximately 20 percent in 2010. Its recorded music business, however, was on life support suffering from a limited number of top-selling acts as well as loss of revenue from piracy. Its market share declined from 13 percent of the recorded music market in 2003 to near 10 percent in 2010 and lagged the other major labels in every year during that period. Loaded with debt and suffering from a decline in record sales, the 2008 collapse of the financial markets made the situation dire.[264]

Additionally, Hands had failed to understand the nature of the music business and the varied world of "creatives." Through the employment of harsh cost-cutting measures in an attempt to right the sinking EMI ship, he alienated several artists on the EMI roster.[265] He had applied a factory widget-making mentality to the personal and sometimes eccentric and creatively sensitive world of the music industry with disastrous results. The label experienced defections from top artists, including Radiohead and the Rolling Stones. Paul McCartney also left to join an independent label. Because of his dissatisfaction with the label, McCartney started avoiding the EMI offices altogether. It seemed as though "everybody at EMI had become a part of the furniture."[266]

In early 2011, Citigroup seized EMI after it failed to meet the loan terms. As owner, it decided that the most profitable strategy would be to sell EMI's recorded-music division to Universal Music Group. The music publishing division was sold in a separate transaction to Sony/ATV.[267] European Union and U.S. regulators approved the transactions despite protests from consumer advocates and independent labels over fears that the sale would give the labels too much leverage in the industry. The concerns appeared valid. Universal represented 29 percent of the recorded-music market prior to the transaction, and EMI represented approximately 10 percent. Sony/ATV's acquisition of EMI's music publishing business brought its market share to near 30 percent, compared to Universal's 23 percent.

Sony/ATV's EMI acquisition brought with it an additional 1.3 million songs in the EMI catalog. Partially financed by private equity firms, the EMI acquisition would give Sony/ATV 15 percent of the net publishing share in exchange for the elimination of nearly $120 million in overhead expenses.[268] In keeping with the private equity acquisition playbook, there is concern that the elimination of the overhead expenses means the loss of over 300 jobs from the EMI publishing workforce.[269]

Interest in music publishing from private equity firms and other investment groups should remain strong in the years ahead. More investors are recognizing the intricacies and quirks that separate the music industry. Music publishing is considered a relatively low-risk investment with the potential for steady cash flow and occasionally high rewards. But with so many investors wanting a piece of the publishing pie, the line between musical creativity and corporate philosophy can be easily blurred.

Does Protecting the Band Mean Protecting the Brand?

The Doors in the Twenty-First Century

Densmore v. Manzarek, 2008 WL 2209993
(Cal. App. 2d Dist. May 29, 2008).

"Riders on the Storm," "L.A. Woman," and "People Are Strange" are just a few of the timeless songs from the legendary rock group, the Doors. Their music created an influential legacy from which several modern musicians can claim inspiration. Active as the original lineup from 1965–1971, the Doors became one of the top rock 'n' roll bands of the twentieth century. Although each band member was talented and contributed to the songwriting, the magnetic and enigmatic lead singer Jim Morrison was the focal point. Their string of hit songs, combined with Morrison's untimely death, thrust the band, and separately Morrison, into icon status. Long after his death in 1971, wall posters, T-shirts, and other paraphernalia continue to be printed and sold with his image.

The Doors, a self-described "band of . . . brothers," came together as a partnership to make joint decisions while navigating the challenges of the music industry.[270] The partnership was fueled by a strong friendship with one another. Even after Morrison's death, the remaining members remained in close contact and made joint decisions to protect the integrity of the band. Then, decades after their meteoric rise to fame, that friendship was put to the test. The members found themselves facing off in court to determine whether the Doors' name could be resurrected and used by a revamped version of the band consisting of just two of the three living original members. Could the new band be marketed as the Doors even though one of the three original members was opposed to it? If so, would it be fair to the fans? The issue was just who, in the twenty-first century, had the right to call themselves the Doors.

The original members of the Doors were Jim Morrison, Ray Manzarek, John Densmore, and Robbie Krieger. Manzarek and Morrison met while they were both film students at UCLA. Morrison had transferred in 1964 from Florida State University to attend film school.[271] Manzarek would later meet John Densmore and Robby Krieger at a transcendental meditation lecture. Shortly afterward, the Doors was born.[272] Morrison did not play an instrument and assumed the role of songwriter and vocalist, while Manzarek assumed keyboard duties and John Densmore took the helm on drums. Although rarely mentioned other than as a guitarist, Robby Krieger was a prolific songwriter, penning classic Doors songs such as "Touch Me," " Love Me Two Times," "Love Her Madly," and "Light My Fire."

The group's formative period was spent playing the L.A. club scene at noteworthy places like the historic Sunset Strip fixture, Whiskey a Go Go.[273] The band eventually signed a six-album deal with Elektra Records, where they released major hits such as

"Strange Days" and "Waiting for the Sun." Their performances were anything but tame, and with Morrison, the unexpected was to be expected. Initially reserved on stage, he soon blossomed into a true rock star, onstage antics included.

An early performance of "Light My Fire" on *The Ed Sullivan Show* shortly after the song's release is firmly etched into the annals of rock history. Sullivan did not want the word "higher" in the lyric "Girl we couldn't get much higher" to be sung on the show, because he was concerned that it was a hidden reference to drugs. The band was asked to change the lyric backstage before the appearance and agreed to do so. During the performance, Morrison sang the original lyric live on the air, infuriating Sullivan, who refused to shake their hands afterward.[274] The Doors were banned from ever performing on *The Ed Sullivan Show* again.

After several successful records, the group decided by mutual agreement to stop performing live for a while. Throughout the group's ascent to fame, Morrison had increasingly been using a variety of drugs and drinking heavily. During the band's indefinite hiatus, Morrison moved to Paris, France, along with his longtime companion, Pamela Courson.[275] Tragedy struck soon after. On July 3, 1971, Courson discovered Morrison dead in the bathtub of their Paris apartment. No autopsy was performed, and the official cause of death was never determined. He was twenty-seven years old. Morrison is buried in Pere Lachaise Cemetery in Paris. He left his entire estate, including his interest in the Doors, to Courson. She died from a heroin overdose in 1974.

After Courson's death, her financial interest in the Doors passed to her parents. There was considerable tension between the two families, as well as within Morrison's own family, from which he had been estranged for several years prior to his death. The frayed relationship was evidenced, in part, by the fact that Morrison left his entire estate to Courson. Morrison's estrangement from his own family was supposedly due largely to his father's lack of support for his career as a performer.[276] His father was in the military and maintained a strict environment in the family. Morrison's distance from his family became so great that he once declined to see his mother and brother backstage after they attended a Washington, D.C., performance. His brother recalled that their mother was in tears the entire ride home that evening.[277] Though the real reason for their estrangement is unclear, his father once suggested that Morrison may have been shielding the family from the spotlight and scrutiny that would have been brought on by his fame.[278] Eventually, the Courson and Morrison families managed to settle their differences and agreed to share Morrison's interest in the band partnership.

The band first entered into a partnership agreement in 1969. It specified that all management decisions and control of the partnership would be effective only with the "unanimous" agreement of all band members. In 1970, the agreement was amended to clarify that no contract, license, or the like was binding on the partnership unless it was first signed by all of the partners. The amendment followed an episode in which Morrison was the only member of the group to vote against the use of a Doors song in a Buick commercial. The other three band members had voted in favor of licensing the song to Buick while Morrison was out of town. Morrison was so furious upon his discovery of the deal that he threatened to sledgehammer a Buick at every concert if the commercial was allowed to proceed.[279] The commercial never happened.

In March 1971, shortly before the start of Morrison's hiatus in France, the band entered into a new agreement, which replicated the terms of the previous one. This new agreement was made retroactive to January 1, 1966, the year the band signed its first record deal with Elektra Records. Three key terms were added to the agreement. The first was a prohibition against any partner entering into any agreement in the name of the Doors without first having prior written consent from all the partners. The second was that the partnership would dissolve upon the death of any partner. The final key term was that no partner would have the right to use the Doors' name for recordings or performances if the partnership were dissolved for any reason other than death.

After Morrison's death, the three remaining band members entered into a third partnership agreement in October 1971. The terms of the previous agreement were repeated. The new agreement further provided a split of the assets among the partnership and specified that decisions were to be made equally among the three living members of the group, along with the families of Morrison and Courson as holders of Jim Morrison's estate.

Manzarek, Krieger, and Densmore produced two albums together after Morrison's death. The albums were modestly successful, but the group was unable to match its previous achievements with Morrison. For many fans, Morrison was the marquee member of the band, and without him the group was unable to sustain the allure that had drawn so many. The surviving members of the Doors later cancelled the record deal with Elektra Records and went their separate ways. They would reunite on only a few occasions in the years that followed. These included an appearance in 1978, when they performed the music that accompanied Morrison reciting his original poetry on a recording entitled *An American Prayer*. They performed it again in 1993, when the Doors were inducted into the Rock and Roll Hall of Fame, and in 2000 on VH1's *Storytellers*.

Although the group could not sustain the success achieved before Morrison's death, their music continued to sell, and the longevity of the band's popularity blossomed into a rock 'n' roll music legacy. Their music has been prominently featured in major motion pictures, including *Apocalypse Now*, *The Lost Boys*, and of course the Oliver Stone–directed biopic *The Doors*, released in 1991. In an extremely lucrative deal, the production company behind the movie *Forrest Gump* paid the band partnership several million dollars to play Doors songs in the film. The group continues to receive offers for song placements.

Major corporations have been among those seeking the Doors' music for their advertising campaigns. Apple, Inc. and Cadillac have made multimillion-dollar offers to use the group's music. Manzarek and the Courson and Morrison estates were in favor of the deals. Krieger was on the fence. Densmore was adamantly against the offers out of what he considered to be respect for Morrison's memory.

Densmore, according to an editorial he wrote for *The Nation* in 2002, had originally been in favor of the offer from Buick in 1967. He was subsequently against the use of the band's songs in advertising campaigns. His objections appeared to be consistent with the Doors' original approach to licensing their music. He has publicly voiced his philosophical objections to the use of rock music in commercial advertising.[280] However, in more recent years he has gone on record stating that if a commercial proposal was "very green" and environmentally friendly enough, as well as in line with the views of the Doors, then he may be open to it.[281]

For years, the remaining members had seemingly been able to manage their catalog successfully and protect the integrity of the Doors' brand. This climate of compatibility began to dissipate slowly in 2002, when motorcycle powerhouse Harley Davidson extended an invitation to the Doors to perform at a concert on Labor Day. The band was offered $150,000 for a two-hour show. All three band members were interested in performing and agreed to do the show. The group recruited Ian Astbury, an English rock vocalist and former lead singer of the Cult, to handle the lead vocals. Astbury, whose look and stage presence is reminiscent of Morrison, has a vocal prowess and timbre that is also similar to Morrison's. As the Labor Day concert drew closer, Densmore believed that his health was not up to the challenge of the concert and decided to pull out. He did, however, give his blessing to the remaining band members to go on with the show. Stewart Copeland, from the mega-group the Police, was brought in to take over drumming duties.

The Labor Day concert came and went with the band delivering a full performance. Shortly thereafter, Densmore read in *Billboard* magazine that this new lineup for the Doors had also performed at a large concert in Canada. He was unaware of that event. The article quoted Manzarek as saying that "Copeland would be drumming from here on out, Ian would be singing and that the foursome was the new Doors line-up for the 21st century."[282]

According to Densmore, neither Manzarek nor Krieger had mentioned anything to him about a touring lineup. As far as he was concerned, his consent had been given for a new lineup for a one-night-only performance. A few weeks after the concert in Canada, Krieger reached out to Densmore, informing him that the band wanted to go on tour and invited him to go with them. Densmore declined the offer but was supportive of the new tour. His support was conditional, however, given in exchange for the fulfillment of two demands. The first was that the new group had to select a name that clearly indicated there was a difference between this new lineup and the original group. The second was that the Doors logo was not to be used in advertisements. Over several conversations, Densmore and Krieger discussed possible names for the new group. When the conversations ended, Densmore believed there was a mutual understanding between himself and Krieger and that the new group would continue to perform while abiding by his two requests.[283]

Several months passed and friends began calling Densmore to congratulate him on the band's re-formation. He later saw an ad in the *Los Angeles Times* for a show scheduled for February 7, 2003, at the Universal Amphitheater in Los Angeles. The first line of the ad read "Witness Rock & Roll History," followed on the next line with "The Doors" in large print. The Doors logo and the terms "21st Century" and "Live" appeared in small print. A picture of the new lineup was also included. Advertisements with a similar design on the Doors' official Web site followed. Densmore was disturbed by the ads because they were not the outcome he had envisioned from his discussions with Krieger. He felt his requests to make a clear distinction in the publicity materials and performances between the original Doors group and the new lineup had not been honored.

Densmore reached out to Krieger and pointed out his concerns. He added that the use of "21st Century" was too small, making it unclear that the new lineup was a new band. Krieger offered some minor edits that were unsuitable to Densmore. Krieger countered Densmore's frustrations by explaining that the ad designs were necessary to attract large crowds.

The new Doors lineup was on a roll. They were booking shows across the country. Advertisements for each show continued to appear with the placement of "21st Century" in small letters and the word "Doors" in large letters. Television advertisements for the concerts featured Jim Morrison's voice singing popular Doors songs. A ticket holder just might even be treated to a special "appearance" by Morrison, because at nearly half of its shows, the group would display Morrison's image on stage for a little over one minute at the beginning of the performance.

Densmore was extremely disappointed by the marketing of the new Doors group. It utilized what he believed were misleading advertisements to promote the new Doors lineup, taking advantage of the recognition and goodwill of the original group. On

Does Protecting the Band Mean Protecting the Brand?

February 4, 2003, a few days before the scheduled Doors appearance at the Los Angeles Amphitheatre, Densmore filed a lawsuit against his former bandmates, Manzarek and Krieger, in the California Superior Court.

About a month later, in March 2003, Densmore notified Manzarek and Krieger in writing that he was terminating the partnership agreement. Under the terms of the agreement, any partner could terminate with thirty days' notice. The agreement also indicated that, at the point of its termination for reasons other than death, all original partners would be barred from using the Doors name. Despite Densmore's notification to terminate the agreement, Manzarek and Krieger continued to perform with the new group.

Densmore sued Manzarek and Krieger on six causes of action, out of which the court found just two in his favor: breach of the 1971 partnership agreement and breach of fiduciary duty toward Densmore. The court ordered Manzarek and Krieger to pay Densmore $82,274 and to pay the partnership $3.2 million. Both amounts would account for profits owed to Densmore and the partnership as a result of income earned with the new lineup's performances.

Manzarek and Krieger responded to Densmore's lawsuit with a countersuit. Among other claims, they alleged that Densmore breached his fiduciary duty toward the partnership by vetoing opportunities for financial gain, such as the lucrative Cadillac and Apple offers. The court found in favor of Krieger and Manzarek, holding that Densmore had breached his fiduciary duty. Out of a total of seven claims against Densmore, the court found in favor of Manzarek and Krieger on three of them.

Densmore's case was consolidated with a similar lawsuit filed jointly by Courson's and Morrison's parents.[284] The Courson and Morrison family lawsuit added a claim of misappropriation of identity, alleging a violation of Morrison's postmortem right of publicity. Unlike some other states, in California, the right of publicity is descendible. The families also sought an accounting and the creation of a constructive trust to manage the profits received from the use of the Doors' name and logo.

The court issued a permanent injunction preventing Manzarek and Krieger from presenting themselves as the Doors or any derivative of that name that may be confusing. On the right of publicity claim, it found that Krieger and Manzarek had violated Jim Morrison's right of publicity by using Morrison's image and voice in advertisements and live performances. In May 2008, the California Court of Appeal affirmed the lower court's decision. Manzarek and Krieger's request for review by the California Supreme Court was denied, thus ending five years of litigation.[285]

Looking toward the future and their ability to perform, Manzarek and Krieger were concerned about the permanent injunction. They felt restricted by an inability to market themselves in a way that would provide adequate fan recognition. They considered the injunction overly broad and a violation of their First Amendment rights. They did not want to have to tour under monikers like "The Doors featuring only Ray Manzarek and Robbie Krieger" or "Two of the Doors."[286] They did have a point, as an advertisement for, say, "An Evening with the Pips, without Gladys" is unlikely to sell many tickets either.

The appellate court attempted to alleviate Manzarek and Krieger's concerns by explaining that they had misinterpreted the injunction. It was not meant to prevent them from publicizing themselves as founding members of the Doors. They could do so, the court stated, as long as their names were listed first and either to the left or above any appearance of the Doors name. Also, the words "original" or "founding" and "members of the Doors" would need to be in the same or smaller font than their names, and "The Doors" could not be displayed in the "wavy-gravy" classic Doors logo style. The court indicated that there was flexibility within the parameters of the injunction, but the most important thing was that under no circumstances could the new Doors incarnation identify themselves solely as the Doors.

The battle over the Doors' name illustrates the high creative and commercial value of a band's name. What began as a meeting of the minds stemming from the best intentions of a self-described "band of brothers" turned into a drawn-out battle in the courts. However, in the fall of 2011, Krieger, Manzarek, and Densmore joined together once again to record a new song with DJ and dub-step producer, Skrillex.[287] The song was part of a documentary film entitled *RE:GENERATION* that paired popular DJs with top musicians in an effort to celebrate the links between various eras in music. Commenting on the recording, Manzarek stated that it was ". . . the first new Doors track of the 21st century."[288] On a final note, Ray Manzarek, the keyboardist whose vision, sound, and seemingly unrelenting enthusiasm helped The Doors reach their iconic status, passed away from cancer on May 20, 2013.

Interlude

Will the Real Temptations Please Stand Up?

If you have ever been to Las Vegas, you probably noticed the large number of entertainment showcases offering performances by well-known musical acts. If you are a fan of Motown or the doo-wop groups of the 1950s and 1960s, you might be particularly aware of the plethora of live music shows featuring acts from these musical eras. At first glance, the group names on the marquee look like the names of the classic groups from that period. However, a closer inspection may reveal something different.

Hypothetically speaking, you may see an advertisement for a group that rose to fame as the Five Doo-Wop Guys only to see that this group is now being advertised as "The Original Back-Up Singers for the Five Doo-Wop Guys Reunion Show." This reunion show lineup may include performers you have never seen, or it may include some performers who were members of the group in previous years but have left for various reasons. If you are lucky, the lineup may include former lead singers and/or founding members. All the performers, original or not, may be talented on their own, but to sell tickets the group relies on the name recognition of the original group.

These reunion-style acts conduct U.S. and international tours. This is not a phenomenon occurring only in tourist locations such as Las Vegas, nor is it limited to Motown and doo-wop groups. To the unsuspecting fan, the opportunity to see a favorite musical group from earlier years is an exciting prospect. Unfortunately, fans are sometimes left less than satisfied if it turns out that the performing group has no recognizable names or faces, as the advertisements might have led them to believe. Such acts can create problems not only for fans but, from a business perspective, they may dilute demand, revenue, and status for the original group.

The nonoriginal performers in these groups understandably need to make a living, and with financial security being far from the norm in the music industry, many performers must continually maximize every possible opportunity to perform. Some performers from the 1950s and 1960s have been particularly concerned about maintaining a flow of income from music, considering that several of them made millions for their labels but received only a fraction of the profits. To add insult to injury, some black performers who had hit songs during that period were not pictured on album covers and had limited television exposure.[289] This left them visually unrecognizable to generations of fans, even though many of their songs have become a part of our American soundtrack.

Original members of some of these musical groups are still touring and performing. Fans typically expect to see at least some of the original members when purchasing a ticket to a show, unless it is made clear beforehand that the performance is by a tribute band. There is concern that the groups advertising themselves as being related to the original acts harm the reputations of the original acts and also cut into their earnings. One such example of this tension involved the Temptations, a Motown supergroup. The Temptations have continued to tour since their heyday in the 1960s and early 1970s. The problem, as the group saw it, was that other groups were touring as derivatives of the Temptations and competing for ticket sales. Adding to the difficulty of determining just who could use the name was the fact that at least nineteen different artists could claim alumni status in the group.[290]

Motown Record Corporation registered the Temptations' name as a trademark and service mark in October 1969. The trademark protected the Temptations' name for use on such items as recordings and merchandise. The service mark protected the right to use the name in conjunction with services such as live performances. Motown owned the trademarks and service marks of several popular groups, including The Supremes.

When it appeared that the Temptations would leave Motown for Atlantic Records in 1977, Motown assigned the rights to use the name *The Temptations* exclusively to original members Otis Williams and David English, commonly known by his stage name, Melvin Franklin. Each member of the Temptations lineup at the time of the assignment—Otis Williams, Richard Street, Glenn Leonard, and Melvin Franklin—signed a partnership agreement specifying that any "leaving member" or the estate of deceased members must relinquish all rights to the name, and that all rights accrue to the remaining partners. Street and Leonard subsequently left the group with signed release agreements, giving up their interests in the Temptations' name and partnership. Franklin later passed away and, per the agreement, his rights in the name were not descendible. Otis Williams was left as the sole owner.

The Temptations were later re-signed by Motown in 1980, and the group's trademark was returned to Motown, giving it the right to use the name on musical recordings and merchandise. Although the specifics of the change in service-mark ownership are unclear, Williams retained the sole right to use the name in live performances and distinguish himself as a marquee member in performance advertisements.[291]

Williams has continued to perform with a new Temptations lineup. He has also turned to the courts for protection of the Temptations' name. In a 1996 lawsuit against Dennis Edwards, a former lead singer of the Temptations, Williams alleged that Edwards infringed on the trademark when he performed under such names as "Dennis Edwards & the New Temptations" and "Dennis Edwards & the Temptations Review." Williams filed the lawsuit along with the estate of Melvin Franklin. A federal court judge ruled in favor of

Does Protecting the Band Mean Protecting the Brand?

Williams and the Franklin estate, granting a permanent injunction prohibiting Edwards from using the group's name in advertisements for his performances.[292]

Dennis Edwards & the New Temptations were not the only Temptations-derivative group. Three former, but not original, members of the group were advertising themselves as "The Legendary Lead Singers of the Temptations." They had been performing together since 2004. The group also billed themselves as "The Temptations Reunion Show." Williams filed a lawsuit against the Legendary Lead Singers of the Temptations in U.S. District Court, Central District of California, on October 26, 2007.[293] The complaint listed as defendants not only the three members of the Legendary Lead Singers of the Temptations but also their managers and some of the venues where they had been performing. Williams's complaint alleged trademark and service-mark infringement, unfair competition, and misrepresentation under the Lanham Act. He requested an injunction against the Legendary Lead Singers of the Temptations to prevent them from performing. The court immediately issued a preliminary injunction to prevent the group from performing.

Williams alleged that the Temptations' trade name and service mark were very well known around the world and that people associated the group name with him. He argued that the use of the derivative or "counterfeit" groups, as Williams referred to them, by music venues misled the public into thinking that the derivative groups were affiliated with and/or endorsed by Williams's Temptations. He further claimed that the derivative groups' practice of accepting "third billing," meaning positions lower than top billing on entertainment showcases, effectively diluted the Temptations' service mark and affected their bargaining power for performance fees. He claimed that when the derivative groups accepted lower performance fees, often at the same venues that the Temptations would play, they unfairly competed against the Temptations. The judge guided the parties toward settlement and issued a permanent injunction against the Legendary Lead Singers of the Temptations. The case was terminated on March 24, 2010. Prior to the injunction, the Legendary Lead Singers of the Temptations had been performing almost nightly for three months at a large Las Vegas venue.

The defendant performers were enjoined from performing under the Temptations name or using the name in any advertising or promotion. The defendant venues were enjoined from infringing on the service mark; using the name "Temptations" in advertising, promotion, or performance of any group that derives its name from "Temptations"; using misleading descriptions to confuse the consuming public by making it appear that the offering is associated with the Temptations; and damaging the reputation and associated goodwill of the Temptations.

The dramatic growth in the number of spin-off and copycat groups has led some states to pass protective laws known as Truth In Music legislation. By 2009, thirty-three states had added such laws to their books. The legislation is reasonably consistent across those states, due in large part to the advocacy efforts of entertainers such as Mary Wilson of The Supremes and Jon "Bowzer" Bauman of Sha Na Na. Advocates also work in conjunction with the Vocal Group Hall of Fame Foundation, an organization honoring and providing advocacy for vocal music groups. The laws specifically prohibit the promotion or production of live musical performances through the use of misleading advertisements. Generally, exceptions are made when the group is the federally registered owner of the service mark, one of the group's members was a member of the original group and has not lost an affiliation with that group, the group advertises itself as a "salute" or "tribute" and uses a name that is not confusing to the consuming public, or has permission in writing from the original group.[294]

When the Fans Sue the Band

Imagine your favorite band is scheduled to play a show tomorrow night. You purchased your ticket months ago when tickets first went on sale. It is tucked away in a safe place so that on the night of the show you can rest assured you are guaranteed to get in. You and your friends have decided on making the five-hour drive to the show. After a good dinner and a round of drinks, you walk across the street to the venue. Everything is perfect and you are ready for the show to begin. Ten minutes before showtime, someone comes onstage and announces that the highly anticipated show has been canceled. No doubt you are upset. Matters are made worse when you learn that the cancellation is due to one of the band members being unable to perform because he partied excessively the night before, or let's call it "exhaustion." All your planning was for nothing, and the money you have spent is now gone with no return. So what do you do now? Get angry and mutter to yourself on the long drive home? For some music fans, the answer is easy. Sue the band.

Several cases against bands have been brought before the courts when fans have been injured at a concert. Though those cases are unfortunate and often involve inexcusable tragedies, it has not been common practice for fans to respond litigiously when the "injury" is a canceled show or a poorly delivered performance. Although the majority of these cases are either dismissed or settled, the few lawsuits that have been filed present some interesting questions. Should fans look to the courts for a remedy when a show has been canceled? What if there is a good reason to cancel the show? Here are a few examples of situations in which the fans have fought back.

In September 2007, Aerosmith, one of the top rock bands around, canceled a concert that was scheduled in Maui, Hawaii. The official reason given by the band's management for the cancellation was that a Chicago show that had been previously postponed was rescheduled for two days prior to the Maui show. The band's management insisted that the Maui concert could not go on as scheduled because the equipment and instruments would not arrive from Chicago in time.[295] The band did, however, go on to play a private show for Toyota in Oahu, Hawaii, three days after the canceled Maui show.

Needless to say, disappointment was rife among ticketholders for the Maui concert, so much so that a class action lawsuit was filed against the band by angry fans. The fans sought monetary compensation for ticket costs, handling fees, and related show expenses in an amount they valued to be, in the aggregate, between $500,000 and $3.5 million. The lawsuit was settled out of court shortly after it was filed. The settlement required Aerosmith to perform a makeup show and specifically required the show to be of the same "quality, type and duration" as standard Aerosmith concerts.[296] The settlement also awarded reimbursements for out-of-pocket travel-related expenses. In this case, the fans' persistence paid off.

In another instance, a fan sued the rock band Rush for canceling a show shortly before it was due to begin. In July 2010, the band was scheduled to take the stage at Charter One Pavilion at Northerly Island in Chicago, an outdoor venue. The self-described "life-long RUSH fan" had flown from New York to Chicago for the concert.[297] He experienced acute disappointment, however, when the show was postponed because of rain. He filed a lawsuit against Live Nation, the concert promoter, and Rush in Cook County Circuit Court. He sought reimbursement of $480 for the six concert tickets he had purchased and for his travel expenses. His argument was that the show should have taken place "rain or shine." After all, the ticket had the words "rain or shine" printed on one side, according to the fan. If the Chicago White Sox could complete a game that same night, which they did, then why couldn't the band he wondered? The fan received a bit of press, as well as some criticism, for the lawsuit. He defended against the criticism by explaining that it was filed because StubHub, the ticket seller, would give refunds only for cancellations, not postponements.[298] The case was dismissed in January 2011.[299]

The lawsuit against Rush was not the first to be filed in Cook County Circuit Court by a disgruntled music fan. In 2003, the rap-metal band Limp Bizkit was the subject of a class action lawsuit filed by fans. More than 170 fans who attended a concert at the Hawthorne Race Course near Chicago, where the band was part of a mega-tour lineup, were seeking reimbursement for a portion of the ticket price after the band refused to play a full set.

The band was appearing as a part of the Summer Sanitarium Tour and was scheduled to play after a set by Linkin Park and before headliner Metallica. As Linkin Park was finishing its set, the band announced to the crowd that Limp Bizkit would soon take the stage. As soon as Limp Bizkit's name was mentioned, it was greeted with boos and jeers from the audience. When the band arrived on the stage, they were heckled and pelted with plastic water bottles and garbage. Fred Durst, the band's lead singer, responded with his own tirade of insults toward the audience. The pelting of garbage and foreign objects became too much for Limp Bizkit, and the band left the stage for good that evening after playing about twenty minutes. There were also reports that a local radio DJ had encouraged audience members to harass the band.[300]

Amid the chorus of boos, however, were some dedicated Limp Bizkit fans. They had come to see the band play a full set but were upset to have received only a twenty-minute show. A Chicago lawyer filed a class action lawsuit in October 2003 on behalf of the 40,000 ticket holders attending the concert.[301] A $25 refund from each $75 ticket purchased was sought. The class action lawsuit was dismissed in March 2004.[302]

Finally, the band Creed, famous for songs such as "With Arms Wide Open," was sued in April 2003 for delivering what was deemed to have been a terrible performance. The show took place on December 29, 2002, in Rosemont, Illinois. Four fans reported that Scott Stapp, the band's lead singer, spent the majority of the show appearing to be heavily under the influence of either drugs, alcohol, or both. He was unable to function and was never able to sing a full song. The fans stated that he "rolled around on the floor of the stage in apparent pain or distress and appeared to pass out while onstage."[303] They claimed the band's management and the concert promoter were aware of Stapp's substance problem and sought $56.75 each as reimbursement for the concert ticket and parking expenses. The fans hoped that the lawsuit would eventually reach class action status, permitting recovery for over 15,000 fans. Unfortunately for the fans, the lawsuit was dismissed in September of 2003.[304] The band did offer an apology for the show, but not a refund.

There appears to be increasing outrage among some music fans over the past few years regarding the rapidly rising cost of concert tickets, poor customer service from major ticket outlets, and sometimes the actions of a band. Suing a band for cancelling a show or delivering a subpar performance may appear to be an extreme response. However, with ticket prices continuing to rise, it is understandable that a fan would be left reeling from the financial impact of a canceled show. Turning to the courts, though, may be a tricky endeavor, because suing the band is one thing, winning the lawsuit is another.

The Politics of It All:

The Presidential Candidate and the Rock Star

Browne v. McCain, 611 F. Supp. 2d 1062
(C.D. Cal 2009) (No. 08-05334).

The 2008 election season was as contentious as any in recent memory. The incumbent president, George W. Bush, was on his way out after serving two terms in office. The election season had already seen surprise developments and several twists and turns on the road to the White House. Senator John McCain was the Republican nominee and Senator Barack Obama was the Democratic nominee.

As is standard in any election campaign, the airwaves were saturated with ads promoting and attacking various candidates. In the months leading up to Election Day, the pace of campaign advertising reached a fever pitch. One of the many ads used by the McCain campaign included a popular song by Jackson Browne, "Running on Empty." Jackson Browne had never given the campaign permission to use his song and was surprised to discover that it was being used. Browne, an outspoken liberal, was less than pleased. A few months before the election, he filed a lawsuit against the McCain campaign in an attempt to have the song removed from the ad.

Jackson Browne has been performing since the late 1960s. His recordings include "Running on Empty," "Somebody's Baby," and the hit 1980s album *Lawyers in Love*. His song "Somebody's Baby" was featured on the soundtrack for the film *Fast Times at Ridgemont High*. He has continued to perform and write music for himself and others over the past few decades. In 2004, he was inducted into the Rock and Roll Hall of Fame and has been nominated for several Grammy awards. Advocacy of environmental and social justice issues is also important to him. He has been recognized for his activism as the recipient of several humanitarian awards and was a past recipient of the John Steinbeck Award, which is given to artists who have demonstrated "a commitment to democratic values and a belief in the dignity of the common man."[305]

Some of the issues topping the candidates' agendas in the 2008 elections were Iraq, immigration, climate change, and of course, the economy. Well into an energy crisis stemming from declining supplies of fossil fuels, the energy policies of the two presidential candidates became hot topics. Choruses of "Drill Baby Drill!" that began in the halls of the 2008 Republican National Convention and continued throughout the remainder of the election season were a call to arms. The chants were a show of support for American domestic offshore drilling and further reliance on fossil fuels, a stance that Senator Obama opposed as a candidate.

In late July 2008, Senator Obama, speaking at a campaign stop in Missouri, responded to the Republican offshore-drilling stance by recommending that energy could be saved if people properly inflated their tires. His message to the crowd was that individuals could help hold down energy costs by keeping their tires inflated.

He then went out on a political limb when he suggested that Americans could save just as much oil from properly inflating their tires as could be produced from offshore drilling. The simplicity of the statement was instant fodder for the conservative pundits, but some media sources pointed out that Obama's suggestion did have a scientific basis.[306] Nevertheless, the attacks continued. The Ohio Republican Party jumped at the opportunity created by the tire-inflation commotion and used it as the theme in an ad to support Senator McCain. The ad spoke in favor of McCain's pro-drilling election stance and painted Senator Obama's proposition of properly inflated tires as being out of touch and ludicrous. A recording of Browne performing "Running on Empty" played in the background.

Soon after the ad began running on television, Browne was contacted by some of his fans and friends. They were surprised to hear his music in an ad for Senator McCain. This was especially perplexing to them, considering their knowledge of Browne's liberal politics and his known support of Senator Obama. The ad was also news to Browne. He had neither given permission for the use of his song nor ever been asked for it.

Permission from Browne, as the song's copyright owner, in the form of a license, was needed by the McCain campaign to include his song in its commercial. The campaign had used the song without taking the necessary step of getting permission. Browne's legal team promptly sent a cease and desist letter to the McCain campaign, demanding that the ad be withdrawn from the airwaves immediately. The letter further requested that Browne's legal team be contacted to discuss compensation.

The cost of a song in a commercial often starts at $75,000 for one year of national use.[307] Well-known songs in a major campaign can cost as much as $1 million or more.[308] The McCain campaign ad was taken off the air, but there was no response from his camp

285

regarding the settlement talks. Instead, the campaign released a statement questioning why Browne would be so upset with the use of his song. According to the campaign, the ad had "given him more airtime than he's had in years."[309]

The McCain camp's lack of a response to discuss compensation caused Browne to file a lawsuit in August of 2008. The lawsuit was filed against John McCain as an individual, the Ohio Republican Party, and the Republican National Committee in the U.S. District Court for the Central District in Los Angeles. Browne sued for copyright infringement and false endorsement under the Lanham Act, and for the inclusion of his voice in the commercial under California's common-law right of publicity. He was seeking an injunction to prohibit McCain from using "Running on Empty" or any musical composition of Browne's in a political ad without a license.

With regard to his claim of copyright infringement, Browne asserted that as the federally registered copyright owner, he was not contacted by any of the defendants about the use of his copyrighted material. Under the Copyright Act, Browne can authorize someone to use his copyrighted material by granting a license.[310] Senator McCain countered by claiming that the use of his song was a fair use. The fair-use exception in copyright law protects the unauthorized use of another's copyrighted material from being considered infringement. Under the accepted four-part test for fair use, McCain believed the use of the song qualified for protection because under the first factor, the purpose and character of the work, McCain claimed that the use was not commercial or transformative. Under the second factor, the nature of the work, McCain argued that the song has been well known for nearly three decades and that its title is now a common expression. Looking at the third factor, the amount and substantiality of the use, McCain argued that the title section of the song was the only part used in the ad. Lastly, with the final factor, the effect of the work's use on the potential market or value of the copyrighted work, the campaign claimed that its use enhances the song's commercial potential rather than damaging it.[311] The campaign also argued the use of the song was a fair use because copyright law should protect a political campaign's usage of copyrighted material in the spirit of a "free flow of ideas."

With regard to the Lanham Act, Browne alleged that the defendants intentionally used his identity, by way of his song, to confuse the public into thinking that he endorsed the advertisement and endorsed Senator McCain. The campaign argued that the advertisement was "political speech" and not commercial speech, noting that the Lanham Act applies only to false endorsements of commercial speech. They further argued that Browne could not rely on the Lanham Act because the commercial clearly identified the Ohio Republican Party as having prepared it, and as such, a likelihood of confusion did not exist.

The court denied Senator McCain's motion to dismiss Browne's Lanham Act claim. Even with the commercial identified as having been prepared by the Ohio Republican Party, the court ruled that confusion might still have existed regarding whether Browne supported Senator McCain. Also, unlike the campaign, the court disagreed that the use of the song was political speech and further doubted its ability to be classified as criticism or commentary, which may have qualified the speech for protection under the fair-use defense.

Finally, the court examined Browne's claim under California's common law right of publicity regarding the inclusion of his voice in the ad. Browne argued that his voice is distinct and identifiable, and that its use in the political advertisement made people connect the ad to him. Senator McCain filed a second motion moving to strike the right of publicity claim under California's anti-SLAPP statute.[312] The purpose of this statute is to provide a defendant with the opportunity to strike a claim when the claim's primary purpose is to chill free speech.[313] To be successful on the motion, the defendant needs to demonstrate that the plaintiff's right of publicity claim stems from an act, performed by the defendant, that is of public interest. If the defendant can do so, then the plaintiff must show that there is a good probability of prevailing on the claim during trial.

McCain believed that Browne would not prevail at trial. However, the court denied the motion to strike the right of publicity claim. It concluded that the defendants had not shown that the use of the song was a matter of public interest. Rather, the court ruled that the song was used primarily to get media attention in support of Senator McCain. The court found in favor of Browne. McCain immediately appealed to the Ninth Circuit over the denial of the anti-SLAPP motion. The Ohio Republican Party was able to remove itself from the case on jurisdictional grounds.

In July 2009, Browne and McCain notified the court that all claims had been resolved and a settlement had been reached. The parties then issued a joint press release announcing that the out-of-court settlement terms included an undisclosed monetary sum. The press release included statements by the Ohio Republican Party, the Republican National Committee, and Senator McCain, whereby they pledged in future election campaigns to "respect and uphold the rights of artists and to obtain permissions and/or licenses for copyrighted works where appropriate."[314] When asked his opinion on the matter, Browne responded, "The settlement is really a great affirmation of what I believed my rights to be, and all writers' rights to be. One would hope that a presidential candidate would not only know the law, but respect it. It was a matter of bringing that issue to bear."[315]

McCain was not alone in raising the ire of an artist due to the use of copyrighted music in political advertisements. Other instances include the use of Sam Moore's "Hold On" by the Obama campaign in 2008, a cloaked reference to Bruce Springsteen's "Born in the U.S.A." by the Ronald Reagan campaign in 1984, Bon Jovi's "Who Says You Can't Go Home" by Sarah Palin's vice-presidential campaign in 2008, Van Halen's "Right Now" by the George W. Bush presidential campaign in 2004, Survivor's "Eye of the Tiger" by Newt Gingrich's 2012 presidential campaign, and K'naan's "Wavin' Flag" by Mitt Romney's presidential campaign in 2012.

The Digital Domain

The proliferation of peer-to-peer networks that has continued since the latter part of the twentieth century is part of the global expansion and social connectivity that has flourished since the Internet, existing in various technological forms since the 1960s, began to be a broadly used network in the late 1980s. However, in the late 1990s, as a growing abundance of content became widely available online, the platforms through which the content was accessed fell under intense scrutiny. The music industry, witnessing a dramatic drop in record sales, honed in on new music-delivery technology, such as peer-to-peer networks like Napster, which they considered a threat to the music business because it facilitated acts of music piracy. Partnering with the film industry in some cases, the music industry ushered in the twenty-first century with a wave of litigation against companies that were making it possible to download music for free through file sharing. To some, these companies represented a bright new frontier in media technology; to others, they have been facilitators of criminal activity through the illegal downloading of music and film. The evolution toward a symbiotic relationship between the advantages of the new technology and the protection of copyrighted material will likely be in process for some time.

In July 1999, Napster, one of the first peer-to-peer networks, was launched online. A file-sharing service, Napster allowed a user to download music for free in the form of MP3s. Shortly after its launch, Napster became immensely popular, particularly among college students. Shawn Fanning, one of the network's three co-creators at age nineteen, was college age himself when the service was launched. Sean Parker, another co-creator, eventually became the first president of the social-networking site Facebook.

Napster made it easy for users to share files with one another via a central server. During this same period, the music industry began suffering a decline in record and CD sales. Many music fans preferred being able to purchase singles instead of entire CDs. Online music-download services like iTunes, which was released in 2001, made this possible. As a free service, Napster was appealing to many.

Just a few months after Napster's launch, the service was hit with a deluge of lawsuits. The Recording Industry Association of America (RIAA) filed a copyright-infringement lawsuit against Napster in 1999.[316] Subsequently, the heavy metal band Metallica discovered that one of its songs was available on the service without authorization. They filed a lawsuit to have it removed. The band also sued several colleges and universities with Internet servers that permitted the swapping of files on Napster. Rap artist Dr. Dre followed Metallica's lawsuit against Napster by filing one of his own to have music removed.

In *A&M Records, Inc. v. Napster, Inc.*, the RIAA was suing Napster on the grounds that it was liable for contributory and vicarious infringement of copyrighted music belonging to various record labels and artists.[317] In May 2000, the U.S. District Court for the Northern District of California ruled that Napster did not qualify for protection under the Digital Millennium Copyright Act's safe harbor provision, designed to protect Internet Service Providers (ISPs), acting as passive central servers, from the infringing activities of their users.[318] Unlike traditional ISPs, Napster's online software enabled users to share files directly with one another instead of through a central server.

Two months later, the district court granted a preliminary injunction against Napster. Though steadily gaining in popularity since its founding, that popularity increased sharply immediately after the injunction ruling, in part due to publicity from the trial. Another reason was that many people wanted to get files from the service before it was shut down. The Ninth Circuit affirmed the trial court's preliminary injunction ruling. In February 2001, the Ninth Circuit affirmed the trial court's injunction but granted a stay of the injunction, a welcome reprieve for Napster while the matter was remanded to the district court. The lower court was instructed by the Ninth Circuit to structure the injunction in a manner that was consistent with the appellate court's ruling.

The appellate court had ruled that the injunction granted by the district court against Napster was too broad, considering that it was required to police all of the material on its system. Napster's structure made this an almost impossible task because its MP3 file index was organized in such a way that validating whether every file was copyrighted was unworkable. On remand, the district court held, in March 2001, that Napster must be responsible for policing its files if it receives notification from a copyright holder charging infringement by the service. Metallica and Dr. Dre settled their claims with Napster shortly after the court's ruling.

Napster was unable to comply with the injunction because the required policing process became too costly. In 2001, just two years after launching, Napster filed for bankruptcy and closed its doors. It would later reemerge as a legal music-downloading service, in 2003. In 2011, it was acquired by Rhapsody, a digital music service, after being sold by its parent company, Best Buy.

The term *peer-to-peer network* is commonly used these days. However, the term describes one category of network under which there are three main subcategories: hybrid, pure, and next generation.[319] Napster is the most famous of the hybrid peer-to-peer networks. The hybrid classification refers to the use of a central server to complete user file-sharing requests. Napster is considered a "first-generation" peer-to-peer network, built upon the hybrid model. With Napster, users, or in other words *peers*, would download its software and register with the service. When the user logged on to Napster, the central server would search the user's hard drive for compatible MP3 files that would then be uploaded onto the server. The files were then made available for download from the central server to other users who had logged in to Napster.

The *pure* peer-to-peer networks were the subsequent generation of file-sharing services that sprang up on the Internet in the wake of Napster's demise as a free service. Pure networks, such as music file-sharing services like Kazaa and Morpheus, are considered second-generation networks, reaching their peaks in the middle of the first decade of the twenty-first century. These services differed from hybrid networks in that they dispensed with the use of a central server. These decentralized networks allowed users to swap files directly with one another's computers, making the swap a true peer-to-peer exchange.

Lastly, the *next-generation* peer-to-peer networks include popular, contemporary networks and protocols such as BitTorrent. Like the second-generation networks, the next-generation peer-to-peer networks were decentralized. However, these networks have advanced beyond the second-generation technology and offer improved efficiency. Some refer to the next-generation networks as "law-defying" networks. This is because they provide increased levels of anonymity, which has given users, in some instances, an additional layer of protection while engaging in illegal activity online.

In June 2005, the Supreme Court announced another groundbreaking decision in the peer-to-peer arena. In *MGM Studios, Inc. v. Grokster, Ltd.*, Grokster, a second-generation peer-to-peer file-sharing service, along with StreamCast and Sharman Networks—the companies behind second-generation peer-to-peer services Morpheus and Kazaa, respectively—were sued by a collective of nearly thirty of the largest entertainment organizations.[320] Sharman was eventually dropped from the case for jurisdictional reasons. The entertainment companies sued the file-sharing companies for copyright infringement. In a surprising move, the U.S. District Court of California ruled in favor of the file sharers, holding that they were not liable for infringement because their software had substantial noninfringing uses. Additionally, it ruled that the companies could not be held liable for the infringing acts of third parties. The Ninth Circuit, again to the dismay of the entertainment industry, affirmed the trial court.

The Supreme Court sought a compromise in its decision and debated the application of *Sony Corp. v. Universal City Studios*, which held that the creator of technology, such as a VCR, that had substantial noninfringing uses could not be held liable for the copyright-infringement activities of the technology's users.[321] In *Grokster*, the Court did not want to deliver a ruling that would "chill" the emergence of new technology. However, it also did not want to rule in a way that permitted the file-sharing companies to escape liability only because their technology structure did not lead to a finding of contributory or vicarious infringement.

The Court found a compromise in the introduction of a new doctrine, inducement liability. As applied to the case, the doctrine of *inducement liability* meant that the file-sharing companies could be held liable if they were found to have promoted infringing activities through their services. Sourced from patent law, this was the first time this doctrine was applied to copyright law. The Court found that both Grokster and StreamCast's Morpheus had marketed their services to the public specifically as alternatives to Napster. As a result, both file-sharing companies could be liable for the infringing activities of their users.

The case was remanded to the trial court. Grokster reached a settlement with the plaintiffs prior to the rehearing, then shuttered its Web site. A message then appeared on its Web site that read,

"There are legal services for downloading music and movies. This service is not one of them." StreamCast, on the other hand, was determined to fight on.

In 2002, Kazaa, Grokster, and Morpheus shared a network, Fast-Track. In February of that year, Morpheus users were no longer able to access the FastTrack network because they had been booted off the system. FastTrack stated that this was due to StreamCast's lack of payment of royalties to use the network. StreamCast, Morpheus's owner, responded quickly and launched new software that was able to connect to another network, Gnutella. However, Morpheus lost a substantial number of users while it was offline, and Kazaa became the leading peer-to-peer service.

Upset by the change in fortune, StreamCast filed a lawsuit against Kazaa on grounds of racketeering. Sharman, Kazaa's parent company, and other related businesses countersued, claiming that an agreement signed early in their business dealings prohibited StreamCast from any litigation against them. Sharman eventually won the lawsuit. Although StreamCast agreed to pay damages, it was unable to do so. As a result, Sharman received a court order freezing StreamCast's assets and spelling the end for the company. It eventually filed for bankruptcy.[322]

Kazaa became a legal music-downloading service in July of 2006. After the entertainment industry waged several court battles against it, the company agreed to pay damages for infringement to the recording industry in the amount of $100 million. It later ceased operations. At its height, prior to becoming a legal service, Kazaa had 4 million users simultaneously. The company's dominance in the peer-to-peer market lasted only a few years. Soon, users began to gravitate toward the next generation of peer-to-peer networks and the realm of BitTorrent.

Bram Cohen, who created BitTorrent, got his inspiration for the concept while developing MojoNation, an open-source, peer-to-peer

Interlude (cont.)

content-sharing system used to share digital content. Confidential files could be separated into encrypted chunks and distributed to computers using MojoNation's software. Users could pass small music files from one computer to another using Napster and other peer-to-peer software. Large files created insurmountable slowdowns. Cohen's revised process, through BitTorrent, separates the files into pieces and places them on users' hard drives. When a request is made for files, such as movies or music, the software identifies the computers closest to the requestor, gathers the pieces, and assembles them at the user's destination. This process results in faster downloads as more users join the network.

Cohen insists it was not developed for infringement purposes and even entered into licensing deals with entertainment companies to distribute copyrighted material legally. The technology has spread rapidly and is frequently used for a variety of infringing and noninfringing purposes.

The conversion of musical content into digital files, distributed for free over the Internet through peer-to-peer file-sharing networks, has been a thorn in the side of the record industry. However, from the industry point of view, there is perhaps progress on the horizon. In 2010, the U.S. District Court for the Southern District of New York ordered peer-to-peer music file-sharing service LimeWire to shut down.[323] In 2011, several record labels reached an out-of-court settlement with LimeWire, resulting in it paying over $100 million to settle infringement claims. Despite this, much of the expected progress against piracy rests on the success of what are considered "legitimate digital music distribution" choices. These include such choices as Rhapsody and Apple's iTunes music store. Nevertheless, the balancing act between innovative noninfringing uses and infringing capabilities of these networks continues to be performed.

Finally Got a (Bigger) Piece of the Pie:

Eminem, Royalties, and Music Downloads

F.B.T. Productions, LLC v. Aftermath Records,
621 F.3d 958 (9th Cir. 2010).

From Detroit's 8 Mile to global superstardom, Marshall Mathers III, known to the world as Eminem, has found his way to the top. His tenacity and skills as a rapper are notorious. Over the years, he has also demonstrated a sharp business acumen. One of the most recent battles dealt with the licensing of his music for permanent downloads. In 2008, his production and music publishing companies filed a lawsuit against Aftermath Records and Universal Music Group seeking a higher royalty rate for permanent music downloads.

Eminem got his professional start in Detroit when F.B.T. Productions, a music production company founded by two brothers, Mark and Jeff Bass, signed him in 1995. F.B.T. was a start-up at that time as well. The agreement with Eminem stipulated that F.B.T., Eminem, and Joel Martin, who was then the managing agent of F.B.T., would share any royalties earned from Eminem's work. Despite having little commercial recording success during his first few years, Eminem continued to hone his skills by entering various talent competitions. He entered a series of local talent contests such as the Rap Olympics, where he placed second. In 1998, Eminem caught the eye of an executive from Interscope Records who arranged a meeting for him with Dr. Dre, the iconic rapper, businessman, and founder of Aftermath Records, based in Los Angeles. The Bass Brothers and Joel Martin were also in attendance. After several days of negotiating, F.B.T. signed an agreement transferring Eminem's exclusive services as a recording artist to Aftermath. Eminem retained a contractual relationship with F.B.T.

The contract was later amended to add two notable provisions: the "Records Sold" provision and the "Masters Licensed" provision. The Records Sold provision provided that, in exchange for granting the exclusive services of Eminem, F.B.T. would receive between 12 percent and 20 percent of the adjusted retail price of all full-price records sold in the United States through "normal retail channels." The Masters Licensed provision provided that F.B.T.'s royalty rate for licenses of Eminem masters to third parties for the manufacture and sale of records *or for any other use* would be 50 percent of Aftermath's net receipts.

Eminem worked well with Dr. Dre and released his first major studio album in 1999, *The Slim Shady LP*, on which Dr. Dre made significant contributions. It was one of the most popular albums of the year, eventually earning triple-platinum status. In May 2000, he released *The Marshall Mathers LP*, which sold 1.76 million copies in its first week, becoming the fastest-selling solo album in U.S. history.

His success led to some changes in his contract with Aftermath. In September 2000, F.B.T. assigned all of its rights to Eminem. Eminem in turn assumed all of F.B.T.'s rights and obligations to Aftermath, and Aftermath assumed all of F.B.T.'s obligations to

Eminem. These changes resulted in Eminem and Dr. Dre having a direct contractual relationship. Under the agreement, F.B.T., Eminem, and Joel Martin would continue to share in the royalties.

In 2002, Universal Music Group, Aftermath's parent company, entered into an agreement with Apple Computer, Inc., that allowed Eminem's master recordings, along with those of many otheer artists, to be sold as permanent downloads through Apple's iTunes store. A permanent download is a digital copy of a master recording that remains on the user's download device, such as a computer or iPod. Master recordings may also be available for streaming, in which case no copy is created on the user's device. Universal later entered agreements with cellular-telephone network carriers to sell sound recordings as ringtones.

After releasing *Encore*, his fourth major album, and trying his hand at acting and producing through his own production company, rumors began to circulate that Eminem was calling it quits as a solo performer. The Detroit Free Press reported that insiders thought he might move his focus to being solely a producer and record-company executive. He denied the rumor but did confirm that he would be taking time off. Within that same time frame in 2005, F.B.T. and Eminem retained an accounting firm to perform a royalty audit of Aftermath's financial records. Although it is widely known that Eminem and Dr. Dre have a very close friendship, it is not uncommon for successful individuals who have both a business and personal relationship to have their lawyers or accountants, for example, look into the other's business affairs or handle negotiations between them.

The audit report, released in early 2006, convinced F.B.T. and Eminem that they had been underpaid, due largely to Aftermath paying royalties on permanent downloads and ring tones based on the Records Sold provision of the agreement instead of the Masters Licensed provision. This was significant because the royalty rate under the Records Sold provision ranges from 12 percent to 20 percent, whereas the rate using the Masters Licensed provision is 50 percent. The total amount underpaid was estimated by F.B.T. to be more than $1 million.[324]

F.B.T. and Em2M LLC, Eminem's record-publishing arm, now run by Joel Martin, filed suit against Universal Music Group on March 6, 2008, in U.S. District Court, Central District of California.[325] Eminem did not participate as an individual in the lawsuit. The list of defendants included Aftermath Records, Interscope Records, Universal Music Group, and others. Each had a direct relationship with Universal Music Group, the largest record company in the United States. The plaintiffs alleged that Aftermath, Universal, and the other defendants breached the agreement made between Aftermath and F.B.T. in 1998 through the nonpayment of royalties at the appropriate rate listed in the agreement, and by not providing adequate accounting records. They argued that the agreement unambiguously stated that the Masters Licensed provision should apply to royalty payments for permanent downloads.

The defendants introduced a motion for summary judgment, asserting that the amendments to the agreement, made in 2004, showed that the parties had intended for the lower royalty rate under the Records Sold provision to be applied to permanent downloads. The motion was denied, and the case went to a jury trial. In 2009, the district court judge dismissed all charges against the defendants, concluding that F.B.T. and Em2M were not entitled to royalties as calculated under the Masters Licensed provision.

Approximately one year later, in 2010, F.B.T. and Em2M appealed to the Ninth Circuit Court of Appeals. The court reversed the district court's decision and remanded the case for further proceedings. The appellate court held that the labels owed F.B.T. and Em2M the 50 percent royalty rate under the Masters Licensed provision of the agreement.

The tension over an artist's share of royalties is not a new issue in the music industry. In 2008, several famous entertainers or their estates filed suit against Universal Music Group for more than $6 million as payment for royalties allegedly owed. The allegation was that Universal had "pervasively and systematically breached" agreements by using accounting tricks since at least since 1998.[326] Included among the plaintiffs were singer Patti Page and the estates of Count Basie, Sarah Vaughan, Woody Herman, Les Brown, Benny Goodman, and the Mills Brothers.

The recording industry has been going through a period of dramatic change since the late 1990s. According to RIAA statistics, the number of CDs sold declined almost 75 percent over the eleven-year period from 2000 to 2011. Digital downloads of singles, on the other hand, increased by more than 800 percent over a seven-year period ending in 2011.[327] After being almost nonexistent prior to 2004, the dollar value of digital-download singles now represents approximately half the dollar value of physical CDs. Primary reasons for the decline in CD sales include the price of CDs, especially during periods of slow economic growth, and being forced to pay for an entire CD when all that is desired is a single track.

In response to the loss of income, several record labels have implemented 360 deals to offset declining CD sales. This model gives the labels a portion of earnings from live performances, merchandise sales, and other retail income generated by the artist. The rapidly fluctuating nature of music-related income sources and the continual emergence of new media platforms for music delivery has forced the industry to constantly reevaluate its profit schemes. Revenue streams such as music downloads have proven very lucrative, and as a result, labels, artists, publishing companies, and others all want a healthy share of the income.

An appeal by Aftermath to the Supreme Court was denied in March 2011. Aftermath and F.B.T. announced they had reached a settlement in October 2012.[328] The details of the settlement have not been made public. However, the fact that the suit was even filed, along with the fact that a settlement agreement was reached, has signaled an opening for even more artists to sue for greater percentages of their digital royalty rates. Several have done so already, including parody rocker Weird Al Yankovic and country singer Kenny Rogers, who filed lawsuits against Sony Music Entertainment in 2012. Eminem's case, according to some, has set a precedent and will influence the way digital royalties are handled in the future.[329]

A change to a 50 percent royalty rate, for example, for permanent downloads would significantly increase the royalty income to some artists and music copyright holders. The increased rate could potentially amount to millions of dollars for F.B.T. and hundreds of millions industrywide if other artists and copyright holders challenge their labels on this issue.[330]

After the Ninth Circuit's decision in favor of F.B.T., a Universal spokesperson expressed the view that the decision would not affect royalty practices for digital downloads. Though that statement may be true, it will be difficult to find many people who believe it. Judging by the actions of numerous artists who have initiated litigation over this issue, it is not a matter of if there will be change but when and how much.

Finale

This book began with chapters about the emergence of new music technology at the beginning of the twentieth century and the struggle to achieve a functioning ecosystem in which the concerns of copyright holders and the need for innovation were valued and well balanced. Over a decade into the twenty-first century, we are in many ways seeing a repeat of the past. The hot topics of the past several years in the music industry have centered around the digital revolution and new scenarios and questions of copyright infringement. Now that the popular music industry has had over a century to grow into itself, it appears that its continual challenge lies in its ability and willingness to adapt, evolve, and innovate. The future of the recorded music side of the industry, which has faced the most challenges over the past decade, still remains to be seen.

The recorded music business began changing with the end of the 1990s. In the year 2000, approximately four years before the industry began ramping up to provide digital products, unit sales of CDs peaked and began a downward trend that remains today. With digital products not yet available, this suggests that the change was due to something other than consumers preferring to buy singles rather than albums. Although it is likely that the weak economy and illegal downloading contributed to the slowdown in music sales, it is also apparent that the industry was caught off guard. In the past, prior to the 21st century, downturns didn't last long and there was always a turnaround as new top-selling artists, music products, and other offerings provided a buffer to overall economic conditions. This time, however, things are different. The recorded music industry has continued to struggle, even in good economic times. There have, however, been glimmers of a rebound with music sales rising in 2012 for the first time since 1999.[331] The sales increase was small and primarily based on digital music. However, it was enough to breathe a sense of optimism in the industry with some declaring that the recording industry was "on the road to recovery."[332] Yet, it's fair to say that the search continues for a business model which is appropriate for this new era.

It is difficult to have a cushion of solvency when the product, CDs, that has historically generated the largest portion of revenue is vanishing before your eyes. Even with layoffs and termination of artists' agreements, big names in some cases, a record company still needs cash to pay for expenses such as recording new music and paying royalties. In this regard, the continued success in the push to digital distribution could be a catch-22. On the one hand, the growing digital revenue will likely one day match the revenue lost to the deterioration of CD sales. Additionally, digital distribution of recorded music is more profitable than physical distribution because there are no, or fewer, manufacturing expenses. On the other hand, however, this is offset by the potential for recording artists' royalty rates increasing from the teens to as much as 50 percent for digital products. The determination may be on a case-by-case basis, making it more expensive to litigate. There will be no shortage of artists filing suit against their labels to get an equitable share of revenue in this new arena.

Looking forward, artists, record labels, and other music copyright holders will be curious to see what the impact of copyright recapture will mean for the industry. Under the Copyright Act, authors may regain control of their work after thirty-five years. This means that starting from 2013 and going forward, an author who transferred his or her copyright to another after 1978 may qualify for copyright recapture. A large turnout of those seeking to regain control would be a benefit for many artists and their estates, whereas it could prove to be devastating to some record labels and music publishers.

Another issue to watch closely is the effect on the withdrawal of digital rights from Performing Rights Organizations (PRO) such as

ASCAP and BMI. The organizations face some risk in their future in this situation where a publisher withdraws its digital rights from the PRO and works directly with the end user, such as a streaming music service Pandora, to maximize revenue. Currently the income from digital licensing is a very small percentage of the total income from public performance licensing; however, it is certain to grow over the next few years. On the surface, the most obvious effect if the withdrawals become widespread would be the loss of revenue to the PROs from managing these digital licenses. Although in some cases PROs have demonstrated a willingness to adapt. Sony/ATV for example withdrew their digital rights from BMI in early 2013. BMI responded by entering into an administrative deal with Sony/ATV in which the publisher would negotiate licensing fees directly with digital services but BMI would collect and distribute royalties to Sony/ATV artists.

Another possible effect of digital rights withdrawal is higher royalty rates charged to licensees because the royalties charged by the individual publishing companies are constrained only by the market. ASCAP and BMI are constrained by consent decrees which effectively limit the amount by which they can raise rates. Finally, for publishing catalogs that withdraw and choose to administer public performance royalties outside of the PROs, there is concern that the artist may suffer because there may no longer be a direct payment of performance royalties as with ASCAP, BMI, and similar organizations.

Additionally, in regards to publishing, it's not possible to look into the future without wondering about the long-term effect of game-changing business models as seen in music publishing companies like Kobalt Music Group. Lauding themselves for their transparent approach to music publishing, Kobalt has introduced a new business model to the industry which offers clients features such as online access and tracking of data, supposedly more accurate and frequent reports, more efficient collection and payment of domestic and global royalties, synch licensing, and online request for advances. The feature which is most attractive to some artists, apparently including Prince, who recently signed with Kobalt, is the ability to maintain ownership and control of their publishing. Artist retention of publishing is a significant feature that differs from the traditional music publishing model where an artist typically relinquished a percentage of their publishing rights in order to be signed to a music publishing deal.

Lastly, it will be interesting to see how other new developments play out in the near future. These include the use of services like Kickstarter, the crowd-funding platform. Through promotional videos and other forms of information dissemination, anyone can request funds to create a project through Kickstarter. Several independent artists have successfully used the platform to fund their recordings. There are many more developments on the horizon for the music industry, and perhaps the only question that needs to be asked is, will the label, the publisher, the artist, and even the lawyer be ready?

So I close with this one thought. Beyond the court battles and the technology debates, what is very clear is that the demand for music, regardless of the form in which it is delivered, is stronger than ever. This is a vibrant time for the music industry. Whether by digital download, vinyl, or live show, people just want to be entertained.

Accelerated Judgment. Dismissal of one or more causes of action based on lack of legal capacity to sue, lack of court jurisdiction, or presence of a release signed by the parties Also known as Summary Judgment

Artists and Repertoire (A&R). Department at a Record Label or Music Publishing Company responsible for signing and developing new artists.

Assignment versus Licensing. *Assignment* of a copyright results in a transfer of ownership. The term may be for a fixed period or the life of the copyright. *Licensing* permits the non-owner to use the copyright with no change of ownership generally in exchange for a fee.

Cease and Desist. An order or request to halt an activity and not take it up again, or face legal action.

Common Law. Established by judicial precedents, that is, previous judicial decisions, rather than by statutes passed by legislative bodies.

Complaint. Document entered by the plaintiff to the court that states one or more specific causes of action against the defendant.

Composition. A musical *composition*, such as a song, consists of music that has been written by a musician and lyrics by a lyricist. In many cases, the composer writes both the music and lyrics. A composition is eligible for copyright protection once it has been fixed in tangible form such as a recording or a musical score.

Constructive Trust. A court ordered measure where a party who has received property unjustly must give it to the appropriate owner. Unlike a traditional trust there is no trustee.

Copyright. A bundle of exclusive rights given to the creator of an original work to distribute, perform, display, license, and develop new material that includes the copyrighted work.

Cover Song. A recording or performance of a song that has previously been recorded.

Defendant. The party responding to the complaint.

Discovery. The pretrial phase in which each party can request documents and other evidence from the other party.

Exclusivity (Recording Contract). During the term of the contract, the artist can record only for the record label unless the artist receives permission from the label to do otherwise.

Fair Use. Limited circumstances, such as parody and non-profit educational uses, under which a person can use another's copyrighted work without permission

Fiduciary. One who holds assets in trust or has a financial relationship with a beneficiary and thus owes that person the highest duty of care, good faith, trust, confidence, and candor. All actions of the fiduciary must be for the benefit of the beneficiary

Fraud. Intentional misrepresentation.

Gold Album. 500,000 albums sold, as certified by the RIAA.

Infringement. The use of a work or part of a work without permission, or the improper use of another's trademark or a confusingly similar mark that creates the appearance of an affiliation with, or of actually being, the other product or service.

Lanham Act. Federal statute that defines and governs trademarks and service marks. It specifically prohibits acts such as trademark infringement, trademark dilution, and false advertising.

License. A formal authorization to do something, such as use the copyrighted works of an author for a fee.

Master Recording. A recording used to replicate additional copies for sale. The record company usually owns the master, unless the parties have agreed otherwise.

Mechanical Royalties. Royalties paid to the copyright owner, usually the publisher, by parties to mechanical licenses who have received permission to record and distribute copyrighted songs on CDs, records, tapes, and certain digital configurations. At the

310

very minimum, the amount is based on a statutorily prescribed royalty rate and the number of copies sold.

Misappropriation. The intentional, illegal use of the property of another for one's own use or an unauthorized purpose.

Music Publisher. Two primary responsibilities: (1) copyright and license administration and (2) financial exploitation of copyrights. Songwriters frequently assign copyrights to publishers in exchange for these services and the payment of royalties.

Negligence. Failure to use the reasonable care that would be expected of a reasonable person in a similar situation.

Performance Royalties. Payment to copyright holder whenever composition is performed publicly.

Permission. A formal approval to do something, usually in written form.

Plaintiff. The party who files a complaint and brings an action in a court of law.

Platinum Album. One million albums sold, as certified by the RIAA.

Recording Contract. Traditionally allows the record company to exploit the sound recordings of the artist through physical sales, such as CDs; digital, such as downloads and ringtones; and performances. In return, the artist is paid a royalty on each unit of sales. The agreement in the sound recording is distinguished from an agreement in the composition, known as the publishing agreement, which addresses the composer's rights in the song.

Recoupment. Some artists are paid advances based on expected future sales. Under the terms of most agreements, these advances must be repaid from the exploitation of music before royalties are paid.

Remand. Return to a lower court for a decision that should incorporate the issues raised by the appeals court.

Rescission. The cancellation of a contract and return of the parties to the positions they would have been in had there been no contract.

Sample. Refers to copying portions of a copyrighted sound recording, which embodies a copyrighted composition, and inserting it into a new song. Permission to do so is required from both the record company, as owner of the sound recording, and the publisher, as owner of the composition.

Sound Recording. According to US copyright law it is "musical, spoken or other sounds" that are fixed in a recording. Sound accompanying movies and other audiovisual creative works, generally other than movie soundtracks, are not considered sound recordings but part of the total work of which they are a part.

Summary Judgment. The party making a motion for summary judgment can show that no material issues of fact are in dispute and the judge has enough information to make a decision without a trial.

Synchronization Rights. Commonly known as "synch" rights. They involve the use of copyrighted music compositions in audiovisual form such as advertisements, television, and film. The rights in the sound recording are licensed by the owner of the master recording, often the record label. The composition is licensed by the owner of the composition copyright, often the music publisher.

Notes

1. Charles Hirschman and Elizabeth Mogford *Immigration and the American Industrial Revolution From 1880 to 1920*, SOCIAL SCIENCE RESEARCH 38, no. 4 (December 1, 2009): 897–920, doi:10.1016/j.ssresearch.2009.04.001.

2. MICHAEL CAMPBELL, POPULAR MUSIC IN AMERICA: THE BEAT GOES ON 28 (Cengage Learning, 2011).

3. Richard Reublin & The Parlor Songs Association, Inc., *The Story of Tin Pan Alley*, PARLOR SONGS ACADEMY, http://parlorsongs.com/insearch/tinpanalley/tinpanalley.php.

4. RANDY POE, MUSIC PUBLISHING: A SONGWRITER'S GUIDE (2d ed., Writer's Digest Books 1997).

5. Nipper's image has also been a logo for associated RCA companies, including RCA Victor, HMV, and EMI.

6. Leeds & Catlin Co. v. Victor Talking Machine Co., 213 U.S. 301 (1909).

7. B. L. ALDRIDGE, THE VICTOR TALKING MACHINE COMPANY 4 (RCA Sales Corporation 1964).

8. JOHN CAIN, TALKING MACHINES 24 (Methuen 1961).

9. Library of Congress, *Emile Berliner*, EMILE BERLINER AND THE BIRTH OF THE RECORDING INDUSTRY, http://memory.loc.gov/ammem/berlhtml/berlemil.html (last visited July 1, 2012).

10. ALDRIDGE, *supra* note 7.

11. Gramophone, U.S. Patent No. 534,543 (filed Mar. 30, 1892) (issued Feb. 19, 1895).

12. *See The Victor Talking Machine Company*, THE DAVID SARNOFF LIBRARY, http://www.davidsarnoff.org/vtm-chapter5.html (last visited Jan. 5, 2013).

13. ALDRIDGE, *supra* note 7, at 32.

14. Although the origin of the Victor name is unclear, some attribute it to being a variation of the name Victoria. The name belonged to the wife of Leon Forrest Douglas, who was a prominent member of the Victor Talking Machine Company team in charge of marketing, sales, and recording at Victor.

15. ALDRIDGE, *supra* note 7, at 33.

16. The Gramophone Company was established as a selling agent for Berliner with an exclusive license to sell Berliner records and gramophones in England.

17. *The Victor Talking Machine Company*, THE DAVID SARNOFF LIBRARY, http://www.davidsarnoff.org/vtm-chapter5.html (last visited Jan. 5, 2013).

18. LISA GITELMAN, SCRIPTS, GROOVES, AND WRITING MACHINES: REPRESENTING TECHNOLOGY IN THE EDISON ERA (Stanford University Press 2000).

19. WALTER LESLIE WELCH & LEAH BRODBECK STENZEL BURT, FROM TINFOIL TO STEREO: THE ACOUSTIC YEARS OF THE RECORDING INDUSTRY, 1877–1929 (University Press of Florida 1994).

20. U.S. Rev. Stat. § 4886, U.S. Comp. Stat. 1901, p. 3382.

21. Leeds & Catlin v. Victor Talking Machine Company (No. 1), 213 U.S. 301, 314 (1909).

22. Leeds & Catlin v. Victor Talking Machine Company (No. 2), 213 U.S. 325, 333 (1909).

23. *What the Victor Company's Victories Mean*, MUSIC TRADE REVIEW, http://mtr.arcade-museum.com/MTR-1907-44-9/MTR-1907-44-9-43.pdf (last visited Jan. 5, 2013).

24. *Leeds & Catlin Co. Fails.*, NEW YORK TIMES, June 22, 1909.

25. White-Smith Music Publ'g Co. v. Apollo Co., 209 U.S. 1, 9 (1908).

26. White-Smith Music Publ'g Co. v. Apollo Co., 147 F. 226, 227 (2d Cir. 1906).

27. U.S. Copyright Act of 1790, 1 Stat. 124.

28. U.S. Copyright Act of 1831, 4 Stat. 436.

29. Act of January 6, 1897, 44th Cong., 2d Sess., 29 Stat. 694.

30. Kennedy v. McTammany, 33 F. 584 (C.C.D. Mass. 1888).

31. Stern v. Rosey, 17 App. D.C. 562 (1901).

32. White-Smith Music Publ'g Co. v. Apollo Co., 209 U.S. 1, 17 (1908).

33. White-Smith Publ'g v. Apollo Co., 209 U.S. 1, 19 (Supreme Court of the United States 1908).

34. *Id.*

35. Richard J. Spelts, *Battle over the Compulsory License: Mechanical Recording of Music*, 36 U. Colo. L. Rev. 504 (1964).

36. Mark Michael Smith, Hearing History: A Reader 284 (University of Georgia Press 2004).

37. U.S. Const. art. I, § 1, cl. 8.

38. Smith, *supra* note 33, at 285.

39. Jenny B. Wahl, *Slavery in the United States*, EH.net, http://eh.net/encyclopedia/article/wahl.slavery.us (last visited Jan. 15, 2013).

40. Ted Gioia, The History of Jazz (2d ed., Oxford University Press, USA, 2011).

41. *Id.*

42. *Id.*

43. Sieglinde Lemke, Primitivist Modernism: Black Culture and the Origins of Transatlantic Modernism (Oxford University Press 1998).

44. Jason Ankeny, *Ralph Peer*, AllMusic, http://www.allmusic.com/artist/ralph-peer-mn0000390252 (last visited Jan. 28, 2013).

45. Lemke, *supra* note 43.

46. Gioia, *supra* note 40.

47. *Id.*

48. *Id.*

49. *Id.*

50. Lemke, *supra* note 43, citing F. Scott Fitzgerald's article "Echoes of the Jazz Age," published by Scribner's Magazine, 1931.

51. Alex Rodriguez, *The Origins of the Word "Jazz*," WBGO.org (Apr. 14, 2011), http://www.wbgo.org/blog/origins-word-jazz.

52. *Id.*

53. Alan Lomax, Mister Jelly Roll: The Fortunes of Jelly Roll Morton, New Orleans Creole and "Inventor of Jazz" 62 (University of California Press 1973).

54. Lionel S. Sobel, *The Music Business and the Sherman Act: An Analysis of the Economic Realities of Blanket Licensing*, 3 Loy. L.A. Entertainment L. Rev., 3 no. 1 (1983).

55. KEN BLOOM, BROADWAY: ITS HISTORY, PEOPLE, AND PLACES: AN ENCYCLOPEDIA 32 (Taylor & Francis 2004).

56. John Church Co. v. Hilliard Hotel Co., 221 F. 229 (2d Cir. 1915).

57. Copyright Act of March 4, 1909, ch. 320, § 1(d), 35 Stat. 1075.

58. Hilliard Hotel Co. v. John Church Co., 136 C.C.A. 639 (n.d.).

59. Eugene Mooney, *Jukebox Exemption, The*, 10 COPYRIGHT LAW SYMPOSIUM (ASCAP) 199 (1959).

60. Copyright Act of March 4, 1909, ch. 320, § 1(e), 35 Stat. 1075.

61. Victor Herbert v. Shanley Co., 143 C.C.A 460 (2d Cir. 1916).

62. Victor Herbert v. Shanley Co., 242 U.S. 591, 595 (1917).

63. *ASCAP History*, ASCAP, http://www.ascap.com/about/history.aspx (last visited July 21, 2012).

64. Victor Herbert v. Shanley Co., 242 U.S. 591, 595 (1917).

65. Dana M. Raymond, *Edwin Howard Armstrong: FM Inventor*, SESSION 4, 3, http://web.archive.org/web/20120311230457/http://www.fathom.com/course/10701020/session4.html (last visited June 27, 2012).

66. Yannis Tsividis, *Edwin Armstrong: Pioneer of the Airwaves*, COLUMBIA UNIVERSITY, http://www.ee.columbia.edu/misc-pages/armstrong_main.html?mode=interactive (last visited Aug. 2, 2012).

67. SUSAN J. DOUGLAS, LISTENING IN: RADIO AND THE AMERICAN IMAGINATION (University of Minnesota Press 2004).

68. *See* Ken Burns, *Empire of the Air: The Men Who Made Radio* (PBS 2004).

69. *Id.*

70. *Id.*

71. E. H. ARMSTRONG, http://users.erols.com/oldradio/eha65.htm (last visited Jan. 5, 2012).

72. CHRISTOPHER H. STERLING AND JOHN M. KITTROSS, STAY TUNED: A HISTORY OF AMERICAN BROADCASTING 252 (Psychology Press 2002). The FCC's decision was apparently based on a flawed recommendation from an FCC engineer.

73. Tsividis, "Edwin Armstrong: Pioneer of the Airwaves." *Supra* note 66.

74. Jorge Amador, *Edwin Armstrong: Genius of FM Radio*, Freeman (Apr. 1, 1990), http://www.thefreemanonline.org/columns/edwin-armstrong-genius-of-fm-radio/, *citing* Erik Barnouw, The Golden Web: A History of Broadcasting in the United States 1933-1953 (Oxford University Press 1968).

75. Tsividis, *supra* note 66.

76. Harold Evans, Gail Buckland & David Lefer, They Made America: From the Steam Engine to the Search Engine: Two Centuries of Innovators (Hachette Digital, Inc. 2009).

77. *Id.*

78. Dana M. Raymond, *Edwin Howard Armstrong: FM Inventor*, Session 1, http://web.archive.org/web/20120316074338/http://www.fathom.com/course/10701020/session1.html (last visited June 27, 2012).

79. Lee C. White, *Musical Copyrights v. the Anti-Trust Laws*, 30 Neb. L. Rev. 62 (1951).

80. E. C. Mills & Neville Miller, *ASCAP-NAB Controversy—The Issues*, 11 Air L. Rev. 399 (1940).

81. Marcus Cohn, *Music, Radio Broadcasters and the Sherman Act*, 29 Georgetown L.J. 424 n.91 (1941). The Department of Justice investigated ASCAP in 1926 but decided not to move forward with a case against it.

82. Mills & Miller, *supra* note 80, at 399.

83. White, *supra* note 79, at 60, *citing* Neb. Rev. Stat. § 59-1301 *et seq.* (1943) (repealed).

84. Buck v. Swanson, 33 F. Supp. 377 (D. Neb. 1939).

85. Marsh v. Buck, 313 U.S. 406 (1941).

86. Remick Music Corp. v. Interstate Hotel Co. of Nebraska, 58 F. Supp. 523 (D. Neb. 1944).

87. White, *supra* note 79, at 61.

88. Mills & Miller, *supra* note 80, at 401.

89. Christopher H. Sterling, Encyclopedia of Radio 393 (Taylor & Francis 2003).

90. *Id.* at 398.

91. Mills & Miller, *supra* note 80. The entire article is composed of opinion pieces from E. C. Mills, Chairman of ASCAP's Administrative Committee, and Neville Miller, President of the National Association of Broadcasters. Each one shares his take on the issues surrounding the boycott.

92. White, *supra* note 79, at 54.

93. Alden-Rochelle v. ASCAP, 80 F. Supp. 888 (S.D.N.Y. 1948).

94. White, *supra* note 79, at 61.

95. Alden-Rochelle v. ASCAP, 80 F. Supp. 888, 893 (S.D.N.Y. 1948).

96. The U.S. District Court for the Southern District of New York has jurisdiction to set licensing-fee rates when a performing rights organization (PRO), such as ASCAP, and a licensee cannot agree on a licensing fee.

97. Cal. Lab. Code § 2855.

98. Cal. Lab. Code § 2855(b).

99. Geffen Records, Inc. v. Love, Civ. No. BC 223364 (L.A. Super. Ct., filed Jan. 19, 2000).

100. *Record Industry Scrutinized by California, Federal Officials*, VH1 News, http://m.vh1.com/news/article.rbml?id=1446484&cid=recco_news_mre&emvcc=-1 (last visited June 10, 2013).

101. Andre Paine, *Virgin Sues 30 Seconds To Mars for $30 Million*, BILLBOARD, http://www.billboard.com/articles/news/1044420/virgin-sues-30-seconds-to-mars-for-30-million (last visited Nov. 1, 2012).

102. Karen Bliss, *30 Seconds to Mars Documentary Wins People's Choice Award in Toronto*, ROLLING STONE (Sept. 18, 2012, 3:25 p.m.), http://www.rollingstone.com/movies/news/30-seconds-to-mars-documentary-wins-peoples-choice-award-in-toronto-20120918.

103. August Brown, *30 Seconds to Mars Soars*, LOS ANGELES TIMES (Nov. 29, 2009), http://articles.latimes.com/2009/nov/29/entertainment/la-ca-30-seconds-to-mars29-2009nov29.

104. Baron v. Leo Feist, 78 F. Supp. 686 (S.D.N.Y. 1948).

105. *Calypso on Trial*, THE RUM AND COCA-COLA READER, http://www.rumandcocacolareader.com/RumAndCocaCola/Calypso_on_Trial.html (last visited Aug. 2, 2012).

106. *Id.*

107. The defendants relied on language in section 5 of the British Copyright Act of 1911 and chapter 31, number 16, of the Revised Ordinances of 1940, Trinidad and Tobago.

108. Baron v. Leo Feist, 78 F. Supp. 686 (S.D.N.Y 1948). Citing Heim v. Universal Pictures Co., 154 F.2d 480 (2d Cir. 1946); Hein v. Harris, 175 F. 875 (C.C.S.D.N.Y.), *aff'd*, 183 F. 107 (2d Cir. 1910).

109. Khan v. Leo Feist, Inc., 165 F.2d 188 (2d Cir. 1948).

110. United States v. One Book Entitled Ulysses by James Joyce, 72 F.2d 705 (2d Cir. 1934).

111. Khan v. Leo Feist, Inc., 70 F. Supp. 450 (S.D.N.Y. 1947).

112. Khan v. Leo Feist, Inc., 165 F.2d 188 (C.A.2 1948).

113. The Paramount Theatre building in Times Square still exists. It has gone through changes, including being shut down and subsequently used as office space. The theater itself was gutted. The building now houses the Hard Rock Café.

114. *The Columbus Day Riot: Frank Sinatra Is Pop's First Star*, THE GUARDIAN (June 11, 2011), http://www.guardian.co.uk/music/2011/jun/11/frank-sinatra-pop-star.

115. *The Sinatra Riots*, THE POP HISTORY DIG, http://www.pophistorydig.com/?tag=teen-idol (last visited Jan. 20, 2013).

116. *The Columbus Day Riot, supra* note 114.

117. *ROCK "N" ROLL*, ENCYCLOPEDIA OF CLEVELAND HISTORY, http://ech.case.edu/cgi/article.pl?id=RR (last visited Oct. 23, 2012).

118. Lorne Manly, *How Payola Went Corporate*, THE NEW YORK TIMES (July 31, 2005), http://www.nytimes.com/2005/07/31/weekinreview/31manly.html.

119. R. H. Coase, *Payola in Radio and Television Broadcasting*, 22 J.L. & ECON. 273 (1979).

120. A.L.A. Schechter Poultry Corp. v. United States, 295 U.S. 495 (1935).

121. GABRIEL ROSSMAN, CLIMBING THE CHARTS: WHAT RADIO AIRPLAY TELLS US ABOUT THE DIFFUSION OF INNOVATION 25 (Princeton University Press 2012).

122. Coase, *supra* note 119, at 292.

123. *This Day in History, Feb. 11, 1960: The Payola Scandal Heats Up*, HISTORY.COM, http://www.history.com/this-day-in-history/the-payola-scandal-heats-up (last visited Nov. 26, 2012).

124. *12-1-1959 Disc Jockey Balks*, THE OFFICIAL HOME OF ALAN FREED, http://www.alanfreed.com/wp/wp-content/uploads/2010/07/12-1-1959-Disk-Jockey-Balks.jpeg (last visited Jan. 20, 2013).

125. *Personal Letter from Alan Freed to ABC*, THE OFFICIAL HOME OF ALAN FREED, http://www.alanfreed.com/wp/wp-content/uploads/2010/07/103-Alan-Freed-ABC-11-21-59.pdf (last visited Jan. 29, 2013).

126. *This Day in History, May 2, 1960: Dick Clark Survives the Payola Scandal*, HISTORY.COM, http://www.history.com/this-day-in-history/dick-clark-survives-the-payola-scandal (last visited Nov. 29, 2012).

127. *Id.*

128. Jeff Carter, *Strictly Business: A Historical Narrative and Commentary on Rock and Roll Business Practices*, 78 TENN. L. REV. 230 (2011).

129. Dean Starkman, *Sony BMG Settles Radio Payola Probe*, THE WASHINGTON POST (July 26, 2005), http://www.washingtonpost.com/wp-dyn/content/article/2005/07/25/AR2005072501624.html.

130. *Biography*, THE OFFICIAL HOME OF ALAN FREED, www.alanfreed.com (last visited Nov. 2, 2012).

131. *See generally* PETER BENJAMINSON, THE LOST SUPREME: THE LIFE OF DREAMGIRL FLORENCE BALLARD (1st ed., Chicago Review Press 2009).

132. Complaint at 11, Chapman v. Ross (Circuit Court, Wayne County, Mich. 1971) (No. 173852).

133. BENJAMINSON, *supra* note 131, at 100.

134. *Id.* at 106.

135. Complaint at 30, Chapman v. Ross (Circuit Court, Wayne County, Mich. 1971) (No. 173852).

136. *Id. at* 8.

137. Chapman v. Ross, 47 Mich. App. 201 (1973).

138. BENJAMINSON, *supra* note 131, at 154.

139. *"Unsung: Florence Ballard" Probes the Life and Death of Supremes Singer*, THE DETROIT NEWS, http://www.detroitnews.com/article/20090626/ENT10/107060001 (last visited Feb. 4, 2013).

140. Bright Tunes Music v. Harrisongs Music, 420 F. Supp. 177 (S.D.N.Y. 1976). Harrison Music, Ltd., Harrisongs Music, Inc., Apple Records, BMI, and Hansen Publishing were also listed as defendants.

141. BOB SPITZ, THE BEATLES: THE BIOGRAPHY 820 (Back Bay Books 2006).

142. Bright Tunes Music v. Harrisongs Music, 420 F. Supp. 177 (S.D.N.Y. 1976).

143. Ringgold v. Black Entertainment Television Inc., 126 F.3d 70 (2d Cir. 1997).

144. Bridgeport Music, Inc. v. Dimension Films, 410 F.3d 792 (6th Cir. 2005).

145. Bright Tunes Music v. Harrisongs Music, 420 F. Supp. 177 (S.D.N.Y. 1976).

146. ABKCO Music, Inc. v. Harrisongs Music, Ltd., 508 F. Supp. 798, 802 (S.D.N.Y. 1981).

147. ABKCO Music, Inc. v. Harrisongs Music, Ltd., 722 F. 2d 988 (2d Cir. 1983).

148. ABKCO Music, Inc. v. Harrisongs Music, Ltd., 944 F. 2d 971 (2d Cir. 1991).

149. *See, e.g.*, Tisi v. Patrick, 97 F. Supp. 2d 539 (S.D.N.Y. 2000).

150. Gaste v. Kaiserman, 863 F.2d 1061, 1068 (2d. Cir. 1988).

151. Sid & Marty Krofft Television Productions, Inc. v. McDonald's Corp., 562 F.2d 1157 (9th Cir. 1977).

152. Swirsky v. Carey, 376 F.3d 841, 845 (9th Cir. 2004).

153. Joe Satriani v. Christopher Martin et al., [Coldplay] No. 08-7987, complaint filed (C.D. Cal. Dec. 4, 2008).

154. *Abe Olman Publisher Award*, SONGWRITERS HALL OF FAME, http://songwritershalloffame.com/ceremony/entry/c3127/5154 (last visited Jan. 10, 2013).

155. Charly Acquisitions Ltd. v. Immediate Records Inc., [2002] EWHC 254 2002 WL 45335 (England, High Court of Justice)

156. BILL WYMAN, STONE ALONE: THE STORY OF A ROCK 'N' ROLL BAND 6 (Da Capo Press 1997).

157. *Farewell Tour—"Thank You, See You at the Reunion,"* THE INDE-PENDENT, http://www.independent.co.uk/arts-entertainment/music/features/farewell-tours--thank-you-see-you-at-the-reunion-2003141.html (last visited Feb. 3, 2013).

158. *International News Report: Rolling Stones Issue Writs Against Manager*, BILLBOARD, August 14, 1971.

159. KEITH RICHARDS & JAMES FOX, LIFE, location 1470, Kindle Edition (Back Bay Books 2011).

160. *Id.* at 4284.

161. *Id.*

162. Motown Record Corp. v. Brockert, 160 Cal. App. 3d 123 (1984).

163. *Id.* at 135.

164. Cal. Lab. Code § 2855(a).

165. Cal. Civ. Code § 3423.

166. Lumley v. Wagner, 42 Eng. Rep. 687 (1852).

167. Foxx v. Williams, 244 Cal. App. 2d 223 (1966).

168. MCA Records, Inc. v. Newton-John, 90 Cal. App. 3d 18 (1979).

169. Motown Record Corp. v. Brockert, 160 Cal. App. 3d 123, 134 (1984).

170. Cal. Civ. Code § 3423(e)(A)(i).

171. Christopher Goffard, *Teena Marie Dies at 54; R&B Singer-Song-writer*, L.A. TIMES (Dec. 26, 2010), http://articles.latimes.com/2010/dec/26/local/la-me-teena-marie-20101227.

172. MARGARET A. BLANCHARD, REVOLUTIONARY SPARKS: FREEDOM OF EXPRESSION IN MODERN AMERICA (1992).

173. McCollum v. CBS, 202 Cal. App. 3d 989 (1988).

174. Brandenburg v. Ohio, 395 U.S. 444 (1969).

175. Hess v. Indiana, 414 U.S. 105 (1973).

176. *POV: Dream Deceivers*, PBS, http://www.pbs.org/pov/dreamdeceivers/ (last visited Feb. 5, 2013).

177. Vance v. Judas Priest, 1990 WL 130920 (Nev. Dist. Ct., 1990).

178. Miller v. California, 413 U.S. 15 (1973).

179. Miller v. California, 413 US 15, 39 (1973).

180. *No More Teen Spirit*, EW.com, http://www.ew.com/ew/article/0,,310283,00.html (last visited Jan. 27, 2013).

181. Aleene MacMinn, *Pop/rock*, L.A. Times (June 25, 1992), http://articles.latimes.com/1992-06-25/entertainment/ca-1108_1_rock-groups.

182. Anne L. Clark, *As Nasty As They Wanna Be: Popular Music on Trial*, 65 N.Y.U. L. Rev. 1496 (1990).

183. Skyywalker Records, Inc. v. Navarro, 739 F. Supp. 578 (S.D. Fla. 1990).

184. Luke Records, Inc. v. Navarro, 960 F.2d 134 (11th Cir. 1992).

185. *Bitter Sweet Triumph*, Rolling Stone, June 1998.

186. *Britpop: Significant Albums, Artists and Songs*, AllMusic, http://www.allmusic.com/style/britpop-ma0000002480 (last visited Jan. 30, 2013).

187. Robert Hilburn, *The Bitter Sweet Smell of Success*, L.A. Times (Mar. 29, 1998), http://articles.latimes.com/1998/mar/29/entertainment/ca-33819.

188. *Id.*

189. *Stones Publisher Says Verve Sample More Than Minimal*, MTV.com, http://www.mtv.com/news/articles/1425045/stones-publisher-verve-sample-more-than-minimal.jhtml (last visited Jan. 30, 2013).

190. Hilburn, *supra* note 188.

191. There has been speculation that "The Last Time" was itself an uncredited cover of a gospel song made famous by the Staple Singers.

192. Hilburn, *supra* note 188.

193. According to the Harry Fox Agency's Songfile database. Available at http://www.harryfox.com/public/songfile.jsp.

194. Hilburn, *supra* note 188.

195. Donald S. Passman, All You Need to Know About the Music Business 241 (7th ed., New York: Free Press 2009).

196. Hilburn, *supra* note 188.

197. *The Verve Sued Again Over "Bitter Sweet Symphony,"* MTV.COM, http://www.mtv.com/news/articles/511079/verve-sued-again-over-symphony.jhtml (last visited Jan. 30, 2013).

198. "Stones Publisher Says Verve Sample More Than Minimal - Music, Celebrity, Artist News | MTV.com.", *supra* note 190.

199. *Id.*

200. *Id.*

201. Neil McCormick, *Allen Klein: Bitter Sweet Symphony*, TELEGRAPH BLOGS (July 6, 2009), http://blogs.telegraph.co.uk/culture/neilmccormick/100001174/allen-klein-Bitter Sweet-symphony/.

202. *Bitter Sweet Triumph, supra* note 186.

203. EQUALITY ON TRIAL, http://www.equalityontrial.com/ (last visited Feb. 4, 2013).

204. *See generally* André Bertrand, *Shostakovich and John Huston: The French Supreme Court on Copyright, Contracts and Moral Rights, in* LANDMARK INTELLECTUAL PROPERTY CASES AND THEIR LEGACY 1–11 (Christopher Heath & Anselm Kamperman Sanders eds., 2010).

205. Mark Fischer, E. Gabriel Perle, and John Taylor Williams, *Perle and Williams on Publishing Law* (Aspen Publishers, 2004).

206. Berne Convention for the Protection of Literary and Artistic Works art. 10(1), as last revised July 24, 1971, amended Oct. 2, 1979, S. Treaty Doc. No. 99-27, 828 U.N.T.S. 221.

207. *Id.*

208. *See* 17 U.S.C. § 104(c).

209. *See* 17 U.S.C. § 106A.

210. *Shostakovich v. Twentieth Century Fox Film Corp.*, 80 N.Y.S.2d 575 (N.Y. Sup. Ct. 1948), *aff'd*, 87 N.Y.S.2d 430 (N.Y. App. Div. 1949).

211. TARA SMITH, MORAL RIGHTS AND POLITICAL FREEDOM 72 (Rowman & Littlefield 1995).

212. Yuri Vielot was replaced by Brother Marquis (Mark Ross) prior to the group's record deal with Campbell.

213. 17 U.S.C. § 107.

214. Campbell v. Acuff-Rose, 972 F.2d 1429 (6th Cir. 1992), *cert. granted*, 507 U.S. 1003 (1993).

215. Benny v. Loew's Inc., 239 F.2d 532 (9th Cir.1956), *aff'd by an equally divided court*, 356 U.S. 43 (1958) (case involved Jack Benny's television parody of the theatrical film *Gaslight*).

216. Campbell v. Acuff-Rose Music, Inc., 510 US 569, 579 (1994). Citing Folsom v. Marsh, 9 F. Cas. 342 (No. 4,901) (CCD Mass. 1841)

217. *Id.* At 582.

218. *Id.* At 586.

219. Sony Corp. of America v. Universal City Studios, Inc., 464 U.S. 417 (1984).

220. Campbell v. Acuff-Rose, 972 F.2d at 592.

221. *Luther Campbell Loses Miami-Dade Mayor Race*, theGrio, http://thegrio.com/2011/05/26/luther-campbell-loses-miami-dade-mayor-race/ (last visited Feb. 4, 2013).

222. *The Lost Boys: How a Pop Sensation Came Undone*, New York Times, http://www.nytimes.com/2002/08/18/arts/music-the-lost-boys-how-a-pop-sensation-came-undone.html?pagewanted=all&src=pm (last visited Jan. 30, 2013).

223. Fred Bronson, The Billboard Book of Number One Hits: Updated and Expanded 732 (5th ed., Random House Digital, Inc. 2003).

224. *The Lost Boys, supra* note 223.

225. Bryan Burrough, *Mad About the Boys*, Vanity Fair, Nov. 1, 2007, at 6, *available at* http://www.vanityfair.com/culture/features/2007/11/pearlman200711.

226. *N Sync Slapped With 150 Million Lawsuit*, Rolling Stone, http://www.rollingstone.com/music/news/n-sync-slapped-with-150-million-lawsuit-19991013 (last visited Feb. 5, 2013).

227. *'N Sync Responds to Trans Con/BMG Suits*, Billboard, Nov. 13, 1999, at 8.

228. Bryan Burrough, *supra* note 226.

229. The two eventually married but later divorced.

230. *Why the Saturn Was the Worst Major Console of All Time*, CNET, http://news.cnet.com/8301-13506_3-9861122-17.html (last visited Jan. 31, 2013).

231. Evan Narcisse, Allie Townsend & Michelle Castillo, *Top 10 Failed Gaming Consoles*, TIME (Nov. 4, 2010), http://techland.time.com/2010/11/04/top-10-failed-gaming-consoles/?hpt=C2/.

232. Joseph Szadkowski, *Dance to the Music of* Space Channel 5, THE WASHINGTON TIMES, June 27, 2000.

233. Kirby v. Sega of America, Inc., 2005 WL 6111153 (Cal. Super. Apr. 28, 2005) (also sued under several unfair competition claims).

234. N.Y. Civ. Rights Law §§ 50–51; Paul Czarnota, *The Right of Publicity in New York and California: A Critical Analysis*, 19 VILL. SPORTS & ENT. L.J. 481 (2012).

235. Cal. Civ. Code § 3344(a).

236. The Lanham Act, 15 U.S.C. §§ 1051, 1125(a).

237. Kirby v. Sega of America, Inc., 144 Cal. App. 4th 47, 56 (2006).

238. Comedy III Productions, Inc. v. Gary Saderup, Inc., 25 Cal. 4th 387 (Cal. 2001).

239. *Id.*

240. Cal. Civ. Code § 3344(a).

241. Guitar Hero *Franchise Just On Hiatus*, G4TV.COM, http://www.g4tv.com/thefeed/blog/post/711783/guitar-hero-franchise-just-on-hiatus-according-to-activision/ (last visited Jan. 31, 2013).

242. *The Romantics Sue Activision Over 'Guitar Hero'*, BILLBOARD (Nov. 21, 2007), http://www.billboard.com/articles/news/1047251/the-romantics-sue-activision-over-guitar-hero.

243. *Biography*, THE ROMANTICS, http://www.romanticsdetroit.com/ (last visited Jan. 15, 2013).

244. The Romantics v. Activision Publ'g Inc., 532 F. Supp. 2d 884, 886–88 (E.D. Mich. 2008).

245. The Romantics v. Activision Publ'g, Inc., 574 F. Supp. 2d 758 (E.D. Mich. 2008).

246. 17 U.S.C. §§ 102(a)(7), 106, 114(b).

247. *Biography, supra* note 244.

248. Ben Sisario, *Sony Plans Major Layoffs of EMI Work Force*, NEW YORK TIMES, Apr. 17, 2012, *available at* http://www.nytimes.com/2012/04/18/business/media/sony-plans-major-layoffs-of-emi-work-force.html.

249. Jeffrey Brabec & Todd Brabec, MUSIC, MONEY AND SUCCESS (6th ed., Music Sales 2008).

250. BOB SPITZ, THE BEATLES: THE BIOGRAPHY 365 (Back Bay Books 2006).

251. *Id.* at 830.

252. *Id.* at 831.

253. *This Day in History, Aug. 14, 1985: Michael Jackson Takes Control of the Beatles' Publishing Rights*, HISTORY.COM, http://www.history.com/this-day-in-history/michael-jackson-takes-control-of-the-beatles-publishing-rights (last visited Jan. 31, 2013).

254. Jordan Valisnky, *"No Big Bust-up" Between Jackson and McCartney*, CNN.COM, http://www.cnn.com/2009/SHOWBIZ/Music/07/16/mccartney.letterman.appearance/index.html (last visited Jan. 16, 2013).

255. *Id.*

256. *Id.*

257. Linnie Rawlinson & Nick Hunt, *Jackson Dies, Almost Takes Internet with Him*, CNN.COM, http://www.cnn.com/2009/TECH/06/26/michael.jackson.internet/ (last visited Jan. 15, 2013).

258. Yinka Adegoke, *Music Publishing's Steady Cash Lures Investors*, REUTERS (Apr. 23, 2009), http://www.reuters.com/article/2009/04/23/us-publishing-analysis-idUSTRE53M6TK20090423.

259. *Id.*

260. *Id.*

261. Simon Meads & Kate Holton, *Special Report: Guy Hands, Citigroup and the Fight for EMI*, REUTERS (June 11, 2010), http://www.reuters.com/article/2010/06/11/us-britain-hands-idUSTRE65A0Q920100611.

262. Yinka Adegoke, *supra* note 259.

263. *Id.*

264. *Terra Firma and EMI: The Magical Misery Tour*, THE ECONOMIST, Feb. 3, 2011, *available at* http://www.economist.com/node/18063824.

265. Devin Leonard, *Battle of the Bands: Citigroup Is Up Next*, N.Y. TIMES, Feb. 7, 2010, *available at* http://www.nytimes.com/2010/02/07/business/07emi.html.

266. Meads & Holton, *supra* note 262.

267. *Universal and Sony Reach Deal to Buy EMI for £2.5bn*, THE GUARDIAN (Nov. 11, 2011), http://www.guardian.co.uk/business/2011/nov/11/emi-sold-to-universal-and-sony.

268. Ben Sisario, *supra* note 249.

269. *Id.*

270. Densmore v. Manzarek, 2008 WL 2209993 (Cal. Ct. App. May 29, 2008).

271. Robert Farley, *Mary and Jim to the End*, ST. PETERSBURG TIMES, http://www.sptimes.com/2005/webspecials05/mary-and-jim/storylinks.shtml (last visited Jan. 2, 2013).

272. *See generally* Densmore v. Manzarek, 2008 WL 2209993 (Cal. App. 2d Dist. 2008), *unpublished/noncitable* (May 29, 2008), *rehearing denied* (June 30, 2008), *review denied* (Aug. 13, 2008) (describing the Doors' history).

273. *See* Susan Hornik, *L.A. Rocks at Whiskey a Go Go: The Doors Celebrate 40th Anniversary*, DISHMAG.COM (Dec. 1, 2006), http://dishmag.com/issue62/music-film/720/l-a-rocks-at-whiskey-a-go-go-the-doors-celebrate-th-anniversary/.

274. *When the Doors Went on Sullivan*, CNN, http://articles.cnn.com/2002-10-03/entertainment/ed.sullivan.sidebar_1_doors-ed-sullivan-steve-and-eydie?_s=PM:SHOWBIZ (last visited Jan. 27, 2013).

275. After Courson's death, her parents provided documentation to show that Courson had been recognized as Morrison's common-law wife under Colorado law.

276. *Jim Morrison's Father Speaks Out*, BBC (Nov. 9, 2006), http://news.bbc.co.uk/2/hi/entertainment/6131518.stm.

277. "Jim Morrison's Death 'Unfortunate' - Dad," *Sydney Morning Herald*, November 9, 2006, sec. Entertainment,Books, http://www.smh.com.au/news/books/jim-morrisons-death-unfortunate--dad/2006/11/09/1162661809788.html.

278. *Jim Morrison's Father Speaks Out, supra* note 279.

279. Geoff Boucher, *Ex-Door Lighting Their Ire*, L.A. TIMES (Oct. 5, 2005), http://articles.latimes.com/2005/oct/05/entertainment/et-doors5/.

280. John Densmore, *Riders on the Storm*, THE NATION, July 8, 2002, *reprinted in* ROLLING STONE, Dec. 26, 2002/Jan. 9, 2003, *available at* http://www.idafan.com/Densmore-TheNation-July8-02.htm.

281. Melinda Newman, *Reopening the Doors: CDs, T-shirts and Vegas Bring Back Morrison and Co.*, BILLBOARD, Apr. 15, 2006.

282. Copeland was soon replaced by drummer Ty Dennis and filed a $1 million lawsuit against the new group, which was settled. According to Manzarek, Copeland "lacked the mystery" they wanted in a drummer.

283. Densmore v. Manzarek, 2008 WL 2209993 at 3–5 (Cal. App. 2d Dist. 2008).

284. *See* Densmore v. Manzarek, Case Nos. BC 289730 and BC 294495 (Cal. Super. Ct. July 21, 2005).

285. Densmore v. Manzarek, 2008 WL 2209993 (Cal. App. 2d Dist. 2008), *unpublished/noncitable* (May 29, 2008), *rehearing denied* (June 30, 2008), *review denied* (Aug. 13, 2008).

286. Densmore v. Manzarek, 2008 WL 2209993 (Cal. App. 2d Dist. 2008).

287. *Remaining Doors Members Record With Skrillex for New Documentary*, ROLLINGSTONE.COM, http://www.rollingstone.com/music/news/remaining-doors-members-record-with-skrillex-for-new-documentary-20111006 (last visited Jan. 27, 2013).

288. *Id.*

289. Julie Mehta, *Long-playing Art: Memorable Album Covers Have Helped Vinyl Records Endure in an Age of CDs and MP3s.*, ART BUSINESS NEWS (August 1, 2003), http://www.highbeam.com/doc/1G1-109905638.html.

290. *Temptin' Fate*, BILLBOARD, July 22, 2000, at 25.

291. Complaint at 30, Otis Williams v. SBE Entertainment Group, No. CV 96-6226-GHK and No. CV 99-09349-GHK (C.C.D. Cal. 2007).

292. Otis Williams et al. v. Dennis Edwards et al., C-No. CV 96-6216-GHK; *see Judge Grants Injunction In Temptations Lawsuit*, BILLBOARD, Jan. 9, 1999.

293. Otis Williams v. SBE Entertainment Group et al., No. 2:2007cv07006 (C.C.D. Cal. filed Oct. 26, 2007).

294. *Truth in Music*, THE VOCAL GROUP HALL OF FAME FOUNDATION, http://www.vocalhalloffame.com/truth.htm (last visited Jan. 20, 2013).

295. *AEROSMITH: Maui Concert Cancellation Explained - Sep. 21, 2007*, BLABBERMOUTH.NET http://www.blabbermouth.net/news.aspx?mode=Article&newsitemID=81213 (last visited Jan. 16, 2013).

296. *Aerosmith to Hold Maui Concert Under Settlement*, THE MAUI NEWS (Apr. 24, 2009), http://www.mauinews.com/page/content.detail/id/517737.html.

297. *RUSH Fan Sues Over Cancelled Concert-July 10, 2010*, BLABBERMOUTH.NET http://blabbermouth.net/news.aspx?mode=Article&newsitemID=142815 (last visited Jan. 31, 2013).

298. *Chris Langone's Explanation - Rush*, THE RUSH FORUM, accessed April 14, 2013, http://www.therushforum.com/index.php?/topic/57537-chris-langones-explanation/.

299. Langone v. Live Nation, 2010-CH-29613 (Cook County Circuit Court, Ill. 2010).

300. Fred Durst was apparently booked at a local Guitar Center the day before to greet fans and sign autographs. He reportedly showed up extremely late and upon arrival stuck his middle finger up at everyone in the store. The radio DJ supposedly egged on concert attendees as a form of retaliation.

301. *172 Limp Bizkit Fans Can't Be Wrong*, THE SMOKING GUN, http://www.thesmokinggun.com/documents/crime/172-limp-bizkit-fans-cant-be-wrong (last visited Jan. 31, 2013).

302. Cario v. Durst, 2003-CH-16762 (Cook County Circuit Court, Ill.).

303. *My Sacrifice*, EW.COM, http://www.ew.com/ew/article/0,,445864,00.html (last visited Jan. 31, 2013).

304. Greg Kot, *Irked by Short Show, Fans to File Lawsuit Against Limp Bizkit*, CHICAGO TRIBUNE (Oct. 8, 2003), http://articles.chicagotribune.

com/2003-10-08/news/0310080339_1_limp-bizkit-audience-exchanged-obscenity-laden-taunts-disc-jockey.

305. *Awards*, STEINBECK CENTER, http://as.sjsu.edu/steinbeck/awards/index.jsp?val=Steinbeck_Award (last visited Nov. 10, 2012).

306. Michael Grunwald, *The Tire-Gauge Solution: No Joke*, TIME, http://www.time.com/time/politics/article/0,8599,1829354,00.html (last visited Feb. 1, 2013).

307. JEFFREY BRABEC AND TODD BRABEC, MUSIC, MONEY AND SUCCESS, 36 (6th ed. Schirmer Trade Books 2008).

308. DONALD S. PASSMAN, ALL YOU NEED TO KNOW ABOUT THE MUSIC BUSINESS 241 (7th ed., New York, Free Press 2009).

309. Brian Baxter, *Election 2008: Jackson Browne Is No Fan of John McCain*, THE AMLAW DAILY, http://amlawdaily.typepad.com/amlawdaily/2008/10/jackson-browne.html (last visited Oct. 15, 2012).

310. 17 U.S.C. § 106.

311. Carl Horowitz, *Jackson Browne Versus John McCain: An Empty Suit*, TOWNHALL.COM, http://townhall.com/columnists/carlhorowitz/2008/12/13/jackson_browne_versus_john_mccain_an_empty_suit (last visited Jan. 9, 2013).

312. Cal. Civ. Proc. Code § 425.16. *SLAPP* stands for Strategic Lawsuit against Public Participation.

313. Cal. Civ. Proc. Code § 425.16(a).

314. *John McCain Settles Jackson Browne Lawsuit, Apologizes for Use of Song*, THE HOLLYWOOD REPORTER, http://www.hollywoodreporter.com/blogs/thr-esq/john-mccain-settles-jackson-browne-63221 (last visited Feb. 1, 2013).

315. *Browne Settles over McCain Song*, BBC (July 21, 2009), http://news.bbc.co.uk/2/hi/entertainment/8161728.stm.

316. *Napster Lawsuit Continues*, BBC (Nov. 1, 2000), http://news.bbc.co.uk/2/hi/business/1000463.stm.

317. A&M Records, Inc. v. Napster, Inc., 239 F.3d 1004 (9th Cir. 2001).

318. 17 U.S.C. § 512.

319. *See generally* MICHAEL SUPPAPPOLA, *END OF THE WORLD AS WE KNOW IT - THE STATE OF DECENTRALIZED PEER-TO-PEER TECHNOLOGIES IN THE WAKE OF THE METRO-GOLDWYN-MAYER STUDIOS V. GROKSTER*, 4 CONN. PUB. INT. L.J. 122 (2005).

320. *In* MGM Studios, Inc. v. Grokster, Ltd., 545 U.S. 913 (2005).

321. Sony Corp. v. Universal City Studios, 464 U.S. 417 (1984).

322. Jon Healey, *StreamCast's Undoing*, L.A. TIMES (May 5, 2008), http://opinion.latimes.com/bitplayer/2008/05/streamcasts-und.html.

323. Arista Records LLC v. Lime Group LLC, 715 F. Supp. 2d 481 (S.D.N.Y. 2010).

324. F.B.T. Productions LLC v. Aftermath Records, 621 F.3d 958 (9th Cir. 2010).

325. *Id.*

326. Peter Edidin, *Universal Royalty Suit*, N.Y. TIMES (Feb. 16, 2008), http://www.nytimes.com/2008/02/16/arts/16arts-UNIVERSALROY_BRF.html.

327. *U.S. Shipment Numbers - February 05, 2013*, RIAA, http://www.riaa.com//keystatistics.php?content_selector=2008-2009-U.S-Shipment-Numbers (last visited Feb. 5, 2013).

328. *Lawsuit Seeking Greater Digital Royalties for Eminem's Music Is Settled*, MEDIA DECODER BLOG, http://mediadecoder.blogs.nytimes.com/2012/10/30/lawsuit-seeking-greater-digital-royalties-for-eminems-music-is-settled/ (last visited Jan. 9, 2013).

329. Christopher Morris, *F.B.T. Settles with UMG, Aftermath*, VARIETY (Oct. 29, 2012), http://www.variety.com/article/VR1118061395/.

330. Eriq Gardner, *Leaked Audit in Eminem Royalty Suit Highlights Huge Stakes for Record Industry*, HOLLYWOOD REPORTER (Feb. 22, 2012), http://www.hollywoodreporter.com/thr-esq/eminem-royalty-lawsuit-aftermath-records-F.B.T.-productions-293881.

331. Eric Pfanner, "Music Industry Reports a Rise in Sales, Crediting Digital," *The New York Times*, February 26, 2013, sec. Technology, http://www.nytimes.com/2013/02/27/technology/music-industry-records-first-revenue-increase-since-1999.html.

332. *Id.*

It was almost impossible to keep these lists short, but the songs below should provide a flavor of the variety of popular music over the decades.

Part One: 1900s – 1930s

Artist	Title
Bessie Smith	Tain't Nobody's Business If I Do
Cab Calloway	Minnie the Moocher
The Carters	Keep on the Sunny Side
Enrico Caruso	Una Furtiva Lagrima
Jelly Roll Morton	The Crave
Judy Garland	Somewhere Over the Rainbow
The Lennon Sisters	Kentucky Babe (1956 version)
Louis Armstrong	Heebie Jeebies
Mamie Smith	Crazy Blues
Tommy Dorsey	Precious Lord

Part Two: 1940s – 1950s

Artist	Title
Benny Goodman	Sing, Sing, Sing
The Chantels	Maybe
Ella Fitzgerald	How High the Moon
Faye Adams	I'll Be True to You
Frank Sinatra	I'll Never Smile Again
The Ink Spots	If I Didn't Care

Artist	Title
Johnny Cash	I Walk the Line
Little Richard	The Girl Can't Help It
Lord Invader	Rum & Coca Cola
Patsy Cline	Crazy
Woody Guthrie	This Land is Your Land

Part Three: 1960s – 1970s

Artist	Title
Alice Cooper	School's Out
The Animals	House of the Rising Sun
The Chiffons	He's So Fine
The Doors	Riders on the Storm
George Harrison	My Sweet Lord
Ike and Tina Turner	A Fool in Love
Otis Redding	Try a Little Tenderness
Parliament	Flash Light
The Rolling Stones	The Last Time
Roberta Flack	First Time Ever I Saw Your Face
The Supremes	Back in My Arms Again
The Temptations	My Girl

Part Four: 1980s – 1990s

Artist	Title
Afrika Bambaataa	Don't Stop…Planet Rock
The Clash	Rock the Casbah
De La Soul	Me, Myself and I
Jane's Addiction	Been Caught Stealing
M People	Moving On Up
Madonna	Borderline
Michael Jackson	Wanna Be Startin' Somethin'
New Edition	Cool It Now
Prince	Purple Rain
Teena Marie	Lover Girl
The Verve	Bittersweet Symphony

Part Five: Twenty-First Century

Artist	Title
Alabama Shakes	Hold On
Amy Winehouse	Back to Black
Beyoncé	Crazy In Love
Dido	White Flag
Fun	We Are Young
Jazmine Sullivan	Bust Your Windows

Artist	Title
Justin Timberlake	What Goes Around Comes Around
Macklemore	Same Love
Norah Jones	Come Away With Me
Old Crow Medicine Show	Wagon Wheel
Rihanna	Umbrella

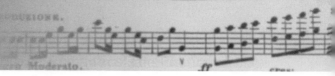

Index

Index

Index

Index